ACTION THERAPY AND ADLERIAN THEORY

Selected Papers by
Walter E. O'Connell, Ph. D.

ALFRED ADLER INSTITUTE
OF CHICAGO

Table of Contents

Part I: The Theory and Technique of Action Therapy
Preface by Bernard H. Shulman, M. D. v

A. Action Techniques in Group Therapy

1. Adlerian Psychodrama with Schizophrenics 1
2. Psychodrama: Involving the Audience 10
3. Stroking and Spitting 19
4. Ward Psychotherapy with Schizophrenics through
   Concerted Encouragement 22
5. Adlerian action therapy technique 36
6. Encouragement 44
7. Elements of encouragement (table) 51
8. Encouragement labs: a didactic-experiential
   approach to courage 52
9. Equality in encounter groups 58

B. The Theory of Action therapy

1. The goals of Action Therapy 62
2. Psychotherapy for everyman: A look at Action Therapy 62
3. Teleodrama 70
4. Adlerian Action Therapy 74
5. Identification and curability of the mental
   hospital patient 81
6. The value of role reversal in psychodrama
   and action therapy (with Brewer, Deanna) 91
7. Skin Jumping Therapy: creating communal cohesion
   (with Wiggins, George, M. D.) 100
8. The addicts "Combo": Building community from
   divergent life styles (with Chorens, Jose; Hiner,
   Darlene and Wiggins, George) 107
9. Natural high model for research and treatment on
   a methadone—maintenance program (with Chorens, Jose;
   Hiner, Darlene and Wiggins, George) 111
10. The glossary 115

Part II: Philosophy and Personality Theory

A. Personality theory
   1. Humanistic identification: A theory of persons 119
   2. Alfred Adler: A psychological heretic 132
   3. Social interest in an operant world: Interaction
      between Skinnerism and Adlerian thinking 140
   4. Sensitivity training and Adlerian theory 154
   5. A criticism of logotherapy 163
   6. The Adlerian-Jungian Sounds of silence 172

B. Psychotherapy and Humor
   1. Humor: The therapeutic impasse 178
   2. The humorous attitude: Research and clinical beginnings 183
   3. The humorist: An ideal for humanistic psychology 198

C. A vision of mankind
   1. The enigma of brotherly love 207
   2. Democracy in human relations 212
   3. Practicing Christianity and humanistic
      identification 215
   4. Humanizing religion, race and sex 229
   5. Humanistic identification: A new translation
      for Gemeinschaftsgefühl 243
   6. Inductive faith: The confluence of religion and
      humanistic psychology 247

PREFACE

A free spirit accompanying a creative intelligence is expected to make original contributions to human life. If one adds to this structure a strong sense of humor, a large *Gemeinschaftsgefühl*, a remarkable psychological understanding and therapeutic skill; the resultant *melange* may well be noteworthy. This large man lives his beliefs:

"What keeps me alive is a very intense and delightful feeling (albeit often temporary) that one's life is worthwhile and has positive meaning. I can contribute to the evolution of the Universe in a small but uniquely valuable and necessary way. And the cost is merely being open to others: Giving, receiving, and encouraging feedback. Without, of course, indulging in the reactive disease of blame and negative self and other abstractions (like Ellis' "negative nonsense"). Just to be open and non-defensive and not worry about being fragile and ephemeral: sharing the "courage to be imperfect," and knowing that this behavior helps all selves grow. Not wanting or caring to prove myself better or even worse than others. Rejecting a timeless, closed, unhearing, unseeing, and angry tightness. Feeling humanistic identification. If only for fleeting moments, being one with the outer and inner universe; yet capable of being responsibly separate: The complexity-consciousness of Teilhard de Chardin . . . experiencing the warm closeness with the spirit, frustrations, and goals of Teilhard, Thomas Merton, Alfred Adler, and Thomas More—yet all the time living my own needs for esteem and outsight. No magical egotistic needs to prove anything . . .

Building my theory of humanistic identification and methods of Action Therapy is fun, not work. It's not just masturbation when I don't avoid the critical scrutiny of the Other and demand complete acceptance. This theory is my existence: I've felt it—molded it from experiences of myself and others. At times I can find experimental proof for the theory, knowing that accepting the conclusions of all experiments is, in one way or another, an Act of Faith. But in wisdom I "trust only movement" (Adler).

The philosophy of Alfred Adler and Teilhard de Chardin provide a substrate for Dr. O'Connell's thinking. The humor of Thomas More (his "favorite saint") permeates his technical devices. He is so much at home with paradox that he unfailingly turns it to his own purposes. The techniques he describes are warm, accepting, encouraging and pointed. At the same time he is direct and severe in his exposure and criticism of self-defeating and self-centered useless and destructive behavior, such as "negative nonsense," "feelings of guilt" and "dehumanization"; calling to mind the way Adler used to describe the "artifice of the neurosis" or the "hesitating attitude" and other such descriptive terms that so well shed light on the mind of man.

This collection brings together some of the best of Doctor O'Connell's thinking and some descriptions of his acutely perceptive techniques. Their wide range of application to all forms of human behavior is quickly apparent. Like Adler and like Dreikurs, O'Connell thinks in broader terms than the usual mental illness—mental health dichotomy. He has something courageous and optimistic to say about all of life and its meaning. He is, above all, an *encourager.*

—Bernard H. Shulman, M. D.

ADLERIAN PSYCHODRAMA WITH SCHIZOPHRENICS

We have come to the concept of Adlerian psychodrama from the observation that whenever a group of people congregate to take concerted rational action for the amelioration of schizophrenia rather than to play descriptive diagnostic games, they will, if successful, soon be following the trail of Adler, whether or not they are aware of their affiliation. This paper attempts to outline such an experience. While psychodrama in combination with Adlerian theory has previously been used in various situations (e.g., 4 and 15-20), this is to our knowledge the first such application with mental hospital patients.

When we started a psychodrama group seeking to adhere to the techniques and theory of J. L. Moreno,[11] we soon found ourselves deviating from these. For one thing, both patient and non-patient participants felt an implacable urge to intervene with various degrees of interpretations and new experiences on the stage, rather than follow automatically the directives of the patient's delusional system until the latter somehow exhausted his repertoire of defensive responses. The directors found Moreno's theory too abstract and his stage accessories too expensive. They then settled for a home-made stage and the effort at "here-and-now" building of patients' self-esteem and social interest via that neglected resource, positive human reinforcement. Interaction with patients was thus predicated upon this solid Adlerian perception of the schizophrenogenic style of life: abysmally low self-esteem, self-defeating fantasy life, and lack of esteem-gaining social skills.[1]

The latest ideas expounded by behavior scientists with Adlerian undertones have continually been incorporated into the group thought and action. Various kinds of double binds[3 9 10] have been used for demonstration and were the topic of short ad-lib lectures by the directors. Mowrer's dictum

Reprinted from *Journal of Individual Psychology*, Vol. 19, 69-76, May 1961.

that it is easier to act one's way into thinking than vice versa[12] has been used as method to stop the escape into abstraction. The A-B-C theory and internalized sentences of Ellis,[5] as well as Arieti's writings on the "referential attitude"[2] of the patient prior to becoming delusional, have been used to help the patient realize that he is not the helpless victim of an impersonal disease process. He is rather actively making decisions, even when he conforms to the "do nothing, say nothing, be nothing" life styles of the chronic schizophrenic and the typical mental hospital. The average patient gradually learns that he reacts to fear with behaviors which, in the long run, only compound future anxiety and rejection.

Organization and Approach

The main psychodrama group was organized two and one-half years ago by a psychiatrist and two psychologists, including the author. Most of the patients are chronic schizophrenics, mainly from the building of the participating psychiatrist. The number of patients is usually between 15-20 males, with 1-17 years of hospitalization, as a rule exceeding five years. Usually about three are in individual psychotherapy with the director, and most of the others in bi-weekly psychotherapy groups. Personnel from all levels of the hospital hierarchy have participated in the weekly sessions as auxiliary egos, i.e., people who play parts to encourage affective interactions and reinforce patients with approval for showing "guts" enough to tell others about their problems and be open to alternative approaches. The number of psychodrama groups has now expanded to three, with seven volunteers (five females and two males) from outside the hospital. The two male volunteers are former patients who were in psychodrama and individual psychotherapy and are now working in the community. They are priceless coaches and mentors for the group, living articulate models of what the problems in living are for the schizophrenic and how they can be faced with help.

A glimpse at the start of a typical session from the eyes of a director might provide a clue as to the interactions involved.

The patients and volunteers are seated in a circle facing the stage. A number of spirited conversations are taking place as the director approaches. In contrast, some of the new or more withdrawn patients sit in isolated silence staring intently at nothing. As the director enters there is a flurry of wit tossed at him. The patients are encouraged to en-

2

joy their moments of indirect hostility, because such actions are only noted when the patients feel strong enough to weather possible retaliation.

PATIENTS. Hey, doctor, where you going all dressed up? Preaching, or dancing? He's going to ask Dr. Leskin for a pass, if he can get to see him. Bet he can't get one . . .

DIRECTOR. Looks like we've got a lively bunch of lads today. Ready to tackle the puzzle of daddies and bosses . . . Let's see how we can do it without stumbling into more trouble. It's not hard to win respect when you don't run away from anxiety . . . Who's going to be the first to take advantage of this rare opportunity to change and to improve on their courage?

Three patients raise their hands and start to talk.

RAY. It's not really a problem . . . But the evening aides push us around . . . like jail . . . .

BILL. I'm going home for three days, and in group Dr. Bell asked me why I never asked to stay home. I'd like to try to convince my mother and stepfather . . .

FRANK. Damn! I never should have been born . . .

DIRECTOR. Good! We've got three guys ready to deal with their problems before us all and see what they can do to solve them, rather than make them worse. Ed and Bill—we've heard from you recently, so we'll take Frank's problem first, OK? Then, we'll get to yours soon. Frank hasn't been up here for a couple of months, but most of us know he's been trying out some approaches to people. That takes real courage. And it seems like he's been getting some bumps, but isn't going to crawl into a hole and hide. Now we're getting some place. Tell us more, Frank.

FRANK. *(getting up on the stage).* I never had a girl, and I don't know how to act . . . They'll laugh at me . . . or yell "rape." I used to stand off . . . and they say I'm a screw-ball.

DIRECTOR. Makes you feel lousy. But you never had a friend, never trusted anyone. No friends, no one to let off steam to—and we'd all be nuts.

SAM. Yea, that's sure our problem . . .

HARRY. Frank's been driving the secretary and OT's (occupational therapists) crazy trying to be nice to them. *Laughter, even from Frank.*

FRANK! They won't marry me . . . They listened to me talk and no one else ever did . . . so I kinda feel . . . *(voice trails off).*

DIRECTOR. If we're anxious, and someone helps, they become important to us. So let's get into it, Frank.

FRANK. When I was home I sneaked out to see if I could find a girl . . . . Mother and father wouldn't like it . . . They'd think I was getting sicker . . . Went to bowling alley. Mrs. Bruck could be a girl .

3

. . and Dr. Leskin and Mike be a couple of these wise guys at home wanting to fight me . . . *(to director)* My mouth's getting dry, maybe I shouldn't . . .

DIRECTOR. Frank, you're going to be nervous. We expect it, but you're going to have to face these situations.

RAY. That's right Frank, go to it.

And so the session starts. Before Frank leaves the stage certain points will be discussed, again and again. Focus will be upon his feelings that people will always do something bad to him, and that he will be overpowered. Eventually his actions which bring negative action from others will be examined and alternative behaviors attempted. When possible, the director will bring in opinions and praises from others, "between the acts."

Outcomes

What has been the value of all this? In spite of the lack of statistics and graphs, all personnel and most patients mention some benefits, with the personnel claiming more. Since we have been trained to question verbal behavior, what about more direct forms of change? First, the patients are much more motivated to attend psychodrama, even though they may be "captives" and enter reluctantly at first, than ordinary group psychotherapy where they sometimes grumble because they are "wasting time" by attending group sessions (when they could be indulging their "avoidance needs" elsewhere). Also, very little wandering off the topic is noted in psychodrama, for attention is focussed upon the real life "play" on the stage.

The psychodrama groups have had a number of successful graduates over the years. They share a characteristic also noted in the majority of individual psychotherapy cases: There is much less of the interminable coming-and-going, of discharge and re-entry, among these patients. It seems that ego autonomy (or "free will") can be a learned ability even in facilities whose motivation for existence is not primarily therapeutic.[6]

Before the groups became a functioning reality, a number of personality quirks, more pronounced with non-patient members, had to be resolved. Initially there was strong reluctance to approach the stage, and the group formed around its old secure conference table. Action was expedited when tables were removed and all chairs placed facing the stage. Next, the

4

protective staff armor was slowly removed and people emerged from behind test equipment and pill bottles to speak in the vernacular rather than in terms of psychiatric entities, fixations, and Freudian mechanisms. The latter two are never used without the director explaining that these are essentially expressions of incapacitating fears that have been learned. And he adds, "It was learned and so it can be unlearned." Such interpretations in terms of learned fears, e. g., fear of assertion, closeness, or even thinking, appear to make more sense to the schizophrenic patient and are more easily incorporated in his thought and action patterns.

The omnipresent fear of co-professionalism among staff members[8] was also tackled until the whole group could accustom itself to freedom-of-speech-and-interpretation for all. While our female volunteers have always been more immune to this reaction, it is a very rare professional in a mental hospital who is not somewhat jolted for a time by the prospect of literally rubbing elbows with and allowing equal interpretative time to his co-worker in psychodrama, the hospitalized chronic schizophrenic.

Of course this democratization of time and space does not mean that patients' interpretations are accepted. The professional therapist is usually the expert, but only because of his typically more plausible and hopeful explanations and not because of irrational prohibitive powers. Even before we were aware of the writings of Szasz[21] a new twist was put on the label of mental illness. As an explanatory concept it was not allowed. For example, one could not solve a problem by invoking the phrase "mental disease," e. g., "I hit her because of bad nerves," or "They say I have mental illness and I'm resting up to overcome it." Anxiety, fear, hatred, and other more colorful common, affective words carry more meaning.

Ongoing Processes

With these premises in mind the group started with everyday superficial transactions to illustrate individual differences, and to encourage assertiveness which was positively reinforced when it appeared problem solving rather than avoiding.

Over the years the staged interactions have always revolved around the patient and the significant problems in his life: family, work, and hospital problems. Many times the esteem-

5

deflating double bind is staged to help the patient recognize it and attempt to break out of it by being less immaturely dependent and defeated. He learns that there are no standard answers for everyone, least of all the implicit psychoanalytic ploy, decried by Mowrer,[13] that there is automatic hostility which must automatically be dumped on someone else for one's mental health. Here Ellis' (5, pp. 215 ff.) fruitful view (the B of the A-B-C), that what the person tells himself about the situation is instrumental in bringing about an emotional response, is of supreme importance. Moreno's "role reversal" technique likewise counteracts the patient's narcissistic static view of others as inveterate rejectors: Through taking the role of the significant other, the patient frequently learns how unreasonable it is to demand changes from another. He is then thrown back upon Ellis' B, with the experience that the greatest potential for change resides within, if he thinks it is possible, and will pay off for him in increased happiness. Another useful technique is the "mirror," employed when the patient is reluctant to approach the stage: If someone else takes his role, it usually is not long before the patient rises and enters into the process, as himself. Moreno's "double" technique (someone behind, speaking the patient's thoughts) was a definite failure. It was not realistic enough, and the patient frequently left the enacted scene to argue with his double.

Contrary to popular psychiatric opinion, the exhibitionistic patient does not benefit from psychodramatic experience as much as the fearful withdrawn individual. The rigidly outgoing person was mainly showing stabilized defenses used to deny problems, but the fearful person generally was not in possession of such hardened methods of avoidance. Too, those with assertive psychopathic traits very often tried to test the strength of staff relationships by attempting to analyze the personalities of the psychiatrist and psychologists. Only when this type of patient could be made to realize his defensiveness, its lack of constructive gains, and the fact that the participants readily admitted to anxiety and refused to "play God" were the slightest improvements forthcoming. The latter ploy was always used to deal with the unrealistic schizophrenic view of himself as monopolizing all the anxiety in the world. (" . . . you'll always have problems and some anxiety. The important thing is what you do about it.")

Volunteers and many hospital workers report that patients become more meaningful to them as people struggling blindly with anxiety. Generally these participants have been exposed to Kraepelinian lectures with a touch of Freudian pessimism. It is oftentimes a long road before these people reach a point where they believe they can add something very positive to the determiners of another person's behavior, e. g., aid in the development of a humanistic identification.

Discussion

The greatest potential for future exploration is naturally that of psychotherapy. Of all the methods extant the approach here presented appears to offer the best setting for increasing self-esteem, teaching of a hopeful theory or philosophy of emotional disturbance, and ensuring that the resulting insights will be practiced.

Psychodrama could be used for both theoretical research and diagnosis, although the former has not yet been attempted here and the latter has been generally frowned upon. It is fairly difficult to make a determined subject-object stance and put the patient under the descriptive diagnostic microscope when one sees the slow improvement in symptoms and is part of this growth process oneself. If we had a standard Adlerian diagnosis combining self-esteem, compensatory fantasy, and social skills, psychodrama would be the ideal setting for this measurement. For which is the better technique for understanding: Asking a patient about his adjustment in a structured interview, or combining this with actual experience with a surrogate?

Yet we do not want to overvalue the influence of this kind of psychodrama. It is merely an hour or two a week in the patient's existence. Unlearning and relearning cannot take place quickly, if at all, in a setting where the influence of learning is hardly mentioned. The patient's internal negative reinforcements, the family's unverbalized neurotic needs,[7] the Babel of theories (mostly accentuating hopelessness), the lack of material and interpersonal rewards and even punishments, . neglect of a program for teaching social skills, the dearth of release alternatives when relatives will not cooperate, and even the national policy to reward materially the continued

7

avoidance of interpersonal relationships (i. e., monetary compensation), all combine to tempt the therapist with the belief that he is Sisyphus reincarnated.

Still, if patients are hospitalized because their behavior bothers others[6] and are usually motivated by their denial-of-relationships with people,[10] what treatment is more appropriate than that which aims to desensitize fears and develop social interest? Mowrer[14] has a point which bears thinking about when he writes that schizophrenics have low self-esteem because their actions merit this. It is true that much of their future feelings of worth will follow from the insight developed in human interactions, some of which will have been afforded by psychodrama. If our mental hospitals were to subscribe to a non- "rejection mechanism"[6] approach without providing personnel trained in an Adlerian orientation, the result would be catastrophic. Merely accepting psychological treatment as the *modus operandi* is no answer. One still must decipher the abstractions (e. g. "get patient to identify with you," "do supportive psychotherapy and strengthen defenses") to realize one's part in developing I-thou encounters.

Summary

Psychodrama groups for hospitalized mental patients are described. Founded on the ideas of Moreno, the original group soon switched to an Adlerian emphasis. The change was motivated by the relative ease in communicating Adlerian premises and the fact that they make sense in treating schizophrenia. Some of Moreno's techniques are still used but the core of the rationale is based upon the Adlerian triad of low self-esteem, avoidance of reality, and poor social skills.

REFERENCES

1. Adler, K. A. Life style in schizophrenia. *J. Indiv. Psychol.*, 1958, 14, 68-72.

2. Arieti, S. Hallucinations, delusion, and ideas of reference treated with psychotherapy. *Amer. J. Psychother.*, 1962, 15, 52-60.

3. Bateson, G., Jackson, D., Haley, J., and Weakland, J., Toward a theory of schizophrenia. *Beh. Sci.*, 1956, 1, 251-264.

4. Corsini, R. J. The method of psychodrama in prison. *Group Psychother.*, 1951, 3, 321-326.

5. Ellis, A. *Reason and emotion in psychotherapy.* New York: Lyle Stuart, 1962.

6. Ewalt, J. *Action for mental health.* New York: Basic Books, 1961.

7. Fleck, S. Family dynamics and origin of schizophrenia. *Psychosom. Med.*, 1960, 22, 333-344.

8. Gallagher, F., and Albert, R. The Gelbdor affair. *Psychiatry*, 1961, 24, 221-227.

9. Haley J. An interactional description of schizophrenia. *Psychiatry*, 1959, 22, 321-332.

10. Haley, J. Control in psychotherapy with schizophrenics. *Arch. gen. Psychiat.*, 1961, 5, 340-353.

11. Moreno, Zerka T. A survey of psychodramatic techniques. *Group Psychother.*, 1959, 12, 5-14.

12. Mowrer, O. H. *The crisis in psychiatry and religion.* Princeton, N.J.: Van Nostrand, 1961.

13. Mowrer, O. H. Even there, thy hand. *Chicago theol. Semin. Register*, 1962, 52, 1-17.

14. Mowrer, O. H. Personal communication. 1962.

15. Shoobs, N. E. The application of Individual Psychology through psychodramatics. *Indiv. Psychol. Bull.*, 1946, 5, 3-21.

16. Shoobs, N. E., Individual Psychology and psychodrama. *Amer. J. Indiv. Psychol.*, 1956, 12, 45-52. Also in K. A. Adler and Danica Deutsch (Eds.), *Essays in Individual Psychology,* New York: Grove Press, 1959. pp. 280-289.

17. Shulman, B. H. A psychodramatically oriented action technique in group psychotherapy. *Group Psychother.*, 1960, 13, 34-39.

18. Starr, Adaline. The role of psychodrama in a child guidance center. *Indiv. Psychol. Bull.*, 1951, 9, 18-24.

19. Starr, Adaline. Psychodrama with a family. *Group Psychother.*, 1959, 12, 27-31.

20. Starr, Adaline and Fogel, E. Training state hospital personnel through psychodrama and sociometry. *Group Psychother.*, 1961, 14, 55-61.

21. Szasz, T. S. The myth of mental illness. *Amer. Psychologist.* 1960, 15, 113-118.

PSYCHODRAMA: INVOLVING THE AUDIENCE

Writings of those who study the behavior of competent psychotherapists agree on at least two important points: the therapist must live an optimist theory, and be motivated to be an exemplary model of the gains of social interest. Many of the well-known psychological views of man attempt to abstract his experiences into concepts of physiological or psychological fatalism. They do not appeal to ordinary man nor do they seek to explain his vicissitudes in his own tongue. If the therapist really believes such dehumanizing views (at least for categorizing his patients, but probably not himself) he is not likely to be a therapeutic influence for those who are unfortunate enough to identify with him.

Our first premise is that actions in the world follow mainly from our habitual responses to *inner reactions*. Subtly we place our meaning on the world and all the "traumata" of life are kept alive by our internalized sentences (or negative nonsense).[2][3][4] As Ellis has aptly put it, many of our problems are engendered by the *B element* of his A-B-C theory (A: external world; B: inner preceptions, internalized sentences; C: reactive behavior). When we make too many demands of people and these are unsatisfied, we experience all the expressions of and defenses against reactive hatred. Of course, this is one of the lessons we never tire of reiterating, since its manifestations are so common, but the B element and goals of behavior go unrecognized.

Our view of behavior problems over the years has been that psychopathology is essentially a denial of responsible living following from a failure to identify with suitable models of behavior (and maintained by internalized sentences). This does not mean that we preach and punish the patient for his past, but rather focus on responsible actions for the future, as a prelude to a more fruitful existence.

Reprinted from Rational Living, 1967, Vol. 2.

In this respect our goals have much in common with Glasser's[7] aim of responsibility as learning to satisfy one's needs without blocking those of others. Shoben's[14] definition of responsibility is similar: Admission of alternative responses rather than fatalism; complying with one's promises; and acceptance of mistakes. (Did you ever realize that there is no room for the primacy of ignorance, stupidity, or panic-inspired behavior—only hostility/sexuality—in psychoanalytic theory?)

In these years there is increasing attention given to this explanation of pathology, to the extent that all the classic schizophrenic symptoms are regarded as elements of the attempted denial of reality.[8] Therefore in our transactions with our patients we seek as much as possible to avoid rewarding these defensive maneuvers of "negative nonsense" by refusing to reject and anger the patient, or to send him off to bed, pill, needle and shock under the guise of necessary treatment. Of course since we are all presumably "simply more human than otherwise" we do have our limits of tolerance.

Our techniques are used as aids to foster new *practices* and more hopeful *experiences* for our patients. They are decidedly secondary to the atmosphere of the group, which cannot in itself be fostered by rote movements but only by open sincerity and warmth. This group-cohesiveness must be one of freedom of discussion, leveling with each other, using whenever possible the words of the patient group. Of course the therapists' tactics should follow as deductions from an optimist theory of social learning. In this fashion, the hypocritical, defensive double-bind method[8] of creating "disease" is avoided, thus lessening the opportunity for the patient to learn to be a disheartened chronic psychotic. The timing is very important to our way of thinking, therefore techniques are not employed merely to show that the director knows them all or to confuse the patients with his "omniscience." We see ourselves as *educators* and the patients as reluctant students clinging to their negative views out of reaction to past interactions.

The *content* of the tutoring is mainly how to work for esteem from others (the basis of self-esteem) rather than suffer from all types of neuroses and psychosis as immature reactions to unfullfilled demands.

11

Adlerian therapy therefore differs from the Moreno type which aims at spontaneity and catharsis. Spontaneity without outsight does not seem to be the hallmark of social living, and its appearance in the therapy group is the result of mutual trust and non-punitiveness. Catharsis (emotional release) is used generally outside of the therapy group, along with a non-directive approach (reflection of the patient's feelings) to stimulate the initial growth of relatedness. In our mode of psychodrama, the patient's difficult situation is enacted, followed by what he could now do if he "felt different and started to practice reaching his goals with people." An Adlerian psychodrama group endeavors to bring many of the members into a discussion of the commonalities of people, and participation in problem-solving activity. By its very nature it is less detached than a group which follows a reductionistic intra-psychic philosophy.

An atmosphere of humor is often mentioned, especially as a precondition for certain techniques.[5][6][9][15] What these therapists seem to mean by "humor" is the playful mood underlying the structured situation.[13] This type of controlled levity seems to work best when the patient's behavior shows he *relates* positively to the therapist; when the material the patient is discussing has been *worked-over* between the therapist and patient, thereby giving the patient at least intellectual awareness of his A-B-C pairings; and when the patient's symptoms seem to be more *habitual* than motivated by panic and extreme anxiety. Under these circumstances, the patient can be an object of wit, provided the therapist will level and play-fair with the patient. He must consent to be the object of wit himself and not double-bind the patient. Or if the wit does hurt, he should be willing to at least discuss the *why's* in a general manner and not subtly reject the patient.

Another form of double-bind which occasionally passes for therapy is noted in encouraging the patient to express feelings, then moralizing against them. This bad communication is a form of "spokemanship" or "mind reading": "Oh, you don't feel that way." To prevent this mistake, we must accept feelings as part of learned responses, and work toward future changes.

Seventeen of the core techniques follow, but one should bear in mind that nothing is sacred about techniques *per se.* In fact the possibility of devising other methods for combatting avoidance, and learning and practicing outsight, are unlimited. Again one should stress to the participants the *learning* of attitudes and behaviors, the expectation of the patient's feeling nervous on stage, and not "do battle" unsuccessfully to get a patient onto the stage. The art of one-upmanship[8] teaches us that to maintain control over an impossible patient one should have an attitude of "If it's your decision, I'll let you," when more positive resources are unavailable.

1) *Role Presentations*—This of course is the crux of the psychodrama; the protagonist (or "star") giving his account, in action, of the problem. He should be encouraged to move about freely and give his description of the physical set-up and people involved in general terms. It is well to have a minimum of chairs on stage until needed; sitting down, in the beginning, might lessen involvement.

2) *Mirror Technique*—A fine device to get recalcitrant patients on stage. He refuses and you offer to play his part. If you do a poor job he generally inches up to take over. If you portray his part according to his perceptions he might say to himself, "He really knows me and doesn't reject me . . . Maybe I can trust him a bit."

3) *Role Reversal*—An excellent device for patients to learn outsight; an awareness of the needs of others, and how to win esteem. Roles are reversed when the patient is involved in demanding behavior. The conversation is continued and reversed when the patient (in another role—say, of the father) makes demands. The patient then responds as patient to demands that he made as father.

4) *Doubling*—A volunteer stands with or behind the patient, verbalizing hidden feelings of defeat, discouragement, failure, triumph, etc. Only the patient is supposed to hear, since the double represents his thoughts; so no one converses with the double. When the patient trusts the group and doesn't show restless and avoiding behavior, this technique can get him moving toward interpersonal problems.

5) *Self-Disclosure*—This behavior is closer to part of a person's style of life than to a practiced technique. In essence, it involves teaching the patient that he is not an isolated, passive victim but is making decisions even if he is unaware of

13

the goals and the action itself. It doesn't imply that one says in effect to the patient "Your problems are really imaginary . . . I had worse ones, but conquered them by myself." The lesson is that others have anxiety, and that repressing and avoiding it only sets up more anxiety and possibly rejection by people in general. Examples: "I don't know about your insomnia, but when I have fear of failure I can't sleep either." "If I didn't have at least one person I could trust, and something to interest me, I'd go crazy, too." "You won't leave the hospital until you experience three months without anxiety? Tell us more about that idea, because anyone who's alive has some anxiety almost everyday." "Sure I have problems, the main one now being that you guys seem to want to sit around for years rather than trust me enough even to yell at me."

6) *Midas Technique*[15]—In a cohesive group, the members satisfy the neurotic and psychotic demands of the patient; either giving him reciprocal demands or getting him to realize that even those won't make life tensionless.

7) *Let's Be Paranoid*[9]—Jackson's method for encouraging patients to *really* look about, to talk of contradictions, and to serve as a behavioral model. The therapist joins the paranoid in looking for evidence of malevolence, but finds more hopeful things as well.

8) *Auxiliaries Acting*—If the group needs direction, auxiliaries portray a double-bind or future projection. Can also be used to show alternative behavior such as "How To Fight Successfully."

9) *Future Projection*—Scenes presented in which the future is enacted. Good for patients who are institutionalized. Overacting to the point of the comic frequently is called for here, as well as in Let's Be Paranoid, Midas, and Paradoxical Intention. Don't give the idea of hopelessness, but the difficulties involved in defensiveness.

10) *Paradoxical Intention*[5] [6]—A method of trying to teach what really amounts to Freudian humor in the phobic patient with anticipatory anxiety. Find out what he is fearful will happen and have him approach the feared symptom as if to excel in it. (e.g. "Drop dead of a heart attack right now, three times.") With the obsessive-compulsive, a chorus of auxiliaries can tell the patient, "To hell with it!" The point here is that

the phobic over-avoids the fearful situation, while the compulsive wears himself out fighting it.

11) *Playing Catch*—During a discussion of non-verbal patients' problems: After the action, others direct questions about the patient to each other, rather than at the balky one. Like the mirror technique, this frequently overcomes resistance and inertia.

12) *Playing-the-Doctor*—This helps a patient to develop outsight into *our* predicaments, and not to see us as arbitrary frustrators. The patient who thinks the doctor should magically cure the patient, or demands that we release all patients, is put into the role of doctor and he interviews others. If he tries to play it easy and give in to all demands of patients, auxiliary egos—playing parents, police, lawyers—dash in to put him down.

13) *Spiking-the-Guns*—Interpretation of the patient's failure to act—as a learned, generalized response to authority figures—now present in the therapy situation: A good antidote for double-binding, since the patient is encouraged to talk to the extent of criticizing the therapist.

14) *The Empty Chair*—When we have families in psychodrama we will have the advantage of seeing the maneuvers by which members confirm or disconfirm each other. Until then, this serves as a device for learning in what way the patient perceives others, and is therefore a good introductory move to start a role presentation. The patient starts conversing with the empty chair. It is surprising how many times patients portray "family disputes" by withdrawal or silence to avoid arguments.

15) *Bind Buster*—This technique is used to dispel the chronic denial-of-denial characteristic of the chronic schizophrenic and engage him in a dialogue in which he will at least implicitly take responsibility for voicing opinions. The director makes extreme generalizations about important groups of people and repeats some until verbal response is forthcoming. For example, one patient said, "I hate to see that doctor's picture on the wall each week." The director remarked, "Don't you know that all doctors are handsome, hard working, and can read minds?" If the patients habituate their formerly-successful frozen silence, the director might retort with a

15

"What's the matter with you guys, just sitting like lumps and letting me get away with such foolish remarks?" The director might then go into a Future Projection (Technique 9) illustrating by action what happens to slaves, even in the best of all possible worlds. All this is aimed at pushing patients out of suffering from—or instigating—double-binds.[8]

16) *How-Easy-It-Is-To-Hate-Everyone*—Nervous paranoids who have been over all their traumata many times in discussions and wonder why they often feel bad are presented with this technique, but this time as a victim. The auxiliary will use the same logic of negative nonsense[4] aloud with the paranoid, which he silently uses on others. The paranoid gets a taste of his own antisocial energizers when he hears, "You are crossing your legs, so you're telling me I'm a queer . . . your hand is doubled up like a fist to hit me . . . your leg is swinging like you want to kick me in the nuts . . ." etc.

17) *Instant Involvement*—This technique was developed by accident, upon the introduction of a patient hospitalized continuously for 18 years. The director played the patient's part, since the withdrawn patient had no "guardian"[11] or anyone whom he accepted. From familiarity with the identification and goals of patients who write pleading and threatening letters to authorities, the director verbalized a defeated life style. The new member became an involved unofficial spokesman, or double, for the director, referring to the latter continuously in the second person—as if he were the detached superego and the therapist his ego. Help was asked from each patient, and the advice given was parried by the director's pointing out unsuccessful examples:

> A Patient: Be neat and clean and do everything the personnel tell you to do.
> Director: But look at Ed! He's neat and clean and nobody gives a damn. He just sits. I need powerful help, and I'll write to president. He's stronger than my father. But I'm afraid to ask, or tell him how I feel about my world. I'll tell him he's going to die . . . But I don't want to kill him. I'm afraid everything is dying. Then I must burn my fingers and punish myself before he punishes me worse . . .

By steering each patient's advice to another patient who either doesn't follow it or does concur, with no apparent results, the whole group is keenly aware of the shared problems.

The patient is spared "being picked on" while others feel safer with their assertion toward the better-known director. The detached superego pours out the details of feared objects and feared negative identities which are reflected in feelings but parried with defensive games of the director-as-patient. All are then turned loose to solve the life style portrayed, with the new patient being given first priority.

Warm-up techniques are not mentioned here, but one recommended method is to let the group develop its own theme and protagonist.

In summary the goal is to overcome *avoidance*, give *encouragement*, teach *outsight* and to give non-punitive *practice* in social skills. We strive to understand the patient according to his learned life style.

REFERENCES

1. Bell, R. Psychodrama techniques. Formal papers presented at psychodrama workshop, VA Hospital, Waco, Texas, April 2-3, 1964.

2. Ellis, A. Rational psychotherapy. *J. Gen. Psychol.*, 1958, 59, 35-49.

3. Ellis, A. Marriage counseling with demasculinizing and demasculinized husbands. *Marriage and Family Living*, 1960, 22, 13-21.

4. Ellis, A. *Reason and emotion in psychotherapy*, N. Y.: Lyle Stuart, 1962.

5. Frankl, V. *Man's search for meaning: an introduction to logotherapy*, N. Y.: Washington Square Press, 1963. (Paperback, 60ᶜ)

6. Gerz, H. The treatment of the phobic and the obsessive-compulsive patient using paradoxical intention. Sec. Viktor E. Frankl. *J. Neuropsychiat.*, 1962, 3, 375-387.

7. Glasser, W. *Reality therapy*. N. Y.: Harper & Row, 1965.

8. Haley, J. *Strategy of psychotherapy*. N. Y.: Grune & Stratton, 1963.

9. Jackson, D. Suggestion for the technical handling of paranoid patients. *Psychiatry*, 1963, 26, 306-307.

10. O'Connell, W. Adlerian psychodrama with schizophrenics. *J. Indiv. Psychol.*, 1963, 19, 69-76.

11. O'Connell, W. Psychotherapy for everyman: A look at action therapy. Formal papers presented at psychodrama workshop, VA Hospital, Waco, Texas, April 2-3, 1964.

12. O'Connell, W. Psychodrama: Communications and life style. Formal papers presented at Psychodrama workshop, VA Hospital, Waco, Texas, April 22-23, 1965.

13. Riessman, F. New approaches to mental health treatment for labor and low income groups. National Institute of Labor Education, 250 West 57th Street, New York 19, New York (50¢).

14. Shoben, E. Personal responsibility, determinism and the burden of understanding. *Pers. and Guid. J.*, 1961, 39, 342-348.

15. Shulman, B. Use of dramatic confrontation in group psychotherapy. *Psychiat. Quart. Supp.*, 1962, 1, Part 1, 1-7.

STROKING AND SPITTING

This is the tale of an "eight year itch," an attempt to introduce methods of Action Therapy which would motivate staff and patients to give up the Blame Game and practice leveling. This is quite a task, for of all the traditions that change rapidly today only the mental hospital seems immune to any radically novel perceptions. Today we still have a horde of "acute" patients fighting for attention and miraculous cures. They are stored in what, historically speaking have usually been warehouses for undesirably behaving people who do not break the written law (or who do so in a "crazy" way).

These panicky people are sandwiched between two isolated classes of vastly different status. The chronic patient is often sufficiently filthy and foul-mouthed to scare others away without triggering an escalation in treatment (e.g., silencing tranquilizing drugs, and shock). He DEMANDS to be left alone to find evidence for his greatness via his circuitous asocial logic. At the opposite end of the continuum is the staff person, oftentimes maintaining the ritual of "running psycho-therapy" and likewise DEMANDING—to be adored passively. One who is in a state of demanding dependency upon another is an apt candidate for a double bind, particularly so when this situation is denied. Therefore at times the doctor may be trapped by the patient whenever the former demands the privilege of being reacted to in a certain way, without "the labor pains" of trying to understand others. Hostility must be expressed very indirectly and irresponsibly by both the master(-slave) and slave(-master) through the incurability myth and "mad" symptoms.

Any mortal who tries to disrupt such games is a fool indeed, but his fate often makes good reading for the next generation.[2][3][4] Believe it or not, however, an active program

Paper presented at the American Society of Adlerian Psychology meetings, New York City, May 1967, under the title of "Team Therapy: An Antidote for the Double Bind."

Reprinted from *The Individual Psychologist*, 1967, 5, 29-31.

did spring up which brought out the best in staff-people and patient-people. Unfortunately, it withered away with the departure of staff who believed there was better "stroking" elsewhere. Of equal-contribution to the defeat was the undemocratic hierarchy which spreads the patient out over many people, only one of which has the mandate to stop or start the flow of patients.

Throughout the life of the Action Therapy program in the traditional setting there was the steady movement of hundreds of patients and scores of personnel. After the first traumatic shock of being together without the techniques of dogma, new tactics of teaching and learning outsight and insight developed slowly. The goals eventually became five in number:

1. *Practice and feedback* on behavior in a social setting.
2. Maintenance of an *authentic team* by mutual working out of goals for patients, feelings toward each other, and acceptance of criticism and failure.
3. *Diagnosis* of patients in current stress or situations.
4. *Training in empathy* or being put in the other guy's spot and bombarded with our own demands.
5. *Theory development.* Even if no one improved, one might be interested in noting the whys.

The team therapy concept was this: that concurrently with giving therapy, staff needs its own. The presence of DEMANDS and reactive frustrations must be examined. Staff as well as patient "negative nonsense" bears watching. This is what is doubled in action learning: Not the repressed hostility" toward "cruel frustrators"—but attitudes, behavior, and goals toward other people.

The therapeutic tactics can best be described as STROKE AND SPIT—and perhaps a bit of unpretentious laughter. It may be that this *simultaneous* stroking and spitting is what makes the good therapist. "Stroking" consists of the therapist giving the patient time and effort "to see with his eyes and listen with his ears"[1] and to reward and encourage signs of courage (active social interest). Correct stroking infers that one also perceives the skillful maneuvers of the patient—as he seeks to avoid intimacy and to hate others. All techniques in this Action Therapy had the goal of exposing the person's childish DEMANDS and the abstract reactive blaming of *himself* ("I'm not good now and forever") and *others* ("people are always unchangeably no damned good") as he tries to avoid future loving transactions.

Only a "stroker and spitter" can flourish in Alice's "Wonderland." This action may be the best operational definition of mature brotherly love that we have available today.

REFERENCES

1. Ansbacher, H. L. and Ansbacher, Rowena (Ed.) *The Individual Psychology of Alfred Adler,* New York: Basic Books, 1958.

2. O'Connell, W. Adlerian Psychodrama with Schizophrenics. *J. Ind. Psychol.,* 19, 69-70.

3. O'Connell, W. Psychotherapy for Everyman: A Look at Action Therapy, *J. Exist.,* 1966, 7, No. 25, 85-91.

4. O'Connell, W. Seventeen Psychodrama Techniques. *Rational Living,* 1967, 2, 22-25.

WARD PSYCHOTHERAPY WITH SCHIZOPHRENICS THROUGH CONCERTED ENCOURAGEMENT

This report represents experiences gained over a five-year period while a mental hospital ward, to which the author was attached as psychologist, gradually changed its program for chronic schizophrenics from custodial care to the beginnings of a continuous treatment system. Motivating this approach was the belief, strongly reinforced by empirical events, that applied humanism is not "do-goodism" but the most appropriate curative agent available for schizophrenic sufferers at the present time.

Here schizophrenia is regarded as an extreme reaction of alienation and isolation, which has for many years been of some value to the patient as defense against catastrophically low self-esteem. Viewing low self-respect as a concomitant of the schizophrenic style of life is not a novel idea, but to regard such as "the hard core" of the reaction is a perception that only recently has found new expression in the literature.[2] [10] [11] [15] [32] [36] [38]

One significant aspect of the approach to be reported here is that the psychologist can serve in the novel role of *therapeutic catalyst*, combining facets hitherto considered incapable of a rational synthesis. In addition to interpreting psychological testing and carrying out psychotherapy, he interacts with line personnel,* functioning as philosopher, scientist, and teacher. This is held to be not only a practical but an essential element in expediting psychotherapeutic success with chronic schizophrenics.

For an isolated hospital psychotherapist the task of attempting to cope with the schizophrenic's insatiable hunger

---

*Line personnel is used as a generic term to include personnel who traditionally maintain face-to-face contacts with patients.[34]

Reprinted from *Journal of Individual Psychology*, Vol. 17, 193-204, Nov. 1961.

(and frequent initial indigestion) for esteem is almost over-whelming. Thus we hold that cooperation and "ultimate concern" of hospital personnel for the patient's self-esteem is paramount for psychotherapeutic success, if it is to be more than a monumental *tour de force.*

Ward Learning Sessions

Formal aspects. Gross misperceptions and biases in the reports of the line personnel, and the excessive number of subtle clashes between personnel and patients, which grew from mutual misinformation and irrational expectations, led to the initiation of a teaching program by the ward psychologist with the constant encouragement and support from the ward psychiatrist.** Weekly sessions were attended by 15-20 personnel, mostly nurses and nursing assistants. Others were occupational, corrective, and recreational therapists, and at times chaplains and trainees in psychology.

Our first attempt, the teaching of elementary psychodynamics, was a definite failure, yet must be considered an invaluable learning experience for us. Group silences and signs of boredom (which vanished when the abstract dynamics were centered around an individual patient) told us that the line personnel can be best engaged by couching lectures in *their* terms about *their* problems.***

We then adopted the following procedure. One patient a month was selected from among those mentioned frequently by the nursing group, and presented to the session to illustrate the operation of psychological concepts and dynamics. The remaining weekly meetings during the month revolved about possible ways of helping this patient find reality worth accepting. Psychological reports were usually available. Social and psychiatric material was also given, frequently by the social worker and the psychiatrist. Two needs became evident here: for the rewording of esoteric reports to fit the lowest common

---

**The writer is deeply indebted to Louis W. Leskin, M. D., for providing a living example of the blessings inherent in wearing the crown of status lightly.

***This lesson has even greater ramifications in terms of hospital, and not patient, rigidities. Most hospital programs, from teaching through psychotherapy and all forms of rehabilitation, are conducted primarily out of the covert needs of those directing the activity, with little attention to the needs of the respondent, be he patient or personnel.

denominator of understanding, and for the tactful handling of confidential psychotherapy communication. An increased discussion of patients' problems within the group, and a halt in the clandestine interchange of gossip pertaining to patients' sexual and hostile behavior, gave some clue that these two needs were met tolerably well.

Fourteen patients, male veterans with chronic schizophrenic diagnoses, participating in individual and group psychotherapies, were given this additional indirect treatment by the didactic-discussion-group approach with personnel. All patients had been treated in the past, without remission, by electro-shock, and two by insulin shock. All were on maintenance dosages of tranquilizers, with the exception of two patients whose medication was discontinued during the study, in a non-crucial test of a clinical hypothesis entertained by the author. Ages ranged from 20-39, hospitalization from one to five years, and no first admissions were in the group.

To start the group meeting, the chief complaint of personnel regarding the patient, the "calling card," was used. For example: "Keeps wanting to change assignments." "His constant stare and silly grin scare me." "Always interrupts any aide and nurse talking. Watches us like a 'peeping-tom,' then grabs us with those clammy hands." "He looks like he's got all the physical assets, but he rushes by us and never looks at us. What have we done to him?" "Always looking for a fight, but complains he's picked on." "Wants to sleep all the time."

Each presentation and the following weekly discussions were designed to illustrate important topics in the psychogenesis of schizophrenia from the life style of the individual patient: Indentifications,[9] [12] [30] [33] communications,[19] [20] [25] [27] chronicity,[7] [8] [17] [20] double binds,[5] [18] [19] [24] manifestation of the "core theory",[23] [38] types of "love",[6] [22] [33] [37] etc.

Psychodynamics were explored mainly in terms of operation in the daily life of the average man and couched in such learning theory terms as to capture the interest of ward personnel. Personnel then interviewed the patient and vice versa, with mutual edification.

Content and theory. This in *essence* is the theory presented in the weekly sessions, in the terminology used.

Whatever the etiology of schizophrenia may be, in many cases a necessary (but perhaps not sufficient) causal factor is a primary family relationship in which the victim learns very definitely and early in life a belief that he is worthless, helpless, hopeless and defenseless against a hostile alien world. Such a lonely *Weltschmerz* develops in a habitual "double binding" atmosphere in which a correct recognition of human motives is never rewarded and massive denial and avoidance become the values of existence.[5] [18] [19] The inner universe of the victim becomes a veritable hell-on-earth, and subsequent catastrophic interpersonal experiences serve strongly to reinforce his rigid myopic philosophy of life. "I am unlovable; I am worthless." Along with such low self-esteem there are failure of a positive, integrated "I feeling," and perceived complete ineffectualness and weakness. It is no wonder that such a nonentity flounders in a morass of excessive demands on others, and reacts with intolerable hostility of which he may be unaware, but which is reflected to others in his bizarre symptoms. He is the proverbial drowning man attempting to clutch at or swallow (and simultaneously avoid) straws of affection. Often, by a highly developed system of denials and compensation, he displays the brittle facade of grandiosity.

Our core concept of schizophrenic dis-ease, then, is an untoward response to a deficiency of essential self-esteem. No substantial improvement can take place without the involvement of this core process. The latest preferred panacea, the tranquilizer, in spite of its value as an antidote to anxiety, has failed to live up to its advanced miracle-drug publicity. In gross terms, temperament or energy out-flow can at present be medically manipulated, but an individual's response to objects, other people, and the self, must initially be learned via reinforcement from others, for the most part.

Our formulation, arrived at empirically and from many other sources, parallels the Adlerian characterization of schizoprenia.

> Due to the greater self-centeredness it engenders, a greater feeling of inferiority interferes with the development of social interest. Such a child . . . will, of necessity, have a hard time in the pursuit of his goals; his mode of operation is based on exploitation of others . . . He is bound to find increasing opposition as soon as he steps outside the limits of his family group. The outside world,

25

therefore, will seem to him increasingly made up of enemies who frustrate his desires. The fictional goal of his self, or his greatness, will become so threatened that he will tend to withdraw from people and real life problems which all demand cooperation for their solutions. Lacking the social feeling of belonging, all people will appear to him as enemies . . . for he cannot, in such a negativistic state, imagine others to be cooperative (2, p. 70).

Effects on Personnel

Understanding the patient. We assume that an individual's behavior is isomorphic with his constructs, meanings, philosophy, or world-design. His actions vis-a-vis chronic schizophrenics are partly decided by what schizophrenia connotes to him. It is my most unequivocal piece of learning from ten years as an aide and psychologist, that in spite of the effort which has been expended in lectures on understanding and accepting patients, the non-therapeutic biases have changed very little, if at all. Line personnel seldom realize the restorative values of *understanding* because the word is isolated from the remainder of the treatment theory, and impersonal, peripheral aspects of training are highlighted. Initially, discussion periods were occupied with observations by personnel of patient behavior worded in abstract phrases. Many times such reports were almost caricatures of psychological reports. But when members of staff and patient populations develop concern for the self-esteem theory and begin to do their "homework" (studious attempts to perceive themselves and others from the core perspective), noticeable and often remarkable changes occur. Peripheral matters of routinized care drop out of discussions, and the penchant for interpretations based on word magic decreases sharply.

The more easily understood self-esteem core theory not only increased healthy interest in the patient, but also gave personnel a more optimistic orientation to patient treatment.

At the same time, discussion groups tended to encourage a healthy detachment from the patient whenever personnel became overly enthusiastic and preoccupied with a particular individual.

Seeing patients like oneself. One function of the unstructured discussion periods was the reduction of a rigid dichotomy between patient and personnel. It is difficult to imagine therapeutic concern emanating from personnel who perceive a vast gulf between themselves and schizophrenia and are so mesmerized by the jargon of professionals as to discount completely their own possible value in the treatment process. When schizophrenia loses some of its mystical aura and becomes more a matter of the patient's "being" than his "having" something (a virus, a communicable disease, etc.), progress is made in the worker's ability to relate to the patient. Research with the dyad[13] and empathy[26] corroborates the view that meaningful relationships are formed not by accident but by perceiving others as being essentially like ourselves.

The discussions brought out that *everyone is alike*, e.g., in the necessity for a certain amount of self-esteem for mental health, based upon satisfaction of psychological and physiological needs through the "loving"[22] concern of the self and/or significant others. Yet in another perspective, *everyone is different*, e.g., possessing varying amounts of self-esteem and different gestalts of learned motives and values.

Joining with staff. Another function of the weekly sessions was to break down the barrier between line personnel and staff. When staff remains exclusive, over-zealous beginning therapists, adjured to achieve an understanding participation with patients, sometimes reverse identification with patients,[27] or develop guilt over a presumed lack of patient progress.[28] When staff and line interact in these discussions, removing exclusiveness, with mutual acceptance of a self-esteem core theory, they both will view their parts in the treatment process more realistically. They will see that one can by his actions enhance patients' self-respect (or self-hatred) but that he is no *deus ex machina.*

Gaining status and stability. The realization of the personnel member's unique contribution to the treatment process should increase his status in his own estimation and in that of patients. One may assume that everyone may potentially be able to establish a satisfying relationship with a patient on a tension-reduction basis, but that a person's significance as a model of secondary identification will vary with his status (earned or reflected) in the eyes of patients.

The program has *quid pro quo* tenets. Personnel attempting to help a patient toward greater stability and maturity, are thereby contributing to their own continuing stability. Humanistic attitudes are good medicine in general, and people

27

fall sick because of the habitual want of such feelings in themselves. The reward from such attitudes is not other-worldly "pie-in-the-sky," but in substantial returns from social hedonism,[16] and understanding and respect for the human foibles in oneself.

Applications, Specific Techniques

We now come to the central question: What can people do to aid others suffering from rigid negative ideation and consequential emotions? Initially, the therapist's total efforts are directed toward reducing tensions and becoming a significant secondary reinforcer.[30] Usually simple acts such as giving information, listening without demanding, displaying various facets of "warmth,"[27] and a thorough faith in the patient's own potential for improvement with the support of others, precipitate rudimentary movements toward people. The successful therapist gives the immediate impression of "strength" and "friendliness,"[38] that is, the ability to satisfy the patient's needs and the inclination to do so.

A complete and simple account of a therapeutic attitude in line with our core theory which is also a part of Adlerian theory can be found in Kurt Adler.

Letting one's foibles show. Personal involvement in the form of anecdotes highlighting the therapist's foibles tends to correct the schizophrenic delusion that sick patients have problems and normals are always happy and omnipotent. These ploys also minimize the transference potentialities encouraged by a shadowy, withholding authority figure. An honest expressive relationship with the patient frequently reduces his delusions that he has no positive impact and a wholly derogatory effect on other people. The disrupting possibilities of the patient expecting too much from the therapist and hating him for perceived neglect, or expecting extreme rejection and cowering from authority, are handled by rapid confrontations. In psychodrama, for example, the psychiatrist or psychologist playing the patient's roles in a double binding, infantilizing family scene might readily admit his feelings of anxiety and hopelessness (e.g. "How can anyone handle this situation except by feeling powerful enough to leave them alone, without hate and loneliness? I sure couldn't live here! Can You?"

Repetition. One of the neglected techniques of psychotherapy, repetition,[14] assumes great importance; e.g. repetition of appropriate segments of the core theory, repetitions of alternative responses to that of "bad"-patient-happy-rejecting-authority compulsion, repetitions of encouragement and rewards for success.

Self-help. When personnel in discussion groups receive the impact of the importance of their own awareness of the context, their feelings and goals, upon their perception of patients' actions, they are wont, like the typical psychotherapy patient, to request oracular assistance from the psychotherapist. They want to be told what to do for, or to, the patient. Rather than refer them to some unconscious motives of their own,[28] we simply offer them encouragement to search their own consciousness for suitable alternatives and, if such are not forthcoming, we give direct answers with appropriate reasons. The hope motivating these tactics is that through increased contacts of this type, line personnel will focus more upon their own personality resources as secondary reinforcers to aid the patient and demand no continuous support from others.

Results

The goal of this pilot approach to spreading therapeutic effectivenes was to inculcate line personnel with a theory of schizophrenia which would motivate them to avoid actions which might compound schizophrenic unworthiness, and to reinforce the patients' struggle to realize human values.

In spite of the lack of conclusive statistics and controls, this tentative approach must be judged successful. Ten of the fourteen patients exposed to this "total psychological push" therapy derived from the core theory of schizophrenia have been making satisfactory extra-hospital adjustment for from one to eighteen months. To be sure, this fact in itself does not demonstrate the efficacy of work with line personnel, for in some instances the changes have come about from efforts by relatives in that direction. More evidence comes from the ward atmosphere, where clashes between patients and line personnel have become less frequent.

A typical case showing the kind of effect achieved with the new understanding by personnel is that of SS. SS was a living composite of classic schizophrenic symptoms. His sensitivity to perceive rebuffs extended to uncontrolled sobbing whenever his name was called for medicine. Like most chronic schizophrenics he never had a friend or developed social skills. His primitive efforts to engage attention (and satisfy other needs as well) included clasping arms of other patients and intruding into any conversation. He soon ran afoul of a nursing assistant who adamantly prohibited such displays of "homosexuality" and precipitated a storm of nail-biting and tearing of clothes by the patient. When the nursing assistant was able to ignore such behavior, mindful of letting be until SS's self-esteem was increased, improvement was more steady. SS has recently entered a foster home and is engaged in community welfare work.

General patient-personnel interaction has increased. A psychodrama group was formed in which personnel have been eager to take part. Another new activity is a monthly picnic of patients and personnel, from psychiatrist to nursing assistant. In this connection the popular remark of the thawing patient is, "Well, so doctors are human after all." To this remark one might add that personnel are making the same inferences about patients.

> . . . the main weapon in combatting the schizophrenic's style of life (is) encouragement, and . . . to cure schizophrenia, first of all, the physician must be more hopeful than the patient. Second, the therapist must become the first meaningful relationship that the patient ever had, by use of the kindliest and friendliest approach and by unfailing, constant cooperation and obvious interest in the patient and his welfare. At the same time, the therapist must be constantly aware of the patient's exaggerated sensitivity to even the slightest hints at humiliation. This approach has to be continued until the patient becomes convinced that fruitful cooperation with another human being is possible, until he becomes more hopeful as to the achievement of some of his goals, and until he learns to feel less of an isolate, and more like a fellow human being (2 p. 72).

As others put it, "Allow the patient self-expression without ever taking away from his impoverished self-esteem, until he can maintain self-esteem in the shared world with others" (36, p. 78).

Emphasize the positive; ignore the negative. When line personnel become sensitive to the fears and anxieties of the individual who regards himself as flagrantly weak, alienated from his own human powers, and uncontrovertibly separated from others, they can also understand how "little things mean a lot" in establishing relationships with such individuals. The frequency of "What's the matter with you?" and "You don't look very good today" decrease, as ward personnel comprehend the potentially destructive influence a few words can have. Once the value of people in treatment becomes a conviction with personnel (still a rarity) and they begin to acquire a rational view on rewards and punishments, they appreciate the maxim of changing what can be changed and ignoring what cannot, i.e., rewarding behavior in which the patient behaves in an essentially human manner, and ignoring untoward incidents. This attitude of letting-be is perhaps best exemplified in the rational psychotherapy of Ellis.[16] Adler put it well in these words:

> It is the greatest mistake to expect an insane person to act as a normal person. Almost everyone is annoyed and irritated because the insane do not respond like ordinary beings. They do not eat, they tear their clothes, and so on. Let them do it. There is no other possibility of helping them (1, pp. 316-317).

If we can precipitate no "good," we should at least not instigate any "bad" through untoward emotion reactions to patient's behavior. A key prohibition is never to reinforce general statements of unworthiness such as "I am bad and cannot change." Line personnel are instructed to ignore such and give attention to more positive responses. Once the initial relationship is solidified, the psychotherapist becomes more adamant in his refusal to brook such defeat-laden statements. As an example, the patient might be informed: "I'm aware you've had these feelings about yourself for a long time. They came about because experiences have led you to think of yourself as worthless and unchangeable. But I won't stand for that kind of talk. Judging from what you say, I like you more than you do. I want to hear good things about you. What do you think of that?" Some of the strongest emotional reactions of futility are emitted by schizophrenic patients when they are encouraged to mention "good things," even among those who were previously considered grandiose and narcissistic.

Humor. The dictum "ignore the behavior and act deaf and blind whenever it occurs," finds much supporting evidence in research and anecdotes,[4] and is perhaps the substrate of humor. Humor in this sense is the way Freud uses the term, as a non-hostile jest in the face of inescapable stress, in contrast to wit which he defines as hostile.[21] The ability to formulate and/or appreciate the humorous retort might be regarded as everyman's *desideratum*.[31] Like wit, it is in some circumstances a relatively innocuous release mechanism for frustration. Even so, humor is an extremly rare and neglected virtue, and its appearance has never been encouraged within the hospital setting. All too frequently the bias of staff personnel has been to analyze away such "acting out" propensities. In small doses this anodyne for tensions frequently leads to the recognition of problems nurtured by institutional life, and thereby precludes destructive double binding by organizations which harbor extensive denials as a *modus operandi*.[5] The remedial device of humor therefore warrants considerable attention.

Discussion

Gains have certainly accrued, but the going has been rough. Anyone familiar with the social structure of traditional mental hospitals must be aware of the terrific inertia to change which can be brought to bear both from the top and the bottom of the hierarchy.[29] The frequent threat to medical omniscience posed by psychology results in chronic double binding from the apex. Sometimes one can almost hear the silent prayer for the "good old days" and for the demise of psychology.[3] [35] There are still wards where psychiatrists will not work with psychologists or social workers, and the main treatment is making the patients swallow pills and push lawn mowers (i.e., "industrial therapy").

From the other end of the totem pole, line personnel can set up their own barriers which are equally difficult to obviate. Evening and night shifts are not available for meetings and have offered much passive resistance. Their brand of omniscience is less glaring but nevertheless formidable. They have had years of "experience," so they know how "to handle" patients. The islands of non-authoritarian treatment where therapists can admit to puzzlement are small and the seas of omnipotence wild and engulfing.

There is no intention here to present therapeutic interventions with schizophrenics as a sinecure. Certainly, when a schizophrenic spends a lifetime derogating himself and the world and fearing retaliation and annihilation, he does not easily slough this view. What is described here is a directive method of psychotherapy which has a goal of moving the schizophrenic back into the world of reality without panic. Providing the patient with gratifying reality experiences and rewards for re-entering the human race is the big challenge and the Gordian knot of any therapy program and provides one of the salient indictments against the conventional mental hospital. Psychotherapy succeeds to the extent it aids in replacing the schizophrenic equivalent of "I am worthless forever and will be annihilated because of my weakness" with "I am human and worthy of living a fairly happy life." The therapist operates as a reinforcer of high incentive value from consistent association with need reduction. Therapeutic strategy calls for obviating generalized and intense self-accusations, and for reinforcing assertion, humor, and all positive human responses in patients (and personnel at times).

Summary

This paper reports on a complex project which includes the following aspects: The ward psychologist's traditional role of tester-therapist *in vacuo* is expanded to include teaching, case presentations, and group work with line personnel. By this method line personnel are instructed in their value as people in the total treatment program. The frame of reference is a core theory of schizophrenia as habitually deflated self-esteem with consequent dependent-reactive hostility. The approach to the patient is general encouragement rather than specific attack on symptoms. Results were judged successful in that 10 out of the 14 patients involved have made good extra-hospital adjustment, ward relations are much improved, and there is more interaction between all the personnel and patients. The paper gives form and content of the training sessions, gains from them for both patients and personnel, and specific therapeutic techniques employed.

REFERENCES

1. Ansbacher, H. L. and Ansbacher, Rowena (Ed.). *The Individual Psychology of Alfred Adler.* New York: Basic Books, 1958.

2. Adler, K. A. Life style in schizophrenia. *J. Indiv. Psychol.*, 1958, 14, 68-72.

3. Ausubel, D. Relationships between psychology and psychiatry: the hidden issues. *Amer. Psychologist*, 1956, 11, 99-105.

33

4. Ayllon, T., and Michael, J. The psychiatric nurse as a behavioral engineer. *J. exp. Anal. Behav.*,1959, 4, 323-334.

5. Bateson, G., Jackson, D., Haley, J., and Weakland, J. Toward a theory of Schizophrenia. *Behav. Sci.*, 1956, 1, 251-264.

6. Bordin, E. S. Inside the therapeutic hour. In E. A. Rubenstein & M. B. Parloff (Eds.), *Research in psychotherapy.* Washington, D. C.: Amer. Psychol. Assoc., 1959. Pp. 235-246.

7. Borman, L. D. The chronic patient in hospital culture. *V. A. Newsltr Coop. Res. Psychol.*, 1960, 2, 7-11.

8. Boverman, M. Rigidity, chronicity, schizophrenia. *AMA Arch. gen. Psychiat.*, 1959, 1, 235-242.

9. Bronfenbrenner, U. Freudian theories of identification and their derivatives. *Child Develpm.*, 1960, 31, 15-40.

10. Brooks, G. W., Deane, W. N. & Ansbacher, H. L. Rehabilitation of Chronic schizophrenic patients for social living. *J. Indiv. Psychol.*, 1960, 16, 189-196.

11. Bullard, D. M. Psychotherapy of paranoid patients. *AMA Arch. gen. Psychiat.*, 1960, 2, 137-141.

12. Burton, R. V., & Whiting, J. W. M. *The absent father: effects on the developing child.* Washington, D. C.: Nat. Inst. Ment. Hlth, 1960.

13. Byrne, D. Interpersonal attraction and attitude dissimilarity. Paper read at Southwest. Psychol. Ass., Galveston, Texas, April, 1960.

14. Cameron, D. Images of tomorrow. *Amer. J. Psychother.*, 1960, 14, 97-103.

15. Davis, T. N. Some principles in the psychotherapy of patients following hospitalization for schizophrenia. *Psychiat. Quart.*, 1958, 32, 110-117.

16. Ellis, A. Rational psychotherapy. *J. gen. Psychol.*, 1958, 59, 35-49.

17. Ferreira, A. J., Psychotherapy with regressed schizophrenics. *Psychiat. Quart.*, 1959, 33, 664-682.

18. Ferreira, A. J. The "double bind" and delinquent behavior. *AMA Arch. gen. Psychiat.*, 1960, 3, 359-367.

19. Ferreira, A. J. The semantics and the context of the schizophrenics' langauge. AMA Arch. gen. Psychiat., 1960, 3, 128-138.

20. Freeman, T., Cameron, J. L., & McGhie. *Chronic schizophrenia.* New York: Int. Univer. Press, 1958.

21. Freud, S. Humor. *Int. J. Psychoanal.*, 1928, 9, 1-6.

22. Fromm. E. *The art of loving.* New York: Harper, 1959.

23. Fromm-Reichmann, Frieda. Basic problems in the psychotherapy of schizophrenia. *Psychiatry*, 1958, 21, 1-6.

24. Fry, W. F. Destructive behavior on hospital wards. *Psychiat. Quart. Suppl.*, 1959, 33, 1-35.

25. Haley, J. An interactional desription of schizophrenia. *Psychiatry*, 1959, 22, 321-332.

26. Halpern, H. M., & Lesser, Leona. Empathy in infants, adults, and psychotherapists. *Psychoanal. psychoanal. Rev.*, 1960, 47, 32-42.

27. Hankoff, L. D. Interaction patterns among military prison personnel. *U. S. Armed Forces med. J.*, 1959, 10, 1416-1427.

28. Hill, L. On being rather than doing in psychotherapy. *Int. J. Group Psychother.*, 1959, 8, 115-122.

29. Ishiyama, T., & Grover, W. The phenomenon of resistance to change in a large psychiatric institution. *Psychiat. Quat. Suppl.*, 1960, 34, 1-11.

30. Mowrer, O. H. Two-factor learning theory reconsidered, with special reference to secondary reinforcement and the concept of habit. *Psychol. Rev.*, 1956, 63, 114-128.

31. O'Connell, W. The adaptive functions of wit and humor. *J. abnorm. soc. Psychol.*, 1960, 61, 263-270.

32. Salzman, L. Paranoid state: theory and therapy. *AMA Arch. gen. Psychiat.*, 1960, 2, 679-693.

33. Shoben, E. J. Love, loneliness, and logic. *J. Indiv. Psychol.*, 1960, 16, 11-24.

34. Sommer, R., & Clancy, I. Ambiguities in the role of clinical psychologist in a mental hospital. *J. clin. Psychol.*, 1958, 14, 264-268.

35. Szasz, T. The uses of naming and the origin of the myth of mental illness. *Amer. Psychologist*, 1961, 16, 59-65.

36. Van Dusen, W., & Ansbacher, H. L. Adler and Binswanger on schizophrenia. *J. Indiv. Psychol.*, 1960, 16, 77-80.

37. Whitman, R. W. & Reece, M. M. "Warmth" and verbal reinforcement. Paper read at Midwest. Psychol. Assoc., St. Louis, April, 1960.

38. Wolman, B. B. Psychotherapy with latent schizophrenics. *Amer. J. Psychother.*, 1959, 13, 343-359.

ADLERIAN ACTION THERAPY TECHNIQUE[1]

Action therapy is a form of group therapy which is focused on what the patient can do for others, rather than on the patient as such (9, 10-18). It is an attempt to put Adler's concept of social interest into action, along lines which over the years have led to some encouraging results with patients.

Development Groups

At the VA Hospital in Houston we have a problem-centered patient group program, called Human Relations Training Laboratory, HRTL.[6] [7] Most participants selected for the program suffer from anxiety and depressive reactions, character disorders, or alcoholism. The problem of therapy is to move the participant from the conviction that he is largely controlled by external forces (external control) to the realization of the initiative that is actually his (internal control). Since people are often remote from where important decisions concerning their lives are made, they are prone to lapse into passivity, and lose enthusiasm, involvement, and a sense of responsibility in handling their own affairs, in planning and executing personal goals, and in managing their lives.[21]

The major vehicle through which internal control is taught is the development group (D-group). That is, in the D-group many patients learn that they can indeed initiate movements which eventuate in positive or negative reinforcements from significant others.[20]

A D-group consists of eight to twelve men who build from "scratch" a miniature society of four weeks duration which sets its own goals and procedures for living together. The men meet five times a week for one and one-half hours without a

Reprinted from *Journal of Individual Psychology*, Vol. 28, 184-191, Nov. 1972.
[1]Paper submitted at Fourth Brief Psychotherapy Conference, Chicago Medical School, Chicago, March 24-25, 1972.

staff member and without a planned agenda. In the remaining program hours, lecturettes are given, mainly by pyschology trainees, in skills related to giving and asking for feedback about behavior. Throughout the four-week period destructive acting out of a member is dealt with by the group, not the staff. A Rules Committee of peers works with the rule breakers to maintain ward justice and harmony. Outside resources, such as a consultant, are available but can be called into the group only through a consensus of all members.

Group members are told that in addition to getting help from other members they are expected to give help in the form of feed-back about their feelings regarding here-and-now behavior of other members. This comes as a surprise to many who never thought that they could help anyone. Since the D-group (historically rooted in Kurt Lewin's work) must rely mostly on its own resources, there is at the start a sense of helplessness; members are frustrated and anxious when they realize that the help they want must come primarily from within their own group.

In such a program it becomes essential to demonstrate their own resources to the members. This may be done during the second week of the D-group sessions through a technique which I developed and have called "action therapy." It is a form of psychodrama, adapted to Adlerian theory, which by demonstrating resourcefulness increases the members' self-esteem and social interest.

In our socio-historical times, everyone, I presume, actively but unwittingly lowers self-esteem and social interest in pursuit of truncated, narrow identification. In such maneuvers we are all only looking for self-esteem through the social actions we consider to have the highest probability of success. The first sparkle of humor comes from a detached realization that we ourselves have crippled our self-esteem through negative nonsense, oughts, shoulds, while demanding unconditional approval from others. In the end, self-esteem is lowered by one's own internalized sentences and the reactive behavior of significant others who have suffered from our demands.

Action Therapy Lecturette

Most patients do not really know why they are in the hospital, that is, in the sense of what in their attitudes has led

37

to behavior which resulted in their being hospitalized. They mainly perceive "nerves" and fear of "loss of control" as causal factors. Therefore, on the first day of the second week I may give them a one-hour lecturette on Adlerian theory of mental disorder, using familiar terms, explaining the mistakes in living which all of us make in varying degrees, and the ways in which we can overcome these errors. An outline of the lecturette is given to each member to implement my attempt to make students out of the patients, and concrete examples of misbehavior in the following days are discussed within the Adlerian frame of reference.

In the action therapy lecturette the need for self-esteem (significance or worth) is constantly reiterated, as is social interest (other-understanding or outsight)—the two "depth" factors to which all other perceptions and actions are ancillary.

The dangers of low self-esteem are illustrated through anecdotes around patient misbehavior as it happens: the failure to risk imperfection, the overcompensatory fantasy life; the strong tendency to be "sensitive" to any mentioning of one's mistakes. One with low self-esteem translates any implied criticism of his behavior as an incontrovertible message of his worthlessness. He rejects even praise, for accepting it could mean added responsibilities, with increased opportunity for failure. Yet the honest, well-intentioned expressions by others of how they see you and feel about you (verbal feedback), are the way to understanding oneself.

The dis-ease of low self-esteem is described as a reactive "willing that which cannot be willed," and a lack of courage to be imperfect, resulting in further humiliation, embarrassment, anxiety, and tension. It is manifested by demanding, blaming, punishing, and by avoiding situations through excuses such as "too nervous," "need time to think," "don't want to be made a fool of." Low self-esteem is usually accompanied by narrow social interest: creating distance from others, being hyperdependent on them, or actively or passively competitive.

A part of the lecturette is concerned with topics which help the director to get the group going, avoiding abstractions and past histories. One such topic is the specific error of lowering self-esteem and narrowing social interest in this present encounter. "We all do this. Why? and how? Why are you doing it right now?" Another topic is anxiety, feeling "certain" that something catastrophic is going to happen to one, beyond one's control. "What do you fear will happen? Tell the group in a fit of openness and honesty. Is it a fear of loneliness, of humiliation, of others detecting imperfections?" Still another topic is knowing another, i.e., understanding how he lowers his self-esteem and social interest in terms of outer and inner (cognitive) movements; knowing his hidden anxieties; understanding the nature of his habitual relationships (hyperdependent, cooperative, or competitive); lastly, knowing how he wants to be confirmed, as "what," and by what types of reinforcements, e.g., as the best speaker, by constant nodding and smiling of others. Ideally, all members know this information about all other members and are willing to share themselves, and confirm others. This builds authentic "community," and each member is able to mirror or double for every other.

Action Therapy Sessions

For the next four days the members have their daily one and one-half hour action therapy session in the morning with the author as director. In the afternoon they view videotape playbacks, with their consultant (not the director) present. Playbacks are uninterrupted presentations of the morning action therapy sessions.

One member at a time volunteers to be the protagonist, one who has the courage to contribute his problems to the group. With the help of the group, which the director actively solicits, the protagonist's low self-esteem is explored along with the "negative nonsense" (arbitrary demanding, blaming, and stigmatizing) which he tells himself,[19] such as "If I show anxiety, I'm not a real man"; "I must never be laughed at or I'm a failure."[4]

While working with the protagonist the director inquires from other members for similarities and understanding. "Why don't you understand Joe?" "What information do you need? What movements does he have to make before you understand him?" "What do you tell yourself about Joe to keep distance from him?" "What have you said or done to Joe to help him tell himself that he is (or you are) inferior as a person?"

The director might ask if others have had similar problems. "Let's see the hands of those who have had sex problems" *(two hands up, ten arms motionless)*. "I see we have two guys with guts and ten liars *(laughter)*. I've had sex problems too. What do you think of that?"

The director can play upon competition itself to precipitate insight into the goals of competition on the useless side and develop group cohesion. One statement might be, "The group's task is to find the most depressed guys. Who is the sickest?"

The director can also capitalize upon competitive power struggles to stimulate sharing and practice of openness. When Harry, a sullen, violently-passive alcoholic, steadfastly refused to play the son who infuriated Harry and led him to drinking behavior, a bet was made with Joe. Joe, also on the stage because the director called for the group to select people with the "best tempers," was told by the director, "I'll bet you two bits you can't get Harry to play his son." Almost immediately the director lost his quarter and the group had a hearty laugh over their power to "defeat" authority. But authority in this case was not defeated since it also laughed and was pleased at the creativity of the group in demonstrating power struggles and provoking movement.

Guessing at another's constricting cognitions highlights the other's "creativity" (albeit of an unexpected negative kind) and focuses on the possibility of his making alternative choices. Guessing in itself is stressed because it is encouraging to realize that no one of us has absolute certainty and guessing is what we are all doing. Guessing at another's creativity also helps to show him a developmental route to the sense of humor through experiencing the tragicomic paradox, e.g., knocking oneself down while crying for help. The humor of unloving the self while demanding pampering from others, the humor of being the best or most perfect self-devaluator, can also be brought out through mirroring and doubling in action therapy.

Through playing the role of doctor or director, the patients may see that the role of the encouraging director can in time be only that of suggesting that the patient strive harder to be more accomplished in his "symptoms." Such a paradox again approaches humor: encouraging symptoms is a benign trick which places the patient in the untenable position of "I won't do what he says ... I'll do the opposite."[5] The ploy illustrates experientially how actively competitive, low self-esteem people create misery. After that it opens the question of "Now what? Shall we practice to be happy and authentic?" At all times the lesson to be highlighted for the patient is: Either stop your negative nonsense, or immediately increase it and learn to enjoy your misery more fully.

Part of the training is desensitization toward psychiatric labeling. Most patients harbor some term (obsessive-compulsive, phobic, psychopathic, etc.) which they apply to themselves as a fearsome prejudicial abstraction, "I am nothing but a hopeless, helpless, lonely . . . " To take the sting out of the word-magic, and to stimulate and develop hope, substitutions are presented, based upon different patient demands and reactions (instead of diseases), such as fighting for super-control over people and events, actively trying to achieve superiority in some ways to all others, avoiding people and events as a method of control. The director may play the patient, while the patient in the role of the doctor experiences the frustrations of a defeated autocrat.

When the director believes the locus for change to be the internal sentences of a patient, he might move to have the peer-group members flood the protagonist with encouragement, relevant to behavior. For example:

DIRECTOR: Joe is good because . . .
PEER: Joe always greets me and has the courage to share his mistakes with us right now.

If Joe should say, "I have no self-esteem, because no one likes me," and if there is validity to it in that others are actually repulsed by him, the question can then be, what movements in what did lead to like-dislike? Esteem comes from positive reinforcement of self and others. If one wishes for esteem from others, he must, for better or worse, at least in the beginning, confirm others in the way they expect to be seen. Arbitrary demanding to "be liked" is only the royal road to mental illness.

Patients on Their Own

The final two weeks of the HRTL program are given over again to D-group functioning. Seeing themselves helpful to others and utilizing help from people like themselves, the participants begin to develop confidence, and experience an increase in self-esteem.[19] Still seeking help from staff, they are less inclined to depend primarily on the "experts." They learn to distribute their dependencies upon themselves, the group, and the staff. Their relationships become interdependent rather than demanding, dependent, or counterdependent.

In the process the participant must assess what parts of his own behavior are effective or ineffective in dealing with others. He must learn to look at his own behavior and try to determine how he perpetuates his problems by believing the negative nonsense he tells himself, clinging to destructive attitudes, and playing habitual, self-defeating games.[1] Psychotherapeutic changes are brought about through mutual helpfulness and tolerance, not by blaming and punishing, but by trying to understand the other person. How does he want to be confirmed? Will he learn to accept a different role in life and a different confirming movement from others?

Concluding Comment

This, then, is a report of an attempt to put into action the Adlerian faith that psychotherapeutic methodology belongs in part to all people, rather than being solely the property of restricted professional guilds.[2] [3] Even beyond that slightly heretical stance is a faith in the person who has been solving his problems poorly yet "creatively"; patients can learn to be therapeutic for each other. After our patients complete their D-group training of four weeks, they are either transferred to other wards or leave the hospital. And it is encouraging to report that of over 200 patients who have in recent years served as protagonists very few have returned to our hospital for further treatment.

REFERENCES

1. Berne, E. *Games people play.* New York: Grove, 1964.

2. Dreikurs, R. *Social equality: the challenge of today.* Chicago: Regnery, 1971.

3. Dreikurs, R., and Soltz, Vicki. *Children: the challenge.* New York: Duell, Sloan & Pearce, 1964.

4. Ellis, A. *Reason and emotion in psychotherapy.* New York: Lyle Stuart, 1962.

5. Haley, J. *Strategies of Psychotherapy.* New York: Grune & Stratton, 1963.

6. Hanson, P. G., Rothaus, P., O'Connell, W. E., & Wiggins, G. Training patients for effective participation in back-home groups. *Amer. J. Psychiat.*, 1969, 126, 857-862.

7. Hanson, P. G., Rothaus, P., O'Connell, W. E., & Wiggins, G. Some basic concepts in human relations training for psychiatric patients. Hosp. Community Psychiat., 1970, 21, 137-143.

8. Moreno, Zerka. A survey of psychodramatic techniques. *Group Psychother.*, 1959, 12, 5-14.

9. Nikelly, A., & O'Connell, W. E. Action oriented methods. In A. Nikelly (Ed.) *Techniques for behavior change: applications of Adlerian theory.* Springfield, Ill.: C. C. Thomas, 1971. Pp. 85-90.

10. O'Connell, W. E. Adlerian psychodrama with chronic schizophrenics. *J. Indiv. Psychol.*, 1963, 19, 69-76.

11. O'Connell, W. E. Psychotherapy for everyman: a look at action therapy. *J. exist.*, 1966, 7(25), 85-91.

12. O'Connell, W. E. Psychodrama: involving the audience. *Rat. Living*, 1967, 2(1), 22-25.

13. O'Connell, W. E. Spitting and stroking. *Invid. Psychologist*, 1967, 5(1), 29-31.

14. O'Connell, W. E. Action therapy is fun. *Voices*, 1969, 5(3), 43.

15. O'Connell, W. E. Teleodrama. *Indiv. Psychologist*, 1969, 6(2), 42-45.

16. O'Connell, W. E. Sensitivity training and Adlerian theory. *J. Indiv. Psychol.*, 1970, 26, 165-166.

17. O'Connell, W. E. Adlerian action therapy. *Voices*, 1971, 7(2), 22-27.

18. O'Connell, W. E., & Brewer, D. The values of role reversal in psychodrama and action therapy. *Handbk int. Sociometry*, 1971, 6, 98-104.

19. O'Connell, W. E., & Hanson, P. G. Patient's cognitive changes in human relations training. *J. Indiv. Psychol.*, 1970, 26, 57-63.

20. O'Connell, W. E., & Hanson, P. G. The protagonist in human relations training. *Grp. Psychotherapy and Psychodrama*, 1970, 23, 45-55.

21. Rotter, J. B. Generalized expectations for internal versus external control of reinforcement. *Psychol. Monogr.*, 1966, No. 609.

ENCOURAGEMENT (1974)

"Normality" of Discouragement

History teaches us that relatively few persons have ever enjoyed, for even a short period of time, a vibrant sense of connectedness with other persons and the world of nature. *Gemeinschaftsgefühl* or the sense of universal interrelatedness — narrowly misinterpreted as "social interest" — has never been formally taught in schools. For much of our recorded history, mankind, even through "democratic" and "religious" institutions, has been preoccupied with the conquest and exploitation of the external world (including people, seen as "objects"). For most of the world, an insane individualism has brought constant misery in its wake. Power and strength are sought through covert and overt exploitative, manipulative, and competitive movements. How different would the world be had our ancestors rejected Descartian dualism, and opted for a humanistic study of eupsychian states.

In addition to the pervasive cultural blindness for interrelatedness for growth and evolution, other formidable barriers to democratic behavior are operating. Low self-esteem individuals do not see themselves as capable of encouraging others, a view often reinforced by autocrats at the top of the bureaucratic power structure. High self-esteemers (with narrow social interest) need to create such hyperdependent "useless" persons to buoy their own sense of worth. In the face of cultural ignorance, discouragement and fierce competition, encouragement remains an unfamiliar skill even though it might be an aswer to the perennial human energy crisis.

Encouragement in the Adlerian system

Encouragement has been a key concept in the Individual Psychology (IP) movement. Practitioners of Adlerian psychology have largely confined themselves to homes and

44

schools, and this existential-humanistic approach is largely absent from the mental hospital scene. Even in the community-at-large when the theory and practice of IP has made the greatest contributions, the dyadic movements of encouragement have not yet been investigated. What often passes as encouragement has not been exposed to the dyadic premises of communication theory: One cannot not communicate; messages are multi-level; and messages sent are not always messages received (Watzlawick, 1964). The basic approach of Dreikurs has been the non-reinforcing of useless goals of misbehavior (attention, power struggles, revenge, and disability displays). Only in the last presentation, before his death, did Dreikurs focus exclusively on the need for a new technology, based on equality and democracy, to encourage cooperation-as-equals (Dreikurs, 1972). Here the focus was on the dyadic movements of the psychic growth process itself; how to encourage each person to maximize his feelings of significance and communal feelings simultaneously.

The theory of humanistic identification (O'Connell, 1965) is based upon dyadic ways of altering mistaken attitudes and actions which have led to low, unstable self-esteem and narrow social interest (or low state of communal feelings). The gestalt of self-induced and ultimately self-defeating movements is clearly illustrated by the cluster of misinformation, ignorance, and delusion practiced by the psychiatric patient as their "explanation" of the process called mental illness.

The intention of the study herein described (Brendel, 1974) was to create an opportunity for the patient in the 4-week HITL (Human Interaction Training Lab) to become more a therapist than a "passive victim," coming to the hospital to be magically cured of "nerves" (Hanson, Rothaus, O'Connell, Wiggins, 1969; O'Connell, 1972). In this design the patient could be called an active encourager, if he was willing and able to understand, assimilate, and practice the outsight necessary for the growth of the other. It is not solely the life style of the patient that makes this self-actualizing altruism unlikely. He is culturally reinforced for his faith in an unyielding illness model which often allows him the opportunity to be a successful "victim" of heredity, environment, pyschic traumas and unknown physiological forces.

45

Encouragement Development Groups (DGs)

The HITL introductory days, one and most of two, were spent with lecturettes about the theory of encouragement. Each lecturette session was then devoted to gathering the information necessary to encourage each group member with the goals of increasing his humanistic identification (sense of personal worth and relatedness to life). In the 90 minute lecturette sessions a here-and-now life style analysis was conducted for each DG member, while the rest of his group provided support and information. A short report was then tacked to the bulletin board in the group room giving the particular patient's life style in dyadic terms. In other words, public notice was given as to how and why the patient *constricted* his life style. The focus was on the *creative* inner and outer movements he had learned to use for power (or influence) but which eventually lowered his self-esteem and narrowed his social interest. Anyone needs the cooperation of others in these constricting ventures: others must provide the reinforcing pampering or rejecting behavior, either willingly or by a subtle provoking "arrangement." The short life style report of about 300 words included a group prescription, since by the premises of humanistic identification, "no man is an island:" we are all constricted, creative, and cooperative in reinforcing the movements and attitudes of others, either wittingly or through being manipulated.

Perhaps for the first time in history, the psychological report was written for the patient and not to comply with institutional rituals. The patient was made aware of his mistakes, along with the realization that no one is to blame, punish, or demand change. Others in the DG were told how to encourage (See "Elements of the Encouragement Process") so they could not wail at the end of the lab, "no one told us what to do." DG disagreements as to possible goals of misbehavior were either argued-out or seen as errors that the authority was also free to make, even in times when hyper-dependent ones lean tragically on professional oracles for magic aphorisms. On occasion an addendum was taped to a report, giving the details of the disagreements as to goals and ways of getting there.

Adler once claimed that he could gather sufficient data for understanding a patient in less than an hour. The life style report offers the same opportunity, often leaving time within the data gathering period for the group to practice encouraging the particular patient who was role-played teleologically by the author (O'Connell, 1969). The life style pattern emerged from watching each patient within the context of his group: What dyadic movements he made as well as those he did not undertake (e.g., how and why he failed to encourage). Others in the group were asked what they learned about the interviewee and why they had not encouraged him. The interviewee was also asked for details of his early recollections and his family constellation. The question aimed at what he hoped to change and why he had not done so. He was questioned about what made him nervous and what he did about it. Answers to "What kind of animal would you like to be—and why?" provide clues as to the goals of behavior. Asking the patient and then his group who was the "best-worst" often gave signs both as to the intensity and meaning of the symptom, and the actions of others which provided reinforcement (e.g., "Is Jim more depressed than Ed?"). Every patient was asked in a matter-of-fact manner how he created his misery. ("How do you go about getting depressed?") Verbal and non-verbal responses showed how aware the patient was of such hidden facets of his useless creativity. If the interviewee continued to answer such questions for long, he found himself noting the "soft" determinism of self-created life style: How he arranged and selected evidence to confirm his constricted views of life (Dreikurs, 1966).

Nuances of Encouragement

One-day encouragement labs have now been conducted in Toronto, Washington, and Houston. Within the VA Hospital, Michelle Brendel (1974) is completing data analysis on the contrast between encouragement groups and the HITL lab groups. At this writing, the only definitive statement that can be made is that participants in the encouragement process do not leave the program arbitrarily as often as regular group members. Further reports will be appearing in the literature of 1974.

Certain clinical statements can be made at this time, in spite of the lack of experimental results. First, the *goal* of the encouragement *process* must be made explicit to avoid confusion with pampering. Encouragement, like many of the labels for the enexplored positive dyadic behaviors, is often seen as a "thing" most people believe they possess. Encouragement is not an inherent trait, so much as a process with a goal to be defined in large part by the reaction of the other. If, for example, I see myself as encouraging while, at the same time, I make movements of tongue, eyes, and limbs which assist the patient in discouraging himself, I have failed, in this particular instance, to be an encourager.

Furthermore, one must be aware that the other probably has learned to define "encouragement" as pampering or rejecting. Until the patient believes that his mistakes are not being pointed out as blame—but that he çan, if he so desires, see blame everywhere as part of his creative moves on the useless side of life—he is "discouraged" by "encouragement." He expects constant "Valentines" from others while he unwittingly makes the pile of crap he sits upon, blaming *ad nauseum*, and constantly creating more crap. Until the patient sees the therapist as a firm friend who will walk 70 times 7 miles in his moccasins there is no progress toward the development of humanistic identification.

Those in the helping professions often make their necks red as a response to "encouragement." The word lacks the Greco-Latin aura usually associated with matters-of-consequence; people routinely see themselves as encouragers, blaming others when they don't instantly ingest the "encouragement" and recover from some ill-defined illness in a miraculous way. Many professionals react with "That person needs to be discouraged!", confusing the "sin" with the "sinner" and showing their faith in the time-honored conservative cosmology that punishment nurtures progress (except in *their* own present situation). Unless such individualists can agree on the importance of constantly learned and maintained self-esteem and social interest, encouragement will always be a mere superficial and "unscientific" word.

True encouragement focuses upon the dyadic situation of sender and receiver. The narrower the humanistic identification of the duo, the more the discouragement (lowering of self-esteem and narrowing of communal feelings). A person attempting to encourage needs to spend more time and movement on what my patients have called "respect"; the first few elements of the encouragement process. Of late I have been listening to the astonishment and shock of graduate students who have experienced the force of encouragement in their life transactions. Uniformly they tell me "it really works . . . without diagnosing or talking about psychopathology . . . but other students and teachers don't believe it." Nevertheless the "sicker" the receiver, the more the sender must stop, look and listen, paraphrase and guess gently at the receiver's feelings, assume attentive postures, and be willing to be open about his own mistakes and feelings in a non-superior, non-demanding way. "Spitting in the soup" is often required: One must anticipate, verbalize, but *not reinforce* the receiver's useless goals or way of influencing others (i.e., power maneuvers). It goes without saying that the sender without humanistic identification is going to be a discouraging dehumanizer, even though he hides his intentions from self and others under the guise of institutional trappings of religion, education, psychotherapy or government. The goal of education is not merely to increase symbolic manipulation (English, mathematics), but to encourage students to resist quietly being manipulated as mere symbols themselves, even if dehumanizing manipulation is attempted by the schools themselves.

REFERENCES

1. Brendel, M. Changes in positive personality traits as a function of teaching encouraging transactions. Unpublished dissertation, University of Houston, 1974.

2. Dreikurs, R. The holistic approach: two points of a line in Dreikurs, R. (Ed), *Education, Guidance, Psychodynamics*. Chicago: Alfred Adler Institute, 1966, pps. 19-24.

3. Dreikurs, R. Toward a technology of human relationship. *Journal of Individual Psychology*, 1972, 28, 127-136.

4. Hanson, P., Rothaus, P., O'Connell, W., and Wiggins, G. Training patients for effective participation in back-home groups. *American Journal of Psychiatry*, 1969, 126, 857-862.

5. O'Connell, W. Humanistic identification, a new translation for Gemeinschaftsgefüehl. *Journal of Individual Psychology*, 1965, 21, 44-47.

6. O'Connell, W. Teleodrama. *Individual Psychologist*, 1969, 6 (2), 42-45.

7. O'Connell, W. Action therapy techniques. *Journal of Individual Psychology*, 1972, 28, 184-191.

8. O'Connell, W., and Hanson, P. Patients' cognitive changes in human relations training. *Journal of Individual Psychology*, 1970, 26, 57-63.

9. Watzlawick, P. *An Anthology of Human Communication*. Palo Alto: Science and Behavior Books, 1964.

ELEMENTS OF THE ENCOURAGEMENT PROCESS

Think and feel dyadically (no units of one). See 3 C's of interdependence.

1. Stop look and listen.

2. Clarify, paraphrase other's messages, guess at feelings.

3. Same or interested postures.

4. Look for similarities.

5. Self-disclosure (open, authentic) of *feelings* and mistakes.

6. Basic feedback—give and ask for
   Specify behavior—feelings about
   Non-judgmental of person
   Close in time
   Behavior over which the individual has control
   Asked for feedback
   Given so other understands
   Freedom of choice

7. Find something good about everyone in the group, even how creatively he arranges for reinforcement of useless goals.

8. Tell how the other person has helped to encourage.

9. How the group and others have helped me . . .

10. How the group could help me more . . .

11. Guess at how I have helped the group . . .

12. Advanced feedback . . . Anticipate and even guess aloud about useless goals—but do not reinforce them.

	Useful	1	2 Useless	3	4
Creative (Arranging Meaning). Search for power (influence)	Cooperation-as-equals	AGM; Attention; Special Service; Excitement	Power Struggles (who is stronger). competition	Revenge	Display of Disability: Hyper-dependency
Cooperative (Rewarding reactions)	Social Approval	Annoyance	Provoked (You can't)	Deeply Hurt	Hopeless-ness

13. Sense of Humor—sense of play
    Doesn't demand . . . pleasures indirect (friendship, sleep, etc.)
    Augustine's Paradox: Whatever you are doing now is of ultimate importance, but if you died now it wouldn't matter.
    Model and reinforce humor.
    LIFE IS TOO IMPORTANT TO BE TAKEN SERIOUSLY.

ENCOURAGEMENT LABS:
A DIDACTIC-EXPERIENTIAL APPROACH
TO COURAGE

Psychiatry's Sociohistorical Movement

The popularity of the many forms of encounter and sensitivity training groups over the last decade might be explained in part by sociohistorical factors. (O'Connell, 1971) In the past, descriptive psychiatry has viewed man as an isolated encapsulated entity. The emphasis has been on the discovery of psychopathology usually induced by unknown biochemical dysfunctions or early psychic traumata. The search for cures was conducted entirely through professional guidance and control, with a there-and-then emphasis upon recovering memories of past, noxious events and the addition of supportive physical treatment. Any incidental and here-and-now focus was to discover and group current symptoms for a psychiatric classification. Critics of this methodology have regarded such a diagnosis as a self-fulfilling prophecy and a precipitating factor in the poor prognosis of the average patient. (O'Connell, 1964)

The encounter devotees, on the other hand, often regard man as purely a transactional creature, a product of social forces, needing beneficial interpersonal experiences but not subservient relationships with well-meaning but autocratic professionals. Whereas the descriptive professional harbors metaphoric premises of man as a rock-like monad, impervious to real change, the "touchy-feely" grouper unwittingly sees man as a "tabula rasa" sponge, lacking a hard core of Being, and at the mercy of vague social forces.

Neither the descriptive nor sensitivity schools of psychiatry have invented well-formulated concepts and behaviors which reflect the goal of treatments and encounters, "mental health." The concept of humanistic identification or HI (O'Connell, 1965) conceives of man as having both a relatively stable inner core (life style or existential-humanistic attitudes) and an innate potential for social intercourse (the need for power, seen as the ability to stimulate or resist interpersonal change). The

Reprinted from *The Individual Psychologist*, 1975, 12, 8-12.

emphasis in HI is focused upon teaching an awareness of one's current inner and outer movements, which are responsible for lowering one's sense of personal worth (or self-esteem) and narrowing one's social interest (or feelings of similarity) with others. Dysfunctional and antisocial behaviors are the result of constriction of self-esteem and social interest, in the services of maintaining one's perceived identity, however inadequate it might be.

At present there seems to be a burgeoning movement within dynamic psychology to search for the positive, and de-emphasize traditional concern with negative behaviors only. At his last professional presentation, the late Rudolf Dreikurs (1972) spoke of the imperative need to invent a technology of interpersonal cooperation. Bullard (1973) perceives the necessity for family study groups to move into the relatively untouched area of defining and learning positive cooperative behavior rather than remain oriented toward negative labeling. In the larger scene of sensitivity training there is a similar emphasis on modeling and reinforcing the positive beyond mere talking about positive concepts (Walter & Miles, 1972). It is entirely conceivable that this will be the next Adlerian concern: "accentuate the positive, to eliminate the negative," to paraphrase slightly the words of a 30 year-old prophetic tune.

Encouragement for what?

All of the efforts of Encouragement Labs are designed to teach the participants, through lecturettes and experiences, that they are not passive victims of their environments. People unwittingly select, "arrange," interpret, and openly react to their milieu. The principal lab premise is that social interest does not emerge full-blown in the absence of psychological complaints (symptoms), but needs to be explicitly taught, especially in a competitive society like ours where there are no institutionalized efforts to teach the movements and responsibilities of love. Social interest in its finest form—courage or active social interest—must be taught from the ground up for along with humor and love, courage as a learned social skill is totally ignored in the academic world.

Encouragement includes in its progressive repertoire of social skills the art of courage: Giving and asking for feedback about peoples' reactions to one's behaviors and guessing at the goals of misbehavior (self and others). Encouragement in its most advanced state includes recognizing the importance of being open and self-disclosing and not provoking and reinforcing inequality (e.g., feelings of insignificance *or* feelings of significance in narrow non-contributory social roles). Encouragement labs point toward knowledge and practice of the humorous attitude, for there is no more encouraging or growth-precipitating person than one with a humorous attitude. Contrary to popular practice, encouragement is definitely not pampering. Yet almost one hundred students, asked to write on how they would encourage authority figures in their lives, gave examples more appropriate to pampering. In these examples, students behaved as if they had no right to give feedback, or if they did it would be ignored or retaliated against: So they made themselves discouraged. Encouragement is not such destructive pampering as telling a person what he wants to hear about how wonderful he is, completely ignoring his motivated mistakes. Encouragement is a process of getting the message across, loudly and clearly, that one is responsible for constricting or expanding his feelings of self-esteem and belonging. To our partners in the ever-continuing human dyads, we are responsible for: (1) giving verbal and nonverbal approval to socially cooperative actions; (2) not reinforcing behaviors in the service of self-esteem on the useless side of life; (3) dissolving the relationship without blame or rancor in the event the dyadic partner gives the impressions of wanting to trap persons in the superior-inferior roles through competitive and/or hyperdependent identity games.

Encouragement labs may be conducted over any period of time, the minimum period being one day. In my opinion labs are best which are flexible, where the director can watch for the need for further theoretical emphasis, or exercises to help participants evaluate their skills as encouragers and the groups alert themselves to signs of democratic group functioning. Groups can observe themselves or pair with another group to observe in group behavior at least the rudiments of democratic functioning: Shared participation (or contributions to group creativity) and consensus by all group members. The longer the lab, the more data generated for feedback, together with greater opportunities for inter-group observations of democratic group atmosphere and interpersonal (and intrapersonal) encouragement.

A one day lab begins with a focus on the participants' feelings and behaviors typical of entering a group of strangers, specifically to understand and help the *other*. The day ends on an exercise to develop the sense of humor, focusing on nondistruptive and uplifting reactions to stress. Stress in humor exercises is often that of separation from others, and even the self through eventual death. The elements of a hypothetical encouragement, subject to change at director and group discretion, follow:

ENCOURAGEMENT LECTURETTES AND EXERCISES

1. **Being Present**
   Mill about nonverbally. Select partner. Build up to two groups.

2. **Think about methods by which you can encourage**
   Group imagery. Director has groups relax, imagine movements of encouragement and possible dangers of encouraging.

3. **Stop, Look and Listen** to the other. "Sunset experience"; you are in awe of Nature's masterpiece and don't try to pick it apart.
   Groups split into dyads. A interviews B on how B wants to be encouraged and fears concerning such. B later interviews A on same theme.
   A's to center, B's observe. A's talk about partners views of encouragement. B's give feedback later on whether A's are correct. Process reversed, with B's in center.

4. **Clarify content, guess at feelings**
   B's interview A's to rate A on self-esteem and social interest. B has already rated self independently. Director calls time periodically to have B's paraphrase A's content, guess at his feelings. Talk about difficulties in following task.
   Share ratings, talk of evidence used and reasons for differences between raters. Reverse process with A interviewing B.

5. **Lecturette on how to lower self-esteem and social interest**
   Behavioral signs and purposes of such. Lecturette on 3 C's of interdependence (O'Connell, Chorens, Wiggins, Hiner, 1973). Lecturettes on feedback and reinforcement of goals of misbehavior.

6. **Natural High**
   Rate self on projected self-esteem and social interest one year from now. A interviews B, later B interviews A to find out what evidence the partner used to convince himself he'll be constricted at a future time. How does partner select and arrange the constricting environment? How can partner move to prevent constriction?

7. **Practice in Reinforcement**

Director plays types of constricted individuals, creatively searching for reinforcement on the useless side. One group tries to encourage, while other group watches and later gives feedback to partners. All groups have a chance for action.

8. **Sense of Humor** (O'Connell and Brewer, 1971).

Counselors in each group write down most stressful situations. Group selects one. Through psychodramatic techniques, director shows inner and outer movements of person which makes situation stressful. Other members model or double humorous responses to the situation to make the scene relatively non-stressful. (O'Connell, 1969).

In this shortened version of an encouragement lab, the stress upon finding something good (success bombardment), even to the point of congratulating creatively-arranged rejections, is eliminated. Similarly eliminated in a compact lab is role playing on four goals of misbehavior in childhood (the former time period is used, unless there has been sufficient information obtained on present group functioning). All kinds of further role playing is also missing. One example would be partners trying to get life style information, then playing negatively significant figures. Through these tasks, participants learn to give encouraging feedback under stress to the "mean SOB," rather than reinforce negative actions. Encouragement labs become so only through the movement of *modeling* behavior expected from others and *reinforcing* socially responsible, encouraging effort by others. We are all our brothers' keepers, in that we easily *keep* discouraging. By learning encouragement we can become our brothers' nurturers instead.

REFERENCES

1. Dreikurs, R. Toward a technology of human relationship. *J. Indiv. Psychol.*, 1972, 38, 127-136.

2. Bullard, M. Four goal tunnel vision. Paper presented at American Society of Adlerian Psychology Association Meeting, Toronto, Canada, 1973.

3. O'Connell, W. The failure of psychotherapy in mental hospitals. *Indiv. Psychol.*, 1964, 2 (1), 24-27.

4. O'Connell, W. Humanistic identification, a new translation for Geheinschaftsgefüehl. *J. Indiv. Psychol.*, 1965, 21, 44-47.

5. O'Connell, W. Teleodrama. *Indiv. Psychol.*, 1969, 6 (2), 42-45.

6. O'Connell, W. Equality in encounter groups. *Indiv. Psychol.*, 1971, 8 (1), 15-17.

7. O'Connell, W. Sensitivity training and Adlerian Theory. *J. Indiv. Psychol.*, 1971, 27, 65-72.

8. O'Connell, W. and Brewer, D. The values of role reversal in psychodrama and action therapy. *Hdbk. Internatl. Sociom.*, 1971, 6, 98-104.

9. O'Connell, W., Chorens, J., Wiggins, G. Natural High Therapy. *Nwsltr. Res. Ment. Health Beh. Sci.*, 1973, 15 (2), 19-21.

10. Walter, G. and Miles R. Essential elements for improving task group membership behaviors. Paper presented at American Psychological Association Meeting, Honolulu, Hawaii, September, 1972.

EQUALITY IN ENCOUNTER GROUPS

The many types of group activities loosely labeled as "encounter" or "sensitivity" owe their existence partially to reactions against the cultural preoccupation with hyperindividuality at the expense of mutuality (O'Connell, 1970). The time-honored de-emphasis upon cooperation-as-equals has spawned this variety of here-and-now verbal and nonverbal techniques which, for the most part, operate without the benefit of logical theoretical considerations. Some encounters only emphasize narcissistic catharsis and lack clinical knowledge as to when such techniques are inappropriate. Other groups wallow in looking for the "real" reasons of behavior, using the hopeless search as a form of one-upmanship ("My fourth ear is better than your third."). Still others try to isolate the self in group, a form of intrapsychic voyage that Dr. Dreikurs calls "psychological masturbation."

Example:

Joe: Ed, may I tell you how I feel when you leave the room just when I start to talk?

Ed: Go ahead! I was just looking for the doctor to find out about sick call. So what?

Joe: Well, I will. But in the past when anyone has been honest with you, this upset you and you started a fight.

Ed: When? Damn you . . . Or, I want to hear.

Joe: I think the only way you feel like you belong in this group is by upsetting the group process. You've never had any practice in cooperating. We have only two more weeks to work on what's bugging us. If you don't open up and level with us what are we all going to do? You're a wonderful group wrecker . . . Am I right?

Ed: (Silence . . . then quietly . . .) Yes . . . I need plenty of help.

Reprinted from *The Individual Psychologist* Vol. VIII, No. 1, May 1971.

A final point here. Encouragement is not mentioned in the traditional feedback conditions. Adlerian encouragement or "stroking" (O'Connell, 1967) communicates worth and decision-making ability to the receiver. A sign that such a view is lacking in here-and-now encounters is to be found in the reactions to weeping in these groups. It is almost ritualistic that participants touch and rub the weeper and perhaps reinforce the weeper's asocial goals— along with their own. Adlerians, I assume, will let the weeper cry as part of the dignity of decision-making, at least until it habitually disrupts group cooperation. Adlerians verbally reinforce efforts at cooperation and only reward persons by nonverbal looking and listening. (The person earns reward simply from being). Through such operations the accent is upon the honest and mutual communication with others, which is the royal road to increasing one's self-esteem and social interest.

Traditional Feedback

Yet, in spite of unsuccessful attempts to maintain instant group joy, there are signs that a seed of democratic process thinking is inherent in some kinds of encounters. The concept of "Feedback" is a prime example of incipient concern for the "other" which Adlerians could help to nurture by their affinity for social interest as the hallmark of maturity. Constructive feedback focuses upon the healing potential present in interpersonal transactions and is superior to narrow concepts of theories which overemphasize "inner" terms (libido, collective unconscious) or "outer" factors (reinforcement). Rather than wholly discount all encounter movements, Adlerians can assist in the democratization of sensitivity groups by searching for aspects of encounter by dialogue.

The concept of feedback presents such an opportunity. Feedback is one of the teachings of the Human Relations (or Patients') Training Laboratory, and Action Therapy is often used as a vehicle for feedback practice (Hanson, Rothaus, O'Connell, and Wiggins, 1969, 1970). The laboratory is a unique workshop (psychiatric ward) in which treatment is built around "leaderless" development groups of patients. The integration of Action Therapy, Adlerian-oriented psychodramatic techniques, has been described earlier in this journal (O'Connell, 1967). The conditions for effective feedback as given by Hanson (1966) are as follows: (a) describing of specific units of overt behavior in contrast to judging the

59

person for "latent" qualities; (b) feedback should be close in time to the behavior which, ideally, is seen by others; (c) authentic feedback, not forced on others, should be motivated by a desire to help; (d) the recipient has freedom of choice to accept or reject the information, and (e) only behavior which a person can control should be included in feedback. The goals of symptoms and the necessity of group discussion of logical consequences are not mentioned (Dreikurs and Grey, 1968).

Adlerian Feedback

Constructive feedback could be considered as an operational definition of social interest in the here-and-now. (Social interest has additional temporal implications—past and future—which are not measured solely by here-and-now feedback.) To qualify as Adlerian, conceptual changes in authentic feedback would have to take place. For example, behavior included in feedback restricted to that which the recipient has under control is meaningless to the Adlerian for all goal-directed behavior is potentially within one's control. It would be better to have the qualification read, "Don't demand immediate change," and "Ask what you can do to assist in the behavioral change, assuming the person *wants* to change." A real Adlerian addition would be, "Anticipate the response of the recipient to your feedback and communicate that *guess* to him." This movement is truly "spitting in the soup" and "taking the wind out of the sails." If patients guess-and-tell purposes of misbehavior when uncooperative moves are "habitually" made, there is less reliance on disturbance-creating attention, power, revenge, and special service plays. Above all, such maneuvers of misbehaviors must not be rewarded: the group must not reinforce, by fight or flight, noncooperative goals, which are really *demands* upon others. To add to the democratic openness the giver of feedback should then ask for feedback to the feedback he has given, instead of assuming (autocratically) that his contribution is "reality" and is automatically received as sent.

Summary

Many Adlerians find sensitivity or encounter groups offensive because of the latter's excessive faith in catharsis alone. The life style cannot change if a person continues to try to maximize his self-esteem by alternative "private logic" behaviors. Incipient concern for the other (social interest) is seen in the concept of authentic feedback, used by the more theoretical and democratic encounter groups. Adlerian contributions to the growth of feedback would emphasize that feedback can be encouraging; that all goal-directed behavior is purposive; that the receiver's response should be openly anticipated; that feedback-to-feedback should be invited.

REFERENCES

1. Dreikurs, R., and Grey, L. *Logical consequences: A new approach to discipline.* New York: Meredith, 1968.

2. Hanson, P. What is feedback? *Participants' notebook.* Houston: Human Relations Training Laboratory, V. A. Hospital, 1966, P. 43.

3. Hanson, P., Rothaus, P., O'Connell, W., and Wiggins, G. Training patients for effective participation in back-home groups. *American Journal of Psychiatry,* 1969, 126, 857-862.

4. Hanson, P., Rothaus, P., O'Connell, W., and Wiggins, G. Some basic concepts in human relations training for patients. *Hospital and Community Psychiatry,* 1970, 21, 137-143.

5. O'Connell, W. Stroking and spitting. *The Individual Psychologist,* 1967, 5 (1), 29-31.

6. O'Connell, W. Sensitivity training and Adlerian theory. *Journal of Individual Psychology,* 1970, 26, 165-166.

THE GOALS OF ACTION THERAPY

Although Action Therapy shares common techniques with psychodrama, the goals of the therapies differ. In Action Therapy the spontaneous release of emotions is not an end in itself, but only the first step in honesty toward self and others. Action Therapy moves toward understanding the other as a unique person, a process called outsight. Symptoms are not always viewed as meaningless, unwanted acts but as hidden methods which elicit *some* esteem from people through attention, provoking mild to severe frustrations in others, and gaining privileged responses. The person is viewed as a decision-making organism, seeking to enhance his self-esteem and worth even by psychotic misery and isolation. The techniques of Action Therapy are used to highlight hidden purposes of misbehavior and to encourage and reinforce more socially responsible motivations.

PSYCHOTHERAPY FOR EVERYMAN:
A LOOK AT ACTION THERAPY

In the event that the Third Psychiatric Revolution[9] sweeps aside the barricades of finances and professional fixations, an even more formidable challenge awaits those who seriously combat "mental illness" (or, the useless styles of life). We need, and need quite badly, a theory for preventing and changing aberrant behaviors currently subsumed under mental illness, a theory acceptable to the "disadvantaged"[18] as well as to the helping therapist. If this defect in our planning is not painfully faced in the present decade, one wonders if all the fussing and fuming over change will merely produce a smaller breed of custodial asylums in more central locations.

For over five years our group of psychologists with the necessary and effective support of a ward psychiatrist, nurse,

Reprinted from *Journal of Existentialism,* Volume VII, Number 25, Fall, 1966.

and community volunteers has been slowly molding a theory of therapeutic intervention, with a view toward incorporating what seems to work now with schizophrenics while maintaining a generalizing eye toward other populations and other possible settings (e.g., family therapy in community settings). We continue to call our weekly groups "psychodrama" yet feel compelled to apologize to Dr. Moreno on the grounds that no member of the group has ever been personally taught by him. We favor the more encompassing Adlerian theory especially since many of our beliefs seem to be shared with that group of workers. The techniques of Moreno[13] as well as the cognitions of the double bind group, [7] [10] [16] [22] have been indispensable to our functioning. Professional relearning has been a necessity, for psychologists as a rule are trained to behave professionally in the dyadic style, stimulated by a mixture of Freudian-Rogerian assumptions[14] not gained from transactions with the desperate denials of the schizophrenic. At least this has been the individual experience of our particular professional example.

Our psychodramas are called Adlerian because of affinity for the following elements implied in the philosophy of that school:

1) Man is not viewed as a mechanistic system powered by a closed source of energy. Feedback and resultant fluctuations in self-esteem better fit our world-view[6] [14] and seem capable of explaining our behavior, a necessary segment of the total treatment field.[17]

2) We have worked ourselves free of intrapsychic overemphasis with its accentuation of infantile and pathological determinism in favor of behavioral responses amenable to change in the here-and-now.

3) The preference is for a diagnosis which attends to self-esteem, compensatory fantasy and extent of humanistic identification abstracted from behavior over time and changing external conditions.

4) Treatment is a process for correction of mistakes and stupidities instead of eliminating impersonal disease processes, and is carried out in a group setting which highlights the creative hypothetico-deductive life style of the individual (e.g., experiences lead to cognitions which are self-reinforced and call forth strong expectations and demands toward others).

Further working hypotheses less distinctively Adlerian will follow an examination of some of the benefits to staff interaction from action therapy (or Adlerian psychodrama) in the here-and-now. Our era is marked (or marred) by considerable professional hullabaloo pertaining to "genuine collaboration" between the helping professions[8] to the extent that ancillaries often translate the term to read "domination."[4] [19] But in the real and non-reified world of people, collaboration is not achieved by edict or a Divine-Right platform. The attributes of the authentic psychiatric team (awareness of motives toward patients and personnel; ability to accept criticism and failure)[3] emerge quite handily in a context where the threat of the naked struggle for the license of omniscience is absent and mutual satisfaction of psychological needs is foremost. This latter pleasant state of affairs is typical of our present functioning, we are told, but enroute to this goal we incurred the wrath of those who want to see eternal verities (and not ephemeral advances) in hospital folkways.

Blueprints for Tactics

Concepts which have emerged and received some clarification from our successes and failures with chronic psychiatric patients are numerous. Only five will be mentioned here under the rubrics of Guardian Principle, Responsibility, Outsight, The Unconscious, and Self-disclosure.

1) *Guardian Principle.* There seems to be both clinical and experimental evidence that we identify with others who reduce our tensions stemming from unfulfilled psychological and/or physiological needs.[14] [2] [15] Myriad questions concerning needs, awareness and secondary reinforcement follow from this premise and cannot be dealt with here.[23] For the purposes of psychodrama with the withdrawn, it seems that every patient should have a "guardian" in the group who seems to understand and accept his feelings and treat him with a personalized dignity. Therefore, whenever possible all patients are participants in individual and/or group psychotherapy, although this rule is often violated.

2) *Responsibility.* Through our example and influence we hope to educate patients to abide by their promises, admit errors openly and feel that man is never an interchangeable unit

in a closed system.[20] Feelings of anxiety and guilt are admittedly uncomfortable but are multiplied by defensive withdrawals and repressions. Such feelings do not automatically lead to predestined behaviors since the latter evolve from the character structure of the individual. Even the symptoms of organic deficit, while decreasing the functioning quality of the organism do not spawn destructive actions *per se*. The "sick role" is also discouraged as an explanation for goal-directed actions. Unfortunately one of the idiosyncracies of our human condition is our failure to feel compassion (and beyond compassion, personalized assistance) for our neighbor unless we label him as sick. Society it seems, as well as patients, can mask culpability with shibboleths and semantic smokescreens.[14]

3) *Outsight*. If one is low in self-esteem, it is highly improbable that he can correct such in a vacuum via tugging on his bootstraps. First there must be earned esteem from others and this, so it seems, must be earned from the learned art of outsight into the motives and feelings of others. If I demand free acceptance from all without doing for others my emotions are still swathed in diapers. Presumed rejections are an ever recurrent topic, so patients are presented with the serious game of "Let's Be Detectives (or Scientists) and Look For Evidence."

Focus is then on three elements:

a) What is your specific evidence for this idea?

b) If the judges (fellow patients) decide the rejection is real, what part did your actions have in the interchange?

c) If there is rejection for no apparent reason, do you need this person's love to live?

Punctiform insight[1] often is seen here: The patient is sensitive to minor "symptoms" or actions of others who are then reacted to as hostile, rejecting, etc. (Hence the antitherapeutic tale that patients communicate with our Unconscious.) His dependency and poor identity magnify the importance of the other for his ultimate existence (and salvation).

4) *The Unconscious*. This term, used so often by patients who have intellectualized their problems, is translated into "awareness" in our lingo. It has no easy trapdoors and

65

pragmatically is equivalent to Ellis's Internalized Sentences and Negative Nonsense.[5] Patients, like the rest of us, find easy access to genetic explanations, ignoring the creative style of life and its heart and soul, the internalized sentences. These realities are much more amenable to therapeutic intervention than Mother-Blaming, even though the ignorance of others may have reinforced self-defeating behaviors. Use of the internalized sentence and outsight as topics of therapy seem a way out of the morass of past pointing. We try to avoid interpretations based on unconscious wishes since these maneuvers add to depersonalization and preceptions of powerlessness.[12] Better to highlight the patient's rigid automatic reactions to internalized sentences as an outgrowth from inferiority complexes.

5) *Self-disclosure.* We do not attempt to imitate the proverbial psychoanalyst, swirling about to confront the prone patient with "Boy, you think you've got problems! . . . " Rather an endeavor is made to unhinge the nonsensical notion that others are carefree and omnipotent. Believing this, the patient with anxiety or guilt hunts the magic of pill or bed rest. Misperceiving and misconstruing the normal, he is too quick to panic over his own essentially normal (or average) feelings. Deviant, unexplained and callous behaviors win for one the title of "crazy," "sick," etc.[11] Therefore, if we would like patients to behave in certain ways, our stimulus-value as identificatory models must be paramount in our actions. There is no place for the maxim, "Do As I Say and Not As I Do!" in an action-oriented psychotherapy.

Techniques for What?

Technical maneuvers in psychotherapy might be defined as learned and practiced interpersonal tactics designed to elicit certain behaviors in patients. As such they must follow from an overview or strategy of psychotherapy. Our philosophy of mental illness is derived from the premise that the patient has been motivated toward the "useless style life" from a lack of appropriate identification models.[2] [15] His internalized sentences have a core of "perceived powerlessness" and he strives to maintain an escalating system of denials and avoidances. All the techniques used are in the service of this theory and might be classified as techniques for establishing relationships, rendering interpretations or rewarding courageous efforts to behave in an insightful-outsightful manner. Psychotherapists who have learned the rudiments of their art at university centers have usually been encouraged to relate in an objective-detached fashion with motivated, verbally facile middle-class clients. Therefore, ways of establishing relationships and rewarding or reinforcing empathic behaviors are grossly overlooked. Yet the success or failure of the Third Revolution, the community-centered program, might rest upon more hopeful theories of psychotherapists which lend themselves to teachable transactional techniques.

The number of techniques employable in action therapy seem infinite.[13] Our five year experience has taught us the recurrent utility of the mirror, double, role reversal, aside and dialogue techniques. The reluctant patient has always, in our experience, become involved in acting upon his problems when a staff member has temporarily enacted his kinetic and verbal reactions through the mirror play. The patient is generally quite astounded that someone seems to know him so well (without retaliating) and is willing to expand time and effort toward one who basically feels so unworthy. The double technique also provides for staff participation, with the protagonist standing behind the patient while verbalizing feelings and "automatic" reactions (e.g., "I feel that I'll be punished for whatever I think or say. I'll try to wriggle my way out by saying something strange. I don't dare try anything more . . . "). Role reversal has remained an excellent vehicle for introducing anyone to his unfruitful arbitrary demands on others then launching the discussion and practice of attending to the needs of others as a means of cementing friendship bonds. In the aside the real feelings and hidden manipulatory games[22] are verbalized although the patient or staff protagonist might be behaving in a defensive self-defeating style. Rather than aim an interpretation toward an uneasy avoiding patient and thereby compounding his lack of self-disclosure, staff or patients may debate the particular patient's motives and goals among themselves. Such an interchange (dialogue) is usually tempered with such overt themes as "We know you've learned this in the past . . . but you can change, if you want to and think it's possible . . . If you think we're wrong tell us . . . " In addition to decreasing defensiveness, the Great Debates provide patients with models for imitation who are more concerned with learning from others than maintaining arbitrary cliches such as "people are no damned good so I must run away but not think about what I'm doing or how I'm feeling . . . !" "I gotta keep a blank mind." Interacting personnel have to keep *behavioral* evidence in mind, for explanation of behavior in terms of the unconscious wish[12] and other abstractions (hostility, dependency) are considered fouls unless well grounded in further evidence. The rules of the psychodrama call for more therapeutic forms of one-upmanship.[7] ("If you're telling me you're a friendlier person than I am, I'll admit such if you prove it to me.")

Because techniques are secondary to theory, any gambit can be incorporated if it assists one to develop a more tolerant understanding of himself and others. For example, Frankl's paradoxical intention[6] has been used successfully with our avoiding patients as has Jackson's technical handling of paranoid patients[10] and Shulman's Midas technique. All of these authors note, of course, that group cohesion and humor must be an integral part of the setting for the technique to be on-target. A priceless catalyst to such a climate is the therapist who believes in the efficacy of his theory but can distantiate at times to jest about his own foibles. As Reissman[18] so aptly remarked, "While the style of the poor probably includes a strong emphasis on informality, humor and warmth, the disadvantaged also like a content that is structured, definite and specific.

REFERENCES

1. Arieti, S. "Hallucinations, delusions, and ideas of reference treated with psychotherapy." *Amer. J. Psychother.*, 1962, 16, 52-60.

2. Bandura, A., D. Ross, & S Ross. "A comparative test of the status envy, social power, and secondary reinforcement theories of identificatory learning." *J. Abn. Soc. Psychol.*, 1963, 67, 527-534.

3. Bierer, J. "The day hospital: therapy in a guided democracy." *Ment. Hosp.*, 1962, 13, 246-252.

4. Bugental, J. "Humanistic psychology: a breakthrough." *Amer. Psychol.*, 1963, 18, 563-567.

5. Ellis, A. *Reason and emotion in psychotherapy.* New York: Lyle Stuart, 1962.

6. Frankl, J. *Man's search for meaning.* New York: Washington Square Press, 1963.

7. Haley, J. "The art of psychoanalysis." In S. Hayakawa (Ed.) *Our language and our world.* New York: Harper & Brothers, 1959, pp. 113-125.

8. Handler, J., et al. "A statement on principles underlying interdisciplinary relations between the professions of psychiatry and psychology." Amer. Psychiat. Assoc., 1964.

9. Hobbs, N. "Mental health's third revolution." Paper read at Amer. Orthopsychiat. Assoc. meetings, Chicago, 1964.

10. Jackson, D. "A suggestion for the technical handling of paranoid patients." *Psychiatry,* 1963, 26, 306-307.

11. Joint Commission on Mental Illness and Health. *Action for mental health.* New York: Basic Books, 1961.

12. Lehrman, N. "Anti-therapeutic and anti-democratic aspects of Freudian dynamic psychiatry." *J. Indiv. Psychol.,* 1963, 19, 167-181.

13. Moreno, Z. "A survey of psychodramatic techniques." *Group Psychother.,* 1959, 12, 5-14.

14. Mowrer, O. *The new group therapy.* New York: D. Van Nostrand, 1963.

15. O'Connell, W. "Identification and curability of the mental hospital patient." *J. Indiv. Psychol.,* 1962, 18, 68-76.

16. ————. "Adlerian psychodrama with schizophrenics." *J. Indiv. Psychol.,* 1963, 19, 69-76.

17. Oliver, W. & A. Landfield. "Reflexibility: an unfaced issue in psychology." *J. Indiv. Psychol.,* 1962, 18, 114-124.

18. Reissman, F. *New approaches to mental health treatment for labor and for low income groups.* New York: National Institute of Labor Education, 1964.

19. Schwartz, E. "A psychoanalytic approach to the mental health team." *Amer. Imago,* 1958, 15, 437-451.

20. Shoben, E. "Personal responsibility, determinism, and the burden of understanding." *Personnel and Guidance J.,* 1961, 39, 342-348.

21. Shulman, B. "Use of dramatic confrontation in group psychotherapy." *Psychiat. Quart. Supp.,* 1962, 1, Part 1, 1-7.

22. Watzlawick, P. *An anthology of human communication.* Palo Alto: Science and Behavior Books, 1964.

23. White, R. "Ego and reality in psychoanalytic theory." *Psychol. Issues,* 1963, 3, 11.

TELEODRAMA

Originally, the search for theory and methods was lumped under the term "Psychodrama," then called various permutations of "Adlerian," "Reality," and "Action." At times this atypical group approach might be called Teleodrama (Rice, 1967)—Brechtian as well as Adlerian. It cannot be called psychodrama for many reasons, only one of which will be mentioned. From even limited experience with the Morenos, one develops great admiration for their tactical presence but the subtle reliance of orthodox psychodrama upon mechanical energies can depersonalize. Therefore patients are often granted easy justification for hating others because of supposedly objective frustrations. But to an Adlerian, "catharsis" can mean a creative relief resulting from finally feeling safe enough to disclose one's "negative nonsense" to others. As such, abreaction is merely the beginning and not the end of treatment.

Much of Bertolt Brecht's genius as a playwriter stemmed from his efforts to portray social interactions in such a way that the audience did not lose itself by complete identification with the actors in an overly aesthetic production (Kantor & Hoffman, 1966). Incongruities of setting and character were employed to highlight hidden truths beneath passively accepted realities. Since Adlerians expect no psychotherapeutic breakthrough from interminable analyses of external and noncentral factors, they share with Brecht this desire to help man overcome his blindness toward his own needs, demands, and goals. Brecht did not favor perfect reproductions of "reality" which led to the audience identifying completely with the actor's overt style and losing the detached onlooker quality. Brecht's unconcern for perfection fits the style of Action Therapy and should help the neophyte therapist whose own drive for perfection usually needs no added reinforcement from the environment.

Reprinted from *The Individual Psychologist*, Vol. VI, No. 2, November, 1969.

A method such as teleodrama in which staff members, by necessity or therapeutic choice, assume all the psychodramatic roles is worthwhile when the audience is avoiding both the process and content necessary for change. These times are quite frequent with what are called "unmotivated" chronic psychiatric patients (Adlerians translate the "unmotivated" to mean motivated to enhance and maintain "sick" self-esteem and social interest by habitual hidden movements toward power, revenge, and special service). When patients are avoiding a commitment to Action Therapy through inaction, the director and auxiliaries can use the benevolent shock techniques of Brecht in teleodrama to show simultaneously the hilarious yet tragic contrast between mere verbal cooperation ("Doctor, I'll do anything to get well 'cause you're my only hope") and hidden goals (an aside: "This Doc looks like a sucker. He needs me more than I need him"). When no movement of the patient is free from a purposive interpretation, the sick role frequently falls victim to the Brechtian distancing effect (which separates a potential audience response of massive sympathy, pampering, and rejection toward patients into respect for their subtle and tragic creativity).

Certain content areas are generally neglected by patients in groups. Homosexuality, for example, is habitually avoided, so the staff can move into the vacuum by acting out the hidden goals of patients (hence the label "teleodrama"). Adlerian theory focusing upon nonsexual and nonconstitutional causes of homosexuality provides the theoretical framework. Psychodramatic techniques (e.g., asides, doubling, mirroring, role reversal) open the hidden goals and fears of all life styles for tender exploration. Patients actively assume doubles and the roles of others, replacing staff, as the teleodramatic plots develop. Frequently a patient will remove himself from his life style presentation in a flood of tears or anger. The alert director will not let these emotions be an excuse for avoidance and will merely ask the patient to please be the double while the director or auxiliary will mirror the patient. As yet there has never been an incident in which a patient did not return to his role as protagonist after the temporary doubling in which a concerned staff member mirrored the patient empathically and teleodramatically. The spirit of mirroring is hopefully democratic. Staff request permission to "see if I know how you

71

are feeling," and add, "Please tell me if I'm wrong when we finish."

Often new staff members become talented in the immediate portrayal of life styles by acquainting themselves with Adlerian writings. For example, all auxiliaries may be given a short summary such as the following from a Dreikurs' book (1957):

"It is quite possible that Mrs. R. is a typical 'drunkard's wife.' Such women are so good that nobody can live up to their standards.. Consequently, the husband feels his deficiency more and more, and then either finds consolation in liquor or uses it to gain the strength to fight back. His drinking is both an expression of discouragement and of rebellion. And Mrs. R, like a typical wife of a drunkard, always gives in again and takes him back. She is too "good' to let him down completely—she just constantly pushes him down a little bit" (P. 97-98).

All actors are told to identify with three facets of the characters they are portraying in teleodrama (Brennan, 1967). In the soliloquy or double, there is animation in words, gestures and postures of hidden life style. That is, the auxiliary speaks of feelings and *purposes* of the behavior. He then moves to the significant others in the scene and tries to maneuver them to reward the style. In the third mode the actor moves throughout the audience, like the Ancient Mariner, trying to justify his behavior to others—usually blaming others, heredity, environment, etc. The actors' reactions to rejection and acceptance elicit much laughter, sufficient to reduce tension, but not enough to negate the message.[1] The members of the audience always have their homemade remedies which they jump up to try. Usually they are based on mechanical solutions, devoid of understanding of the actor's purposes. The main message is that individuals can select from almost any behavior their "reasons" to justify hatred, rejection, hopelessness—and unfortunately the rarity, social interest. This Adlerian approach fits in so well with the Brechtian distancing effect and Brecht's belief that the smallest social unit was not one person that I am wondering if anyone has tried to use Brechtian techniques in an Adlerian frame.

[1]While on the subject of laughter it is appropriate to note that Adlerian theory gives wit its due. The therapist, not being bound by the pity inherent in the view of the patient as a passive victim, is free to shock

72

benevolently and educate by witty behavior. Once mutual respect and cooperation have been developed in the therapy situation, the therapist has freedom to playfully over-and under-reflect in his guessing at the patients' efforts to hide and enhance low self-esteem and narrow social interest. Wit and humor in the therapy interaction are our most neglected interactions. Wit might be assumed to arise when the patient with expanded self-esteem and social interest suddenly experiences the simultaneous presence of two conflicting actions at the same time. As he pleads passive victimizations he realizes his foolish and delusional fashioning of the world to suit his desires to put others in his will. The incongruity in a nonthreatening world blossoms into laughter.

ADLERIAN ACTION THERAPY

People are taught concepts, but they are not taught or confronted with the experience which corresponds to these concepts. They see, as the Zen Buddhists say, the finger which points to the moon and mistake the finger for the moon."[1]

Action therapy tries to separate the finger from the moon. The finger is the sterile concept, the isolated, reified nouns without verbs. It is the authority without empathy, with unquestioned faith that all persons are alike: Little Mugs passively awaiting the nourishment of the Big Pitcher. Only cracked or warped mugs fail to change their behaviors after the Pitcher's decree. Action therapy on the other hand operates with a democratic respect for the individual's choices. Its only "demands" are that we listen to one another and try to experience the life style of the other person. Its hope is that people can experience alternative attitudes and actions to isolated, unrewarding suffering.

For over ten years the emphasis in action therapy has been upon behavior, not reified concepts, and has focused upon understanding the creative life style. Attempts to expand empathy have been by social learning situations for *all* rather than a paternalistic "giving" of therapy to inferior breeds. (Isn't it strange that no one has studied the *superior* skills of the insane?) Ideally the process has been to transform zombies (people who, with consummate skill, work for esteem through irresponsible noncooperative and "victimized" styles) into angels (those who communicate empathy to the "sinner" and humorously point out stupid, short-sighted goals of symptoms, without being controlled by others).

A number of papers have been written earlier describing action therapy, its theoretical background, techniques, and rationale. The present paper elaborates on prior efforts, specifical-

---

Adapted from a paper presented at American Psychological Association Convention, Washington, D.C., September, 1969, as part of a symposium entitled "Psychodrama and Science: Theoretical Approaches."
Reprinted from Voices: Summer, 1971.

ly on problems that psychiatric staff and patients share covertly, and on initial research efforts to test the value of so-called therapeutic endeavors.

The Winning Team: Staff functioning is maximized when it becomes democratized. That is, the patient is then respectfully allowed to be "sick" if he openly chooses an environment which will not esteem him as a person and compounds this mistake with self- and other-derogation for a crazy kind of esteem. But even democratic psychiatric teams are not things which function smoothly and effortlessly like a perpetual motion machine. All human activities have a purpose from veiled magical-egotistical ones to social growth-seeking. Frequently the typical psychiatric team follows bureaucratic strictures without ever examining the personalized meaning of "disease" and "cure."[2] Action therapy was born out of an attempt to create staff involvement in its behavioral orientation. The typical session pulls together some shared ideas of what staff can do and how patients might block this. The patient and his keepers are seen as a system, each element with its own demands. These demands should, for optimal functioning, be made overt (e.g., "I demand patients stay awake or I will not direct action therapy"). Implicit demands are examined openly to detect heightened needs for attention, power, revenge, and special service. If the latter are present the next move is "What thoughts and perceptions do I *select* to make myself so demanding and hyperdependent upon others?" The mature one, it seems, can give time and effort quite selflessly because he doesn't create his own unworthiness.

It is probably quite rare that a psychotherapist ever develops in his working situation a close relationship with a colleague who functions as a cotherapist and gives honest positive and negative feedback. If the therapist does find one co-human for this purpose he is a very lucky guy. In the psychotherapeutic relationship the general trend has been for the authoritarian therapist, who sees with the third eye and hears with the third ear, to sharpen this skill in competition with fellow therapists (whom he probably never sees in action). And competition doesn't lead to cooperative feedback. In contrast, imagine a democratic scene where all participants, patients, directors, auxiliaries are expected to give feedback (yet, of course, very often choose to do otherwise). In an egalitarian

75

system the director models the kind of behavior he seeks in patients. In this setting, one does not, as a rule, confuse "the finger and the moon." "Do as I say and not as I do!" may suit the pre-electronic era of passive listening but not the times of active watching.

"Tensions Go When Pretentions Fall:"[3] The most difficult task for neophyte directors and auxiliaries to learn is the ability to share responsibility and admit defeat (e.g., when patients' defensive skill exceeds therapists' tolerance level). Their self-ideals seem to revolve about complete independence and utter perfection. One is on the road to democratic directorship when he can say, "I really don't know what to do now. Will you please help me? How do you feel about my asking you for assistance?" or "I'm in a crazy situation. I'm like a baseball coach who wants his team to practice, but after saying you want to be good players you tell me, 'I can't practice because I may make a mistake . . . or not hit a home run every time . . . ' or 'I got a hit yesterday so I never have to practice again . . .' Now I think that damned funny!" The learner in the helping profession often, it seems, wants to be godlike (as a reaction to low self-esteem?) and declares the patient or the therapy useless, too sick, or a complete failure if volunteers do not come forth in droves and change their behavior because the therapist merely wishes it to be so. Because of this "commonest neurosis" of striving for perfection, student therapists often would rather assume the role of the private practitioner and be the unquestioned authority, commenting in splendid isolation upon frictionless events of other times and other places.

It is really funny, but potentially tragic if not noted and commented upon, that the beginning director asks for action and is angry and frustrated if he gets it or does not get it. This is a double bind situation if the therapist, instead of disclosing his feelings for purposes of mutual exploration, blames the patient subtly for anything he does. This leads to the second point of difficulty, what to do when the patient moves. And this is where the therapy becomes more Adlerian than ever. That is, the *consistency* and the *creativity* of the life style[4] gives clues as to what the director selects for the problem the group will attempt to solve. He is attuned to negative nonsense or statements which express a hopeless disdain for self and others. That is, the subtle retreats from social responsibility which gain the patient minor esteem (which is all he thinks he can hope for) are major clues the director pursues.

Consistency is used to help the director from getting mired in factual debates about people, places, and things. From patient behavior the director can infer attitudes toward the self and others and can use this information to go beyond past situations. Action therapy might be compared at times to the Brechtian theater. Its aim is to stimulate an active puzzlement in people who believe humans are depersonalized, mechanized objects with whom they can never have favorable influence without brute force. "To transform himself from general passive acceptance . . . (a man) needs to develop that detached eye with which the great Galileo observed a swinging chandelier,"[5] and many techniques can be used for that end. Consistency of the person allows generalization from one modality to another (attitudes to behavior and vice versa). Thinking about the inventive tenacity of the life style gives the director impetus into the future. He can imagine probable stress situations, and implicit goals of the protagonist who, like the rest of us, seeks rewards and reinforcements congruent with his life style. So from the use of the psychodramatic techniques of the soliloquy and the empty chair[6], for example, the Adlerian-minded director can exponentially increase working knowledge about protagonists. In summary, the successful growing director works his way free from unproductive verbal stalemates. He experiences the non-fatal effect of admitting imperfection and he looks for evidence of negative nonsense in verbal and nonverbal communications. These are then generalized into a consistent holistic picture of the person's life style. The creative power of the self- and other-attitudes is taught by experience and empathy through the use of asides, mirroring, doubling.

Once a director is free of the dis-ease of trying to be perfect and carry the therapeutic load alone, a remarkable flexibility grows. From an Adlerian view the protagonist is not a passive victim. He is capable of changing his life style but purposively, yet unwittingly exaggerates his symptoms, feelings of victimization and powerlessness. In everyday life, similar under- and overstatements are mechanisms of wit and humor.[7] Hyperboles-in-action are exemplified by Mark Twain's examples of braggarts (the bungling little men who attempt to convince the world of personal greatness) as well as by the phenomenology of "the mentally ill." The English propensity for underestimating situations (called "miosis") brings laughter, too. So would the movements of therapy patients to attenuate their social worth and responsibility *if* we could see them simultaneously in a non-victimized orientation and *if* we didn't believe patients would construe our laughter as "hostility." Wit and humor are used in action therapy, and good sessions are characterized by heightened attention and laughter. The veteran director often uses laughter for group tension-reduction by pointing to ludicrous actions (but never to communicate inferiority of person).

An especially useful experiential technique combines role reversal and mirroring. When a patient *demands* esteem from others—without outsight and cooperation—he is told to reverse roles and play the other. The director warms the patient up to play this significant other, then selects an auxiliary to mirror the patient. The latter is then faced with interacting with "himself," a situation never experienced in daily living. The mirror should caricature the patient's demands and movements in condensed form (condensation is another mechanism of wit). The mirror, by exaggerating, understating, and condensing, gets the point across with a merry performance. The protagonist, now playing the "rejecting" significant other, hears a rapid condensation of paradoxes. For example, "I love you and want you to be happy but raise the kids anyway. But do as I say and don't let me know you're making decisions. Tell me everything you do and how great I am but don't bother me or I'll shut up and think about things that will make me depressed . .. " Condensing all the protagonist's contradictory, defeating attitudes and demands is without equal in getting a point across with laughter.

Successful therapy teaches the patient a sense of humor. Frankl's paradoxical intention is one technique for developing this.[7] Its use implies that the patient himself is not derogated, even if his actions are. When we move from Freud's idea of gallows humor, where the person in *objective* stress responds with jests, to the action therapy situation a new phenomenological field is encountered. The protagonist there is faced with stress which he had unwittingly created by isolated reactions to low self-esteem and social interest. He can, with help, learn to find esteem in more socially cooperative ways. Faith in the Adlerian life style gets the therapist out of the rut of cloying pity for the patient, who is not a lower-order nit-wit, as a rule. Educating the patient in humor increases that of the therapist and is a sparkling and rare example of social synergy.

Patient Commitment to Treatment: In the traditional mental hospital setting both staff and patient population have trouble maintaining an "active social interest" (courage, in Adler's terms). Both groups model and reward mutual withdrawal.[8] Action therapy was designed with the indifference of both groups in mind, knowing that a change in element of the system can reciprocally alter the action of the other.

In pre-chemotherapy days patients disrupted hospital well-being with active violence. Today the disruption stems from passive violence, the patient who will not follow the treatment regime, yet will not openly admit his denials. This silent rebel gains less attention, power, revenge, or special service than his more volatile predecessor, but his uncooperative behavior still disturbs, disrupts, and destroys therapeutic programs.

Persons engaged in action therapy programs have for long had strong faith, based upon clinical evidence, that protagonists who risk openness before a group lead a fuller posthospital existence with less frequent rehospitalization and social isolation. As with all therapies which can be subsumed under the generic term psychodrama, almost no "hard" research data has been available of the life styles of protagonists. Some are now being gathered which will be only partially reported here. For a five-month period those patients who either volunteered themselves or were volunteered by their groups to be principals in action therapy were classified as members of the protagonist group (N equals 42), while those who were not selected or subtly resisted the selection of pleas of anxiety, noncompetence, or "no problems" were called the non-protagonist group (N equals 151). All patients were exposed to the month-long leaderless groups, instrumented laboratory exercises, and semiweekly action therapy sessions of the Patients' Training Laboratory at the Houston VA Hospital.[9] This research ward has a here-and-now group orientation in which the giving and receiving of feedback relative to behaviors is paramount. As part of the data gathering all patients were given the Personal Beliefs Inventory (PBI) pre- and post-laboratory experience. The PBI is a 60-item test of "negative nonsense,"[10] high scores indicating irrational thinking (e.g., "Punishing oneself for all errors will help prevent future mistakes.")[11]

At this point, some facts regarding patient commitment become clear. Only 104 nonprotagonists, as compared to 39 protagonists were available for posttesting. Forty-seven nonprotagonists and two protagonists dropped out of the program for various reasons. The difference, favoring protagonists' commitment to the program until termination would be expected to occur by chance only five times in a thousand (chi square of 8.64).

The combined sample of nonprotagonists and protagonists showed a decrease in "negative nonsense" (F equals 38.1, $p <$ .0001). The protagonist group showed a greater reduction in faulty thinking than the nonprotagonist group (F equals 2.3, $p < .12$). (Some purists who hold the .05 probability sacred will object to the use of the .12 level of probability, being victims of a dogma inherited, we are told, from agronomy. This higher chance level was risked because the protagonist group was mixed with nonvolunteers, only one session was allowed per protagonist, some of the treatment given was organized by inexperienced directors, and some members of the nonprotagonist group actually spent more time on the stage as doubles and role-players than the protagonists. In other words, with groups and treatment not clearly delineated, less striking results were expected. These circumstances lead one to be happy to find significance even if it could occur spuriously 12 times out of 100).

So either because of or in spite of action therapy, some people seem to be experiencing the moon and not merely describing their fingers.

IDENTIFICATION AND CURABILITY
OF THE
MENTAL HOSPITAL PATIENT

The mental hospital microcosm is now passing through an age of what we fervently hope is a burgeoning maturity. Not so many years ago we had no doubts, no anxieties, and were blithely turning to oracular authorities for assuring answers. We learned the dogmas all too well: The high priest was the medical man and the psychologist an insecure acolyte; or, in more modern sophisticated analogy, the psychiatric team of psychiatrist, psychologist, and social worker was the personification of authoritarian father, rebellious son, and doting mother.[18] Psychoanalysis was the treatment of choice "for all God's chill'un;" and the "incurability myth"[4] was an inviolate truth. Furthermore, psychotherapeutic ceremonials were only valid when practiced by those with proper and respectable degrees. The couch, the one-to-one encounter, and other manifestations of "one-upmanship"[10] were prized. Group methods had their secondary places of honor in the therapeutic armamentarium, depending for their appraisal upon whether the acknowledged leader was medical or psychological, social, or a mere aide. In the latter cases, the appellation "psychotherapy" was never uttered. The quest was for insight and, like the mythical unicorn, it was only hunted by certain people at appropriate times.

Now all this has been seriously questioned, and the mental hospital ethos is experiencing the "strain and stress" of inquiries into those premises upon which so much time and energy has been based. It is the writer's hope and belief that mental hospitals will profit from such experiences by responding with increased anecdotal and experimental research, rather than regressing to their old stultifying "incestuous fixations"[8] and concomitant multiple hostilities. The purpose of this paper is to point in one hopefully fruitful direction.

Reprinted from *Journal of Individual Psychology*, 1962, 18, 68-76.

The Passing Mental Hospital Scene

The domain of medicine. Psychological treatments, predicated upon neurotic problems, have never deeply impressed the decision makers in the small world of the disenfranchized schizophrenic. The biological substratum has been paramount in mental hospital mentation. Obviously it offers a more palpable and somewhat more measurable approach than the psychological. The millennium seemed to have arrived with the tranquilizer. The medical man's image was enhanced, and he was able to spend his time indulging in medical matters: searching endless combinations of drugs, and combating their side effects. The "ancillary" personnel's role seemed even more futile, drone-like, and unrewarding than before.[13] But the surcease and pleasant hopes proved only temporary.

The failure of psychoanalysis. The psychoanalytic mode of thought is second only to the organic frame of reference as the favorite hypothetic and deductive system of professionals in the mental hospital field. Studies of defense mechanisms and id-derivatives may have been of assistance to the eventual understanding of human problems, but unfortunately as far as treatment of the schizophrenic is concerned, there is little or nothing to be gained from following the psychoanalytic model. Certainly one can translate phenomena of treatment into psychoanalytic terms by a Procrustean squeeze, but these terms have been based on "uncommon sense" observations in the first place. Many psychoanalytic deductions contribute to the pall of hopelessness which has been one aspect of the "style of life" of neuropsychiatric institutions: The basic unfavorable view of psychoanalytic treatment for schizophrenics; too much attention to biological, energic concepts at the expense of observing the therapeutic effect of people, especially in the formation of primary and secondary narcissism;[3][8] a narrow view of love as debilitating rather than enriching the ego;[3][8] an insistence upon a kabbalistic relationship;[2] esoteric jargon as a necessity for a real cure; and the injunction that patients' problems are never to be discussed outside the therapy hour by patients, for this constitutes wanton defensiveness and dissipation of the optimal therapeutic tension.

When we grasped at the straws of somatogenesis and psychoanalysis, and refused to let go, the treatment aspects of mental hospitalization were forthwith temporarily doomed.

Although the organic and psychoanalytic theories seem incompatible to the novice, they are both essentially constitutional, biological viewpoints sentencing the schizophrenic to poor prognosis and eventual chronicity.

The "incurability" of schizophrenia. When one incorporates the incurability myth into his attitudes, he becomes a living example of R. K. Merton's uniquely human "self-fulfilling prophecy."[11] Physical laws operate beyond our thought control, but the laws of behavioral sciences must allow for the operation of the individual's universe of attitudes upon resultant behaviors. In other words, if I believe the incurability myth, I will act towards patients "as if" they were really impossible cases or objects, and, if this reaction is mirrored in many others, the patient becomes essentially incurable. The patient has been deprived of the interest of others, and is made to believe also by rejection that he is incurable. The phenomenon of chronicity as man-made rather than the end result of an endogenous disease process, has been ably reported by discerning psychiatrists.[4] [5] [6] [13] [14]

To the hospital's error of incurability one might add the process of infantilizing "understanding" and the inculcating and reinforcing of the "sick role" and all its conditioned responses, e.g., enhancing somatizations and passive waiting for cures.

Incipient dissatisfactions with custodial care and psychoanalytic methodology as ways of solving the mental-health problem have brought back a host of ancient concepts and frames of reference. Values, sin and responsibility, free will and determinism have been resuscitated. Some value may be realized in time from their reexamination, yet it is difficult to judge what, if anything, has accrued from all this to benefit treatment of schizophrenics.

The existential trend has certainly highlighted the defects of psychoanalytic dogma. But it encourages another error in the neglect of etiological determinants. That is, responsibility, free will, and the like do not just grow like Topsy but have laws which govern their appearance. There is determinism—although Mazer[15] reports that psychiatrists subscribe to this law only during their office appointments — and the psychotherapist's task remains that of contributing something positive to the determiners.

Identification, A Way Out

The process of identification enters here. It can be conceived as just such a positive determiner, and the application of this concept may make our mental hospitals worthwhile institutions for re-socialization. But first its value must be recognized, its operation carefully reported, and eventually its experimental variables manipulated.

There have been a number of serious psychological studies on identification,[7] [12] [16] but these have been far removed from the psychotherapy of schizophrenics. Despite his brilliant research and incisive thought on identification, Mowrer[16] seems to have compartmentalized this work as he tackles the problem of schizophrenia. His thought here commences where we leave off: the ability of a patient to confess and take responsibility for transgressions. It is hoped that as Mowrer deals with more regressed patients, he will take into account his enlightening views on the identification process as a learning relationship based upon tension-reduction premises.

Some attention is paid to the concept of identification in psychotherapy at the present time. But this is mostly according to psychoanalytic thought, limited to the value which accrues from identification with a shadowy withholding authority, and amounts to lip service only.

Schizophrenics need much more than that. A first premise will be that the schizophrenic does suffer from a lack of adequate identification models. In his life he has had a paucity of significant others to aid in the development of a consistent sense of identity. He has never been helped to achieve the firm belief that he is a worthwhile unique person, with roots in the past, and a future in which he can make an important contribution to the lives of others. The schizophrenic feels that he does not really exist. He feels like a confused, unworthy appendage of someone powerful, or like nothing at all—a microscopic bit of plankton on an infinite stormy sea. He cannot assert himself normally because of fear of imminent cataclysm; so he talks and aggresses in a circuitous manner which he fears might be decoded by a potentially overpowering person.

In other words, the schizophrenic is one who suffers from extremely low self-esteem, the core theory of schizophrenia,[17] and from lack of social relatedness. Thus the appropriate therapy is one of encouragement and socialization. If the patient cannot learn to socialize in the hospital, he has no alternative but to become a chronic patient. Before the icing of insight can be added, a stable bilateral relationship must be formed between the patient and the therapist.

Within the framework of such a view, identification implies the slow development of Adlerian social interest, an "evaluative attitude toward life *(Lebensform)*," actively encouraged by the therapist.

The ability to identify must be trained, and it can be trained only if one grows up in relation to others and feels a part of the whole. One must sense that not only the comforts of life belong to one, but also the discomforts. One must feel at home on this earth with all its advantages and disadvantages . . . The capacity for identification, which alone makes us capable of friendship, love of mankind, sympathy, occupation, and love, is the basis of social interest and can be practiced and exercised only in conjunction with others. In this intended assimilation to another person or a situation lies the whole meaning of comprehension (1, p. 136).

Identification in Hospital Therapy

Regarding the place of identification in therapy, perhaps it would be well to distinguish between the social interest of process schizophrenics and of reactive schizophrenics.

The hallmark of the process schizophrenic, who is highlighted here, is a preoccupation with personal panics to the exclusion of a positive interest in others—others who are in his eyes uniformly withholding, tantalizing, and tempting. There is no place for nondirectiveness here; such a patient must be taught social skills from the ground up and be rewarded for his essential humanness which he does not see.

This throws a tremendous burden of responsibility upon the therapist, from which he is sheltered by the organic and the "50 minute hour toward insight" approaches. He must be a *real* person with strong feelings of worth, hope, and unburdened by residual hatred. The therapist must be active and consistent in rewarding courage and in blocking generalized self-disparagement. For how can a patient incorporate attitudes which are seldom or only subtly and ambiguously expressed? The therapist must be able to venture into self-disclosure as a model for identification and to counteract the schizophrenics' perception of him as an omnipotent authority.

Double binding[17] must be minimized. Again this requires an active therapist who must be certain that the patient is not misinterpreting in silence. The act of double binding presupposes a dependent "victim" and authorities who communicate incongruous messages and will not allow discussion of the contradictions. Repeated exposure to such treatment is one method of inculcating low self-esteem in people, and is sometimes a sickness of the hospital itself. An example of institutional double binding is seen in cases where the patient learns to communicate more openly in group psychotherapy, yet at the same time his awkwardness is not tolerated by ward personnel, and he is restrained by physical or chemical means.

In the reactive schizophrenic there may be partial identification with others, and high self-esteem for a particular infantile image which the world outside of the primary group will not accept or reward. Social skills are more developed but without a mature attitude of mutuality. The role of the therapist here requires less "mothering" but more flexible "fathering."[8]

Identification with any real people, regardless of professional status, is the essential process of psychotherapy. Lack of acceptance of this is partly responsible for the dilemmas of co-professionalism and social intrusion, even in progressive humane hospitals.[9] In fact, not only boundaries of the hierarchy of the professions but also the patient-professional boundary are here often still inviolate, and identification goes on in the one-up-and-one-down relationship of the circumscribed hour. When the therapist feels threatened by the patient, he believes that academic degrees and information necessarily keep an iron curtain operating between himself and the patient; the therapist seems to feel that growth and maturity in the patient will cost him so much libido as to leave him vulnerable. Actually, the therapist should know that the true differentiation between himself and the patient is his capacity for humanistic identification and his self-esteem, which the patient cannot take from him.

An Example

There is no doubt that being a real person, in the above sense, involved in ordering the confused world of another, is more taxing for the therapist than other models of therapy available. The difficulties with patient CC will illustrate what happens when the defensive social barrier goes down.

CC had been a member of group psychotherapy for over a year. He is a typical process schizophrenic with all the social gaucheries implied. His mother has been a mental patient for over 20 years, and his father is probably a paranoid schizophrenic uneasily tolerated by the community. CC was humorless, dogmatic, and handicapped by a borderline IQ. In the group he glowered silently at the members and appeared on the verge of fights many times. He later became very tremulous in psychodrama and started to derogate authorities and females indiscriminantly. These displays resulted in the application of many chemical restraints. When he went on initial group-therapy outings, he started to learn the value of some of the social niceties and received increased attention and reward for such. Shortly afterward he began to discuss sexual prowess in the group but wanted a pill to relieve these sins. Then a therapeutic dilemma reared its ugly head. The patient began to punch the therapist lightly and push him around whenever they met.

The typical attitude expressed by psychologically-oriented personnel was that the patient could not help such behavior and was expressing sexual and hostile bullying impulses. Such interpretations did not halt the patient's behavior. But when the therapist drew the line, the patient noted the anger easily, blamed the behavior on the result of past ECT ("made me like a child"), then loudly threatened suicide. The therapist's approach was to admit his anger and state emphatically that the patient was capable of acting differently and not destroying himself. He pointed out that his anger was a sign of interest in the patient, and there was to be no rescinding of the patient's privileges. This elicited many expressions of hope and fear from the patient, which he had not expressed previously. The punching by the patient ceased, but his lack of social skills still kept him in close contact with chemical restraints.

CC's behavior is an excellent illustration not only of the difficulties precipitated by social contact, but also of the necessity of blending "objective" and phenomenal interpretations of the patient's behavior. Whereas the observers believed this to be the eruption of hostile and sexual responses, the patient stated that he was being friendly, "like the boys on the ward taught me." The latter pictures infantile expression more vividly.

87

Reward and Punishment

More active, identification-based psychotherapy undoubtedly requires more setting of limits, without double binding. Such tactics might sound spuriously like punishment, but are they? There is no taking away of privileges, no threat of lowering the self-esteem. This is not to say that all punishment is out of order, for it is a device in socializing the child and the schizophrenic. There are times when noncorporeal punishment is required in the raising of a child and his emotional counterpart, the regressed schizophrenic. The patient, like the child, is not allowed to harm physically either partner in a relationship, and harmful solutions are negatively reinforced. Punishment is frequently necessary in the daily routine of the ward. Personnel are chronically puzzled over the manipulations of rewards, especially the non-material interpersonal varieties. What to reward and with what? At times tension must be fostered in the patient to insure tension reduction, learning, and a creation of significance for the therapist, who schools the patient in the art of reducing tension and anxiety in the most efficacious style.

Failure to realize the potential incentive and reward value of the therapist as a real person, has encouraged us to continue glibly with an encapsuled abstract need-system philosophy. This awesome view of determinism has led to the cul-de-sac of subtly neglecting the patient ("he needs to be that way"), until personnel frustration explodes in arbitrary acts of mechanical restraint and withholding of privileges, leaving the patient no chance for queries. That is, we temporarily tolerate the patient's behavior as an expression of inexorable needs, without examining two important points: (a) Is the patient's behavior really need inspired, or simply habitual and therefore more amenable to change if someone encourages him without embarking upon emotional strangulation? (b) What influence can we bring to bear to alter the acceptance of such destructive determinism in favor of a more personally satisfying determinism?

A remark by SC, paraphrased by many other schizophrenics, will serve as an abrupt close. "I hated my mother because she'd say, 'Do what you want, dear,' but she'd never assist me to develop any skills except listen quietly as she read fairy tales to me. But at times when I thought I knew

what to do, she said, 'Do what I say and don't talk about it!' "
Are we in the mental hospital perpetuating the traumata?

Summary

Psychotherapy with hospitalized schizophrenic patients has been tethered by treating it as the medical man's domain exclusively, by the tacit incorporation of psychoanalytic frames of thoughts, and by assuming the incurability of schizophrenia. If there is any truth in the premise that regressed schizophrenics are unsocialized and childlike, more active, extensive approaches must be employed in therapy, working toward the growth of humanistic identification on the part of the patients, in Adler's sense of identification as "intended assimilation to another person." Such proposed treatment would highlight the development of social interest in patients through the active support and understanding of therapeutic personnel who are skilled in "mothering" and "fathering," rather than simply observing and reporting symptoms. Difficulties involved in this approach would represent a necessary stage in the growth of mental hospitals and must be faced maturely if such institutions are to become treatment-oriented rather than remain custodial in nature.

REFERENCES

1. Ansbacher, H. L. and Ansbacher, Rowena (Ed.) *The Individual Psychology of Alfred Adler.* New York: Basic Books, 1958.

2. Bakan, D. *Sigmund Freud and the Jewish mystical tradition.* Princeton, N. J.: Van Nostrand, 1958.

3. Benda, C. "Narcissism" in psychoanalysis and the "love for oneself" in existential psychotherapy. *Dis nerv. sys. Monogr. Suppl.,* 1961, 22, 1-9.

4. Bockoven, J. Moral treatment in American psychiatry. *J. nerv. ment. Dis.,* 1956, 124, 167-194, 292-321.

5. Borman, L. D. The chronic patient in hospital culture. *VA Newsltr coop. Res. Psychol.* 1960, 2, 7-11.

6. Boverman, M. Rigidity, chronicity, schizophrenia. *AMA Arch. gen. Psychiat.,* 1959, 1, 235-242.

7. Bronfenbrenner, U. Freudian theories of identification and their derivatives. *Child Develpm.,* 1960, 31, 15-40.

8. Fromm, E. *The art of loving.* New York: Harper, 1959.

9. Gallagher, E., and Albert, R. The Gelbdorf affair. *Psychiatry,* 1961, 24, 221-227.

10. Haley, J. The art of psychoanalysis. *Etc.,* 1958, 15, 3-11.

11. Hardin, G. Three classes of truth: their implications for the behavioral sciences. *Etc.,* 1961, 18, 5-20.

12. Hill, W. Learning theory and the acquisition of values. *Psychol. Rev.,* 1960, 67, 317-331.

13. Lefton, M., Dinitz, S., and Pasamanick, B. Decision-making in a mental hospital: real, perceived, and ideal. *Amer. sociol. Rev.,* 1959, 24, 822-829.

14. Lehrman, N. Do our hospitals help make acute schizophrenics chronic? *Dis. nerv. Sys.,* 1961, 22, 1-5.

15. Mazer, M. The therapeutic function of the belief in will. *Psychiatry,* 1960, 23, 45-52.

16. Mowrer, O. Identification: a link between learning theory and psychotherapy. In *Learning theory and personality dynamics.* New York: Ronald, 1950. Pp. 573-616.

17. O'Connell, W. Ward psychotherapy with schizophrenics through concerted encouragement. *J. Indiv. Psychol.,* 1961, 17, 193-204.

18. Schwartz, E. A psychoanalytic approach to the mental health team. *Amer. Imago,* 1958, 15, 437-451.

THE VALUES OF ROLE REVERSAL IN PSYCHODRAMA AND ACTION THERAPY*

(with Deanna Brewer)

Far too many practitioners of psychotherapy have forgotten (if they have ever been aware of) the fact that psychotherapeutic techniques are meaningful in terms of lessons to be taught and/or behaviors to be practiced. Like the symptoms of the patient, techniques cannot be studied in isolation and are understood only in terms of their goals for human behavior change.

Role Reversal (RR), the most valuable technique in the psychodramatic armamentarium, is no exception to the rule that techniques are used for definite purposes. Ofttimes directors of psychodrama use RR to demonstrate unwittingly the range and facility of their competitive skills. Others switch to RR to diagnose and/or teach the client a certain amount of flexibility in his movements and relationships. At times RR may be selected for a cathartic effect, the director selecting a type of role which could achieve maximum emotional release for the protagonist. But catharsis as an end result has many critics both theoretical and experimental (Berkowitz, 1970). In essence the critics report that the benefits of abreaction are slight when compared to the negative effects of reinforcement of destructive interpersonal acts. In authentic psychodrama and Action Therapy catharsis is used not for emotional release only but as a first step toward outsight and authenticity (O'Connell, 1966).

Often what appears in literature as RR is not so in the holistic systematic sense. Psychodrama and Action Therapy are both socially embedded methods, so the roles to be reversed are those of the self and a significant other in dyadic interaction. As an example of a narrow view of RR, Rothaus,

*Paper presented at the 79th Annual Meeting of the Amercian Psychological Association, September 3-7, 1971, Washington, D. C.

Reprinted from *Handbook of International Sociometry*, 1971, Vol. VI

Johnson, and Lyle (1964) isolated a dimension of behavior (passive-active) for reversal. The "role" reversed was actually only speeding up or slowing down of movements without reference to the hidden goals of the patient or his dyadic other. Role reversal as defined above, while of interest to the therapist, represents at best a rudimentary aspect of role reversal and not the most powerful insight- and outsight-producing source.

Psychodrama

According to Moreno, there is creativity in man's organization of his world. In order to relieve himself of some of the frustrating burden of spontaneously creating appropriate responses for each event as if it were perpetually new, man has developed behavior patterns which ideally release new spontaneity and creativity and help him derive some sense of world order (Bishof, 1970). When behavior patterns are used more for their promise of security from unpredictability, spontaneity and creativity diminish and role rigidity takes their place. Moreno calls such set patterns of behavior, cultural conserves. Should they be abused, role reversal can be used as a technique to regenerate flexibility and spontaneity by allowing practice and change toward new behaviors.

Cultural conserves serve an important function in the development of a civilization by preserving the values of its culture. One of the ways we learn our language is through cultural conserves such as language games. To have some order to our communication we have learned to expect and depend on people to play language games. Most of us know what "stop" means and that "red" is associated with "stop" in our traffic laws. However, such action does point out how we depend on cultural conserves to organize and give structure to our lives.

The expectations of and dependency on such cultural conserves can shape our destiny and our lives. Take, for example, the language game of a patient who walks into a therapist's office, and is asked the question, "How are you today?" Now the appropriate response for the patient to make would be something like, "I'm fine," or "I'm not doing too well," or even "A little out of breath from running up the stairs." But what if the patient returns with the comment, "The plane ran down the tracks." More than likely and especially if he continued to give such inappropriate responses, he would be diagnosed as a schizophrenic.

Sources of Role Confusion

In much the same sense, Moreno (1959) discusses the social appropriateness of roles. We learn at an early age the confusion between role and identity through cultural conserves and language development. Consider, for example, an adult who asks his four-year-old son what he would like to be when he grows up. The little boy has already learned a certain art in making socially appropriate responses so he says, "I want to be a fireman." The father might then follow with a reinforcing response like, "Oh, how cute. You'll be such a good fireman."

Along with languages games, one of the very subtle catalysts for role-identity confusion is the toy industry. Very few toys reflect core identity teachings. Most focus on roles, e.g., military toys, toys for "little mothers," toys for "little doctors and nurses," etc.

Just as Moreno uses the idea of the social atom to describe the social constellation of the individual, the distinction between role and identity can also be seen as analogous to the atom where the identity corresponds to the nucleus and the roles correspond to the electrons. It is the electrons that give the atom character and allow the atom to attract other atoms just as roles function for people. And, as the nucleus and electrons have both similar and dissimilar functions working together to provide for the atom as an integrated unit, so do the roles and identity work together for the person. Yet, it is felt that a distinction made between role and identity is worth expansion as an explanation for role rigidity. A person who is trying to give up a role to take on another does not see the giving up as such a threat when a distinction between role and identity has been made and he does not feel he is giving up a part of his identity along with the role. If, however, an individual structures his roles to the point where he does not deviate from a set pattern of behavior (role rigidity), he will inadvertently lose his spontaneity; and, eventually, he will lose his ability to develop himself to his fullest.

Role Playing and Role Reversal

Psychodramatic role reversal allows practice in taking on a variety of roles while being rewarded and encouraged for such behavior. Moreno describes role reversal as a technique of socialization and self-integration through the act of taking into oneself the role of another. He further emphasizes RR as a technique to help the patient act spontaneously in the here-and-now while utilizing his abilities to make socially acceptable adjustments to "reality."

To examine how role rigidity can effect role reversal, take, for illustration, a little boy who gets angry with his baby sister for pestering him, and he hits her to show her he means business. The mother, hearing the screams and cries of her little girl, rushes to the scene and finds out what has gone on. One of the most common ways for mothers to deal with such a problem is to try to get the boy to see what he has done and to feel the pain he has inflicted on his baby sister. The mother might say, "Shame on you for doing that to your sister. For your punishment, I am going to let her hit you so you will know just how she feels."

This is one of the first forms of RR an individual experiences, and it is easy to see how this could contribute to role rigidity, too. Not only was the boy faced with punishment as he takes on the role of his sister (feel what she was feeling), but also his perception of the incident was arbitrarily overruled. Perhaps this can be used to explain why a man who is angry with his wife has a hard time reversing roles with her. By doing so he is encouraged to understand her life style demands and in contrast his needs may become secondary, at least temporarily. Yet, by reversing roles, he might be able to alter his valuation of her and in turn change his perception of the relationship.

Action Therapy

In Action Therapy the final goal is to increase the person's self-esteem, hopefully in harmony with a widening social interest. Operationally, this goal is defined by well-developed skills in giving and receiving feedback (O'Connell, 1971a, 1971b). Widening social interest and increasing self-esteem are difficult movements to teach for the adult patient's life style is no *tabula rasa* but, among other things, a creative system of "negative certainties" (Beecher, 1966). Therefore, types of "replacement therapy" are doomed in advance. With adults, symptomatic behaviors have usually been highly practiced over time. Even more stable are the attitudes toward self, others and life situations which motivate feelings and actions. There are no flexible mature persons whose sources of esteem and social interest are purely external and who live as recipients of passively received esteem by transplantation or replacement. In fact, the appearance of such demands and their certain frustrations is the hallmark of the disturbed and disturbing person.

Techniques are used in Action Therapy to show to the patient that changes in his errors-in-living, "negative nonsense," are his responsibility. If he desires to pursue minimal self-esteem via defective social interest, the natural consequences are misery for the patient— and those dependent upon him. Self-esteem is chronically deflated by self-blame in the pursuit of the only esteem the patient thinks is available to him. Patients in Action Therapy experience "how" and "why" they narrow their lives and are given a chance to practice alternative behaviors, if they wish.

The theory of humanistic identification (O'Connell, 1968) and its methodology for change is definitely focused upon incorporating into onself- and other-transactions a more hopeful optimistic theory of the other, which then becomes its own self-fulfilling prophecy. As a prerequiste for peak experiences and mature autonomy, one learns to give, receive and encourage authentic feedback (O'Connell, 1971b), and not to become hyperdependent on others so that feedback is impossible. Chronic dependency eventuates in interpersonal demands, usually unconscious, to be pampered, rejected, or simply left alone. Demands differ from expectations mainly in the extreme frustration, blame and "negative nonsense" (Ellis, 1962) which follow unsatisfied demands. A polar opposite of the pathological demand is the sense of humor. The humorist feels the shock of frustration but has outsight into the needs of others. He can disinvolve himself sufficiently from his space and time malaise to develop a "god's-eye view" (Munro, 1951). A habitual sense of humor hinges on adequate self-esteem, social interest and a playful aloofness from the seductive security of polarities, dualities, and abstractions (e.g., "Kill the commies . . . devils . . . Blacks . . . yellows . . . whites, etc.,

etc.,"). The humorous attitude, the epitome of love, respect and independence can be taught. Action Therapy takes a small step toward teaching humor—through the models of the director, the auxiliaries and the technique of role reversal.

Role Reversal in Action Therapy

With all forms of mental illness self- and/or other-blame is paramount in maintaining misery. Patient-types go through the endless cycle of demands, frustrations, blame and negative "proof"-seeking. All persons, I assume, are creative enough to find "reasons" for maintaining the premises of their life styles, no matter how self-punishing the consequences. The premises are maintained, that is, until significant others give adequate feedback and do not reward behavior which is in the service of useless goals. For a happy change, the protagonist must experience the pervasive demands he creates—which are so commonplace as to be ignored by him as a cause of his failures (e.g., "I want to know the *real deep* reason which makes me .."").

Our philosophy of therapy is becoming so other-oriented, albeit undoubtedly self-centered, that we have habitually and gently tried to manipulate each patient into the role of his *Gegenspieler* (Adler's term for the self-created enemy, purposively selected to maintain and enhance life style attitudes). The fantasy RR is accomplished with questions focused on feelings, demands, frustrations, and pains of the other (the therapist might ask Joe, the patient: "What does Helen say to herself that makes her feel so miserable," then, "I wonder what Helen tells herself that Joe does to help Helen feel so miserable?"). Hopefully, this imagery RR, if its use helps the patient attain dignity and worth, will be further practiced to the extent of becoming an autopsychodrama, a way of the other into the patient's previously locked-in demand system, or even a preliminary step to humor development.

A rudimentary type of RR has been described. Now a more advanced technique will be mentioned. This method, which has no name, brings play— one of the few human movements which has yet to be well incorporated—into the medical model. (Incidentally, I am reminded of the neglect of play when I become so engrossed in teaching the patients to practice feedback that the whole "interactional-dance" loses any zestful variations of rhythm.) This kind of RR needs a happy auxiliary who does not see the patient as a passive victim. Female volunteers from the community are therefore much better at this activity than hospital personnel. The auxiliary will act out the patient's life style demands (the purposes of his symptoms, his muffled cry for magic and its eventual frustration). In the beginning of the scene she will probably be interacting with the patient as a significant other, in the way the patient reports seeing this person. As the patient's demands increase, the reversal is made. The auxiliary now caricatures the patient, the latter is faced with the impossible task of relating to his own demands, and the director keeps him in role and reflecting on the trapped feelings of the patient forced to interact with his own double binds. A marvelous psychedelic experience, provided that the auxiliary and director are skillful at emotional tutoring, is in the making.

A question frequently asked by new auxiliaries concerns the authenticity of the antagonist, as if the other has some immutable real qualities free from value judgment. For example, "Is Joe's wife *really* that way?" (What can one answer except "no"?) Frank Haronian (1967) has a very interesting way of resolving this question. His approach starts with his observation that friendship, generosity and tenderness have no essential place in Freudian theory since they all supposedly reflect the vagaries of real sexual-hostile urges. He then reports on Dr. Hanscarl Leuner's Guided Affective Imagery (GAI) as a way out of a narcissistic, selfish orientation. In GAI both patient (or protagonist) and antagonist purportedly are benefited, and the self-other dualism is vitiated. The GAI can be continued in fantasy in Action Therapy via an empty chair technique (O'Connell, 1967) or with an auxiliary portraying the antagonist or terrifying object. Leuner's patient is to a degree dealing with the projections of earlier introjections, in psychoanalytic terms. By learning to feed, accept and eventually make movements of love toward the terrifying other in his daydreams and fantasies, the protagonist learns to accept himself and thereby reintegrate his own projections. The other is freed from living as an inkblot and can have an existence all his own and be accepted for that.

In this context, the old adage "People we can't tease, we can't love" comes to mind. If we think of persons in terms of

97

psychic processes rather than isolated entities, it might be possible to conceive of a type of projection less fatal than the paranoid type. It would appear at a point in the development of self-esteem and social interest at which the person is playfully and not seriously projecting his impulses. Later on, he accepts them but for a time they are playfully projected upon positively significant others—before the development of a true sense of humor, at which time projection is nonexistent or subliminal. This phenomenon has been seen in intensive RR, as the protagonist learns to accept and cooperate with himself and later others, while the need for the *Gegenspieler* diminishes, perhaps forever.

REFERENCES

1. Beecher, W., & Beecher, M. *Beyond Success and Failure.* New York: Julian, 1966.

2. Berkowitz, L. Experimental investigations of hostility catharsis. *Journal of Consulting and Clinical Psychology,* 1970, 35, 1-7.

3. Bishof, L. *Interpreting Personality Theories.* New York: Harper & Row, 1970.

4. Ellis, A. *Reason and Emotion in Psychotherapy.* New York: Lyle Stuart, 1962.

5. Haronian, F. "The ethical relevance of a psychotherapeutic technique," *Journal of Religion and Health,* 1967, 6, 1-7.

6. Moreno, J, & Moreno, Z. *Psychodrama.* Vol. II. New York: Beacon, 1969.

7. Munro, D. *Argument of Laughter.* Melbourne : Melbourne University Press, 1951.

8. O'Connell, W. "Psychotherapy for everyman: A look at action therapy," *Journal of Existentialism,* 1966, 7(25), 85-91.

9. O'Connell, W. Psychodrama: "Involving the audience," *Rational Living,* 1967, 2(1), 22-25.

10. O'Connell, W. Humanizing religion, race, and sex. In W. Pew (Ed.), *The War Between the Generations*. Minneapolis: Alfred Adler Institute, 1968.

11. O'Connell, W. "Sensitivity training and Adlerian theory," *Journal of Individual Psychology*, 1971, 27, 65-72. (a)

12. O'Connell, W. "Equality in encounter groups," *The Individual Psychologist*, 1971, 8(1), 15-17. (b)

13. Rothaus, P., Johnson, D., & Lyle, F. "Group participation training for psychiatric patients," *Journal of Counseling Psychology*, 1964, 11, 230-238.

SKIN-JUMPING THERAPY: CREATING COMMUNAL COHESION

(with George Wiggins, M.D.)

The goals and techniques of the outpatient division of the Drug Abuse Program at the Veterans Administration Hospital, Houston, are shaped for the most part by the inner and outer experiences and beliefs of the authors of this paper. Lacking a better label, the psychiatric orientation of the clinic might be called existential--humanistic, with the treatment of choice being small groups (or communities) led by ex-addict counselors.[1] The treatment facility fits the definition of a methadone maintenance program, since almost 60% of over 300 outpatients are receiving regular doses of methadone. The Houston outpatients program[2][3] has evolved well beyond the original Dole-Nyswander model, which assumed no prior psychological or social etiological factors and which aimed at high dosages of methadone to overcome an unexamined metabolic deficiency, with an assumed "blocking" effect.[4] At the opposite extreme, our philosophy of treatment is to seek a methadone level for each patient at a point below which the patient would give physiological and/or psychological distress signals, and to aim for community contribution instead of quietment. All patients are expected to participate in group counseling twice a week. Such treatment plans give rise to many problems concerning therapy, techniques, training, and motivation—only a few of which will be examined here.

Community or Tourism

Both authors have been pioneers in group techniques for over twenty years.[5][6][7][8] One facet of this therapeutic thrust has been faith in "Everyman" as a potential community builder and group counselor . . . provided, of course, that he has developed the necessary hopeful, optimistic theory of life style change. Our Everyman is armed with a few techniques

Reprinted from *Medical Surgical Journal*, St. Joseph Hospital, Houston, March 1974, Vol. 9, No. 1.

for overcoming the passive-victim stance, low self-esteem, and lack of communal feelings and is granted opportunities to self-disclose his own mistaken feelings and actions and to practice encouraging interpersonal movements. Skin jumping, as will be noted later, serves as a training session on all counts.[9]

The outpatient treatment for the drug addict focuses upon the patient's constriction of communal feelings (whether the cause or the effect of drug addiction) as a target for therapeutic intervention. Some professionals feel that they lack power or influence in such a program. When they see the ex-addict counselor demonstrate unusual talent in dealing with patients, their "helping" treatment philosophy is threatened. In our program, professional power is gained by helping staff and patient grow in self-esteem and social interest. The core of the treatment regime is abandonment of passive-victim stances and, instead, construction of communities through common interests, experiences, motives, rituals, and ceremonies. Too much professionalism spoils the broth. In the real world of interpersonal transactions, professionals in the helping sciences often run rampant over patients, demanding special service and power while reinforcing hyperdependent and distance-creating maneuvers of the patients. At times the "objective" professional is the objectionable tourist, watching with a disinterested, pessimistic third eye for signs of certain failure.

With professional therapists, for better or worse, absent from the treatment and used mainly as tutors of counselors, there is a resulting void in the therapists' ranks. In our program, six ex-addicts, former patients who successfully completed the inpatient program, have served with distinction as catalysts for community building and group cohesion. If only six ex-addicts were given the counseling mandate, they would soon be inundated, as would any professional group, by the quantity and quality of drug patients. This pressing problem of leadership among peers is being approached by exposing both the ex-addict counselor and his assistant (the lay therapist) to patient skin-jumping experience. Although still a patient, the lay therapist offers much needed support while serving as a co-therapist or counselor trainee. Too many patients with too much motivation away from authentic growth communities is the chronic nightmare of methadone maintenance programs. A common sight in drug programs going through the pains of defeated autocratic "leadership," passive confusion, and intense professional competition is the large group of patients coming together only to disseminate drug-taking motivations. The untrained and unconfident group counselor abdicates or involves himself in a losing power struggle, and the group process degenerates into a competitive peer-contest over who has experienced more pleasure or pain or has gathered more knowledge in the drug world. Drugs and violence are commonly the only preoccupation of such useless life styles.

The authors believe that the chronic addict has less sense of community influence than even the schizophrenic patient. The latter may exhibit a tremendous fear and avoidance of closeness, whereas the addict often discounts the community except as a vehicle for quick satisfaction of creature needs and the chemical ingredients of self esteem. Actualized persons, on the other hand, are those who are attuned to encouragement of self and others; they do not suffer from sitting on a self-created dung heap, complaining in thought and action of the horrible, incapacitating odor. To prevent such anti-therapeutic mob scenes (*Greyhound* or *depot* groups*) skin jumping was devised as a training method to tutor individuals in developing and maintaining a therapeutic personhood, while teaching specific group techniques. We believe that a teaching procedure such as skin jumping can be a way of learning theories and techniques of behavior therapy and at the same time serve as one answer to the lack of professional therapists.

Skin Jumping as a Structured, Simplified Psychodrama

Skin jumping is a didactic-experiential approach at its best. All participants are learners, and learning is growth as well as simple ingestion of words. Skin jumping has evolved from the authors' long experience with psychodramatic techniques. O'Connell, in particular, with his Action Therapy[5] [7] [8] [10] has modified the theory and practice of psychodrama into the operation of an encouraging democratic community and away

---

*So-called because these individuals are simply waiting passively to be moved about by circumstances, rather than actively looking within themselves for solutions to their problems.

from the charismatic-healer and suffering-victim mode of therapy. This distinction is an important one for the nurturing of cooperation-of-equals, because the counselor, his lay assistants (who are still patients, often co-therapists, and always candidates for counseling positions), and professional tutors are all in it together in weekly or semiweekly skin-jumping sessions.

Community has always been constructed through walking a mile in someone's moccasins or walking two miles with him instead of just one: feeling-with, without the blaming, hopeless judgments of such negative nonsense as *hopeless, wicked,* and *can't change.* Skin jumping was invented to present the addict with a simple, elementary dose of community: a heart-to-heart talk where everyone is involved in putting himself in the skin of another, perhaps only for a few seconds. How else can community begin?

As a part of staff therapy and teaching, eight participants are involved in the training group. Real life problems provide the content of the session. Directors are rotated among the group and learn—by making mistakes—the techniques of finding a dyadic problem (the heart-to-heart), setting the scene, the role presentation, the role reversal, the lights-out soliloquy, and the sharing aftermath. Skin jumping reaches its goal when the director moves the players along quickly to consummate the production within an hour. Such movements, rather than words-words-words, appeal to the "tell it" and action life styles of the blue collar addict.

Techniques of Skin Jumping

The salient points of the technique have been described elsewhere.[9] The strategy is to provide each person with an opportunity to jump into another's skin. Suppose O'Connell is having a problem with Wiggins: O'Connell becomes the protagonist and Wiggins the significant other. The director gets O'Connell to set the scene in order to involve his imagination in therapeutic play, an area in which the addict is supposedly unskilled.[1] The director may then decide to use Wiggins as the actual significant other or have someone else (who is like Wiggins or who needs to experience "Wigginising") play Wiggins. The director may believe that the significant other needs to view himself at a distance, or perhaps in actual therapy the significant other is too paralyzed with fear to play himself. The empty chair technique is a good way to present roles if no one knows the protagonist and the significant other. By playing both roles in a heart-to-heart, the protagonist shows, in his verbal and nonverbal movements, the way in which he structures this dyad. When the director feels that the demands of the protagonist, his frustrations, and his methods of resolving them have been demonstrated, role reversal is in order. In our opinion, role reversal is the most potent single technique in therapy.[8]

Role reversal in the hands of a firm and friendly director gives the protagonist a chance to feel and experience the other, in the latter's skin. In this case, O'Connell would play Wiggins, making an effort to see with his eyes, hear with his ears, and feel along with him. O'Connell would also experience facing himself if Wiggins (now playing O'Connell) and the director were to exaggerate O'Connell's demands. In this way, the psychic seal is broken; the protagonist in role reversal (e.g. O'Connell) might *experience* in dyadic form how he looks for evidence, and then creates, provokes, arranges it to continue useless blaming movements as a way of influencing others (getting power).

Once the role reversal takes place, the protagonist continues to play the significant other, staying and feeling "in his moccasins" throughout the skin jumping. All the other participants then assume, in turn, the protagonist's role, handling it as *they* would act. People will watch actions, whereas words by themselves would seem preachy and uninvolved. Participants immediately experience whether or not their solution would work. Usually suggestions are ineffective because they are not thought out in terms of the life style demands of the duo. The solution-giver faces the problem of how to encourage the protagonist (without blame, naturally) to try the novel approach. In this way each participant is responsible both for encouraging others and for the effect of his own behavior (his attempted movements of encouragement). After each participant has been in the protagonist's shoes and the protagonist has experienced, over and over again, the situation of his frustrating (and frustrated) significant other, the roles may be reversed to the original ones. The protagonist (O'Connell) now plays himself and the director selects someone to play the significant other in the *most frustrating* style. Often a protagonist shows that he now can handle the stressor without flight or fight (a tremendous boost to self-esteem and feelings of competence), whereas in the beginning of the session he was immobilized, or a mass of giggles.

The lights-out soliloquy follows next, starting with the director and ending with the protagonist. Each participant tries to verbalize the hopes, fears, frustrations, and goals of the protagonist while moving about the room, intently inner-focusing on the other rather than reacting to the expressions of the audience. With the lights back on, there is a sharing period. This step is mainly a future orientation on how one can encourage the protagonist toward external interpersonal problem-solving rather than continuation of his sideshow of blaming and competing.

Contraindications

Skin jumping, like any potent drug, is not without danger. We have all experienced the actual vertigo which comes with exposing oneself to multiple impulses and viewpoints before we have induced and experienced trust and intellectual assimilation. Therefore the group must move gently, the participants not using the session to prove themselves superior or inferior, but rather to stop, look, listen, and encourage the others. O'Connell[10] has long believed that many of the techniques of psychodrama (like doubling) can be ways of crowd pleasing (the "one-upmanship" ploy) and so has eliminated them in situations where well trained auxiliaries are absent. Wiggins has learned that directors develop slowly and only with shared practice on simple fundamentals of movement, almost like learning to dance (e.g. setting the scene). One cannot push the average street addict into directorship until his passivity and community *ignor-ance* and avoidance have been altered.

Summary

The problem of addiction has been reviewed as a reflection, in part, of the more virulent and resistant *dis-ease* of community *ignor-ance*. The hope is that eventually education in the field of addiction will encompass the chemistry of community encouragement. The only goal that cannot stultify, discourage, or derange is the growth-experience of trying always to understand and encourage community within oneself.

REFERENCES

1. O'Connell W: Social interest in an operant world: the interaction between Skinnerian and existential-humanistic thought. *Voices: The Art and Science of Psychotherapy* 9(3):42-49, 1973.

2. O'Connell W., Chorens J, Wiggens G, Hiner D: Natural high model for research and treatment on a methadone maintenance ward. *Newsletter for Res in Ment Health and Behav Sci* 15(2):19-21, 1973.

3. Wiggins G, O'Connell W, Hiner D, Chorens J: The addicts' combo: Building community from divergent life styles. *Newsletter for Res in Ment Health and Behav Sci* 15(3):49-51, 1973.

4. Brill L, Lieberman L(eds): *Major Modalities in the Treatment of Drug Abuse*. New York, Behavioral Publications, 1972.

5. O'Connell W: Psychotherapy for everyman: a look at action therapy. *J of Existentialism* 7(25):85-91, 1966.

6. Hanson P, Rothaus P, O'Connell W, Wiggins G: Training patients for effective participation in back-home groups. *Am J. Psychiatry* 126:857-862, 1969.

7. O'Connell W: Action therapy techniques. *J. of Individ Psychol* 28:184-191, 1972.

8. O'Connell W, Brewer D: The values of role reversal. *Int Handbook of Sociometry* 6:98-104, 1971.

9. O'Connell W, Wiggins G: Skin-Jumping therapy: One road from skin-popping to communal feelings. *Voices: The Art and Science of Psychotherapy* 10(1):in press, 1974.

10. O'Connell W: Adlerian psychodrama with chronic schizophrenics. *J. of Individ. Psychol.* 19:69-73, 1963.

11. Van Kaam A: The addictive personality. *Insight* 4(2):23-28, 1965.

THE ADDICTS' "COMBO": BUILDING COMMUNITY FROM DIVERGENT LIFE STYLES

(with George Wiggins, Darlene Hiner & Jose Chorens)

Psychiatry has been faced for a number of years with the question of the relevancy of its labeling process. The diagnosing of mental illness, once considered the chief methodology for discovering regularity and differential treatment, is now regarded by many workers as negatively self-fulfilling, overlooking social, economic, and political factors, and oblivious to positive change.[4] The conflict over labeling is especially pronounced in the area of drug addiction, where some patients, lacking in extended communal feelings, might be eager to receive and retain an illness label and subsequent financial compensation.

This paper is an effort to look for a dimension of creative labeling; one in which the active social movements of the life style are not neglected.[6] We hope to share clinical impressions and thereby generate hypotheses which might enrich the helper-helped dyad in the drug world. Specifically, two divergent life styles will be defined and their transactions described. A thereapeutic use of this competitive duo will then be outlined.

The combo stands for a combination of "doctors' pet" and "street addict" (or junkie). Both types are representative of the addictive "radius of action" previously part of our ex-addict counselors' lives, when they were under the duress of addiction. The pet and the junkie combination in our program is a composite "minute man," called into action by group leaders to meet as a trio with the problem addict, mediating and prescribing for major violations of therapeutic contracts.[1] The contrasting movements, feelings, and goals of both addictive types could be discussed at length. The limited purpose here is

Reprinted from Newsletter for Research in Mental Health and Behavioral Sciences 1B 15-5, Vol. XV, #3, Aug. 1973 to postulate a sharp difference in terms of movements in relation to the medical authority. These movements often lend themselves to destructively active and passive competition on treatment wards, yet can be used to foster community if handled wisely.

The doctors' pet is defined as an ex-addict counselor who, during his habit, made definite approach movements toward the medical authority. He conned, pampered, and often became a significant other to the medical man even to the extent of sharing addictions. An oasis was discovered by the pet who in turn reinforced the doctor's need for esteem and power by any ploy which "worked." The pet's former tropism toward the doctor can now be turned to therapeutic advantage if the doctor does not become addicted to "strokes" from the pet. When encouraged and recognized as an asset to a drug program, the doctors' pets champion the wider social transactions of the therapeutic community, serve with distinction in ward drug surveillance and stimulate the growth of intra- and extra-hospital interpersonal relationships (e.g., work with volunteers, prisons).

The street addict's movement toward the doctor was nonexistent or negative, designed to stimulate power struggles and revenge reactions from authority. Whenever the street addict is responded to with annoyance, power struggles, deep hurt, and hopelessness by the medical man and his surrogates, the disdain and avoidance is all the more reinforced.[5] If the active beneficial cooperation of the patient is required, there must be a continuous base of recognition of cooperation-as-equals (e.g., "I want to tell you how you've helped me to become more open and encouraging"). To avoid reinforcement of useless behavior, the counselor with a robust sense of humor and self-esteem can congratulate the patient on his skill in defeating all therapeutic efforts (but with an honest smile and not rancor and sarcasm). (Such unexpected behavior should at least temporarily "blow a mind" and upset some traps.) Street addicts, who seem to vastly outnumber the doctors' pets, are suitable for outreach training, attracting a new supply of addicts to the clinic for treatment. A sharing of the street experience and mutual knowledge of the survival skills of the street jungle can be used to advantage to develop significant relationships. A similar situation of shared experiences exists for the doctors' pets and their smaller number patient counterparts. As a rule though, the street addicts recruit and the doctors' pets set communal limits on aberrant behavior, giving to the patient his choice of involvement or leaving the program.

When the combos are functioning flexibly enough to assist a program violator developing behavioral consequences and responsible restitution for destructive acts, group counselors are less burdened with addicts striving for power and esteem on the useless "private-logic" side of life. The counselors are less likely to reinforce self- and other-defeating behavior of patients by reacting with chronic annoyance, power stances, deep hurt and conclusions of hopelessness to addicts' demands. As the members of the combos secure encouragement for their efforts, they no longer do battle with each other by avoiding, fighting, and depreciating other counselors by "arranging" invidious comparisons. Such warfare is to be anticipated initially in the contrasting combo life styles. There is little doubt that the combos can be catalysts toward cooperative communications and decreased acting-out (or acting-in) behaviors. Working together responsibly on the program problems, their mutual animosity soon disappears. After members of the combos learn not to be provoked into unnecessary combat by the sullen problem patient, they may informally begin the latter's therapy. In other words, when the duo can calmly guess together about the purposes of misbehavior and consequences which would benefit the community, "as if" the non-cooperative sullen addict were not present, the offender's tantrums are not being reinforced.[3] Eventually, he will discuss his own restitutive behavior, after explaining the purposes of his antisocial episodes to the disinterested "pet" and "street" counselor. The counselors, representing the forces of communal feeling and a profound awareness of the subtle habitual street games, are the keystones of a therapeutic atmosphere for the growth of any drug program.

When combos function well, with staff encouragement, the psychiatric staff may begin to look beyond their traditional diagnostic and therapy roles. If they have hopeful and dynamic attitudes, group therapists can teach the ex-addict counselors in simplified terms, the techniques and theories of life style change. Making relevant the abstract concepts may benefit the professional therapist as well as the novice group counselor. It is possible for the conceptual traffic to flow in the opposite direction as well. Nonverbalized insight of ex-addict counselors might be put into systematic form for teaching and research by interested and attentive team members.[2] After all, if someone wasn't curious about how admission counselors made successful counselor-patient matchings, this paper on the catalystic combo would not have been written.

The biggest stumbling block to the combo may be the institution itself, for the combo does not fit into an authoritarian, autocratic professional-helper model. When patients are unofficially avoided, tranquilized into non-persons, or seen as necessarily sick forever ("in remission"), they are not likely to be given an opportunity for self- and peer-treatment of their self-induced diseases. The program then becomes a jealously-guarded staff prerogative; patients rebel in a million-and-one passive and active ways; and we're all back to the point we were too fearful to leave anyway.

*

REFERENCES

1. Bell, R. The Glass Ark: A drug abuse treatment program. *Newsletter for Research in Psychology*, 1972, 14(4), 41-43.

2. O'Connell, W. Ward psychotherapy with schizophrenics through concerted encouragement. *Journal of Individual Psychology*, 1961, 17, 193-204.

3. O'Connell, W. Psychodrama: Involving the audience. *Rational Living*, 1967, 2(1), 22-25.

4. O'Connell, W. Failures of mental hospitals—or of society. *Psychiatric Opinion*, 1970, 7(5), 8-12.

5. O'Connell, W. *Social Interest in an Operant World*. Paper presented at the American Society of Adlerian Psychology meeting, Houston, Texas, May 1972.

6. O'Connell, W., Chorens, J., Wiggins, G., & Hiner, D. "Natural High" model for research and treatment on a methadone maintenance ward. *Newsletter for Research in Mental Health and Behavioral Sciences*, 1973, 15(2), 19-21.

NATURAL HIGH MODEL FOR RESEARCH AND TREATMENT ON A METHADONE-MAINTENANCE PROGRAM
(with Jose A. Chorens, George E. Wiggins, & Darlene M. Hiner)

Lennard, Epstein, Bernstein, & Ransom[1] state that the unequivocal message behind prescriptive drugs is a tragic labeling of dysjunctive emotions as illnesses to be cured by passive pill-popping, rather than through open and loving movements of mind and body. We do not hold such an extreme avoidance of physical solutions. Such a bias would panic many of our patients who still fear the loss of a trusted support. Natural High therapy is simply offered as an additional therapeutic approach to be combined with methadone as a cure for hyperdependence (on pills and/or people).

Natural High therapy aims to develop in the addict the responsibility for the consequences of his own behaviors rather than a static, isolated, and passive sense of life. He learns how and why he restricts his self-esteem and social interest by discouraging himself and others with his outer and inner (internalized sentences) actions. Natural High therapy inherits all the action techniques of action therapy.[2] Uniquely, it adds a constant search for techniques which will help the addict realize that he has constricted his humanistic identification by lowering his self-esteem and narrowing his social interest through habitual blame and fatalistic premises about anxiety, life, and death. We believe that the addict, on the road to social responsibility, benefits from learning the theory and practice of his own therapy. The purposes of our Drug Addiction Unit have been described elsewhere,[3] so only rudiments of such a tutoring in mature interdependence will be given.

In our times, mental anguish is often created by a desire to be in constant and complete control of feelings through complete independence or passive resignation. In Natural High

Reprinted from Newsletter for Research in Mental Health and Behavioral Sciences, IB 15-5, Vol. XV#2, May 1973 therapy the focus is upon our lost connections with mankind and nature and our ability to assist in the evolutionary process. The 3 C's of interdependence—constriction, creativity, cooperation—are taught verbally and through the therapist's nonverbal examples. If this interdependence—the opposite of dehumanizing "negative nonsense"[4] —is truly believed, the result is a person who does strive for instant self-esteem through drugs. Basically, he is no longer preoccupied with searching for proof that he is an isolated individual or a passive nonperson. All people have the interpersonal power to elicit reactions from others, although too often just the negative reactions are seen, which are then insanely generalized into timeless blame of self and others. Constriction means all people have less than optimal self-esteem (feelings of worth or significance) and social interest (feelings of accepted similarity with all mankind: past, present, and future). Therefore, no one can honestly place himself above or below others as a person. Creativity means that we all search for "reasons" for our life style attitudes and are generally resourceful enough to find proof or manipulate others into behaving in such a way as to furnish this proof for our preconceived views. Cooperation signifies that life takes place in dyads or units-of-two. Whatever my loving or hating behaviors, the reactions of others (even though interpreted or "filtered" through my life style) are needed to reinforce my behavior. In a very real sense, I am the precipitate of the reactive approvals, annoyances, demands, hurts, and hopeless reactions of significant others. If I am lucky, or rather honest and hopeful, I will work for encouraging transactions in the here-and-now. I will ask for (and give) feedback without blame[5] about my discouraged search for power on the useless side of life. My true friends will seldom reinforce my useless movements of discouragement, but will gently guess at how and why I search for discouragement at this present moment.

The following figure (or life style road map) is given to addicts to plot their own routes to a "natural high." The dimensions are self-esteem, power (the ability to influence others, positively or negatively) and social interest. Hoffman[6] has noted that the addict lacks good objects in his ego to maintain symbolic sources of self-esteem. Therefore he returns to primitive physiological methods of obtaining feelings of warmth and goodness. May[7] describes the sense of powerlessness of the addict and his discomfort of perpetually feeling weak, which is temporarily alleviated by drugs and the purposive search for physiological euphoria. Van Kaam[8] has considered the powerless passivity of the addiction-prone personality as oriented toward effortless fulfillment, away from the possibilities of anxiety and failure. Adlerians have seen the addict as a weak, pampered individual, without social interest, angrily exploiting others.[9] Social interest combined with self-esteem equals *courage* or active social interest according to Adler.[10] May sees the addicts blocked "angry energy" as an ally of therapy, if the direction of the therapeutic program is toward Adler's ideal of social interest.

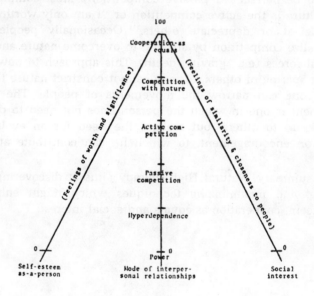

Figure 1. Natural High

Our research has through time found a positive relationship between self-esteem and participation.[11] Theorists and researchers have overlooked a very important clinical phenomenon in this area. Addicts can get self-esteem from a very narrow role (e.g., mother's hyperdependent "child") and

113

have high esteem in that role, as long as the reinforcer is actively relating. Because such persons usually lack social interest and skill in other power maneuvers, they panic when acting outside of their circumscribed roles. In Natural High therapy the goal is courage (active social interest) through cooperation-as-equals, operationally defined as the ability to give and receive feedback, encouraging cooperation and *not* to be a reinforcer of discouragement.

Power, the habitual life style movement toward others, is often reinforced through hyperdependent relationships ("I am only worthwhile if loved by a powerful one"). Power also is gained at the expense of potential self-esteem and social interest through avoidance of situations seen as failure ("the need to be perfect" or passive competition). Most common in our culture is the active competition or "I am only worthwhile if I defeat or depreciate others." Occasionally people depersonalize competition by striving to overcome nature and existential forces (e.g., gravity, death). This approach to power is at least sparing of others, for one cannot constrict nature to the degree one can narrow the movements of people. The ideal movement is one in which the person does not need to defeat or look up to others, but realizes the need for an evolution based on encouragement, to which he can contribute at any time.

In summary, Natural High therapy aims at discovering, inventing, and maximinzing techniques which might enhance self-esteem, cooperation-as-equals and social interest.

REFERENCES

1. Lennard, H. L., Epstein, Bernstein, & Ransom *Mystification and Drug Misuse.* San Francisco: Jossey-Bass, 1971.

2. O'Connell, W. & Brewer, D. *Hdbk. Internat'l Sociomet.,* 1971, 6, 98-104.

3. Bell, R. *Newsletter for Research in Psychology,* 1972, 14(4), 41-43.

4. Ellis, A. *Reason and Emotion in Psychotherapy.* New York: Lyle Stuart, 1962.

5. O'Connell, W. *J. Indiv. Psychol.,* 1971, 27, 65-72.

6. Hoffman, *Comp. Psychiat.*, 1964, 5, 262-270.

7. May, R. *Power and Innocence: A search for the sources of violence.* New York: Norton, 1972.

8. Van Kaam, *Insight*, 1965, 4(2), 23-28.

9. Beecher, M. & Beecher, W. *The Mark of Cain: An anatomy of jealousy.* New York: Harper & Row, 1971.

10. Adler, A. The Individual Psychology of Alfred Adler. New York: Basic Books, 1956.

11. O'Connell, W., Baker, R., Hanson, P., & Ermalinski, R. *Int. J. Soc. Psychiat.*, 1974, 20, 122-127.

DEFINITIONS FOR HUMANISTIC IDENTIFICATION

1. **COMPETITION**—can be seen in the actions of those who derive self-esteem and power by the external source of *comparison* with others, rather than by helping solve external social problems. Competition can be *active*: "I feel worthwhile when I am better than or above others." Passive competition is more subtle, and is noted in the avoidance of the possibility of failure ("I feel significant only if I never fail at anything. I know I'm not good enough to be really skilled.")

2. **COOPERATION-AS-EQUALS**—is present in dyads when partners interact as persons of dignity and worth. Both are considered responsible for non-fatal consequences of their behaviors and have a right (but not a demand) to be seen and heard.

3. **COURAGE**—active social interest. High self-esteem leads to movement in its role behavior. Therefore courage implies self-esteem in the role of loving dyads: giving and receiving encouragement. Although courage and social interest are often considered absolutes (all or nothing), both can apply to *any* number of relationships.

4. **DEMANDS**—subtle attitudes of "You must . . ." or "You must not . . ." usually not expressed verbally and hence operating unconsciously. Demands are inferred from movements which reflect the blame and negative nonsense which follow goal frustrations.

5. **DISCOURAGEMENT**—interpreting actions to mean that one is incapable of learning to love and to improve his life style attitudes. In discouragement one has the bad faith that he is hopeless forever, in all things, or hopeless without an omnipotent mind-reader or spokesman. The crux of dehumanization.

6. **DYAD**—the most simple but extensive unit of human relations. Socially there is no unit of one person. All our transactions, overt and covert, take place in dyads or twosomes. Our attention span and interpersonal needs keep us focused on only one dyad at any *one* time. Think about that one!

7. **ENCOURAGEMENT**—a process which in its fullest expression communicates the message that one is ultimately responsible for (and capable of) expanding his own self-esteem and social interest and that no other person, event, or force is to blame for one's decisions. To start encouragement with discouraged persons it is often necessary to begin with simple unobtrusive presence, or praise of possession or skill, even to the extent of lauding one's creative craziness (e.g., "What skill you must have. Please tell me how you get yourself depressed whenever you think of me!"). An advanced form of encouragement and openness is to tell the other how he has or can help you to a "natural high" by giving encouraging feedback.

8. **EXPECTATIONS**—often frustrated in each of us. We learn to expect certain behaviors from others because even the most self-actualizing person has some power and esteem needs from others (the more mature, the more encouraging or giving is our orientation). When expectations are frustrated and we give honest, open (and hence nondemanding) feedback, we won't get into negative nonsense. Feedback can be loud and animated, simply because we're humans, not perfect angels.

9. **FEEDBACK**—pertains to expression of feelings (basic feedback) or guesses at goals of others (advanced feedback). Authentic feedback should be undemanding and nonjudgmental of the person, close in time to specific behaviors, expressed so the receiver understands (see "Taking the Wind Out of the Sails"). If you are afraid to give feedback you may have victimized yourself into a hyperdependent relationship. Feedback (other than inauthentic and destructive) is likewise lacking in competitive situations where you believe you must beat or put down the other to feel worthwhile.

10. **"FEELINGS OF GUILT"**—a label which a person puts on bodily feelings (which may be no different in nature from fear or anxiety) for the purposes of increasing his status, and avoiding punishment or acknowledgments of imperfections. Guilt feelings may be used to continue offensive behaviors while the offender gains esteem by communicating that he is better than those who express no, or less, guilt feelings. One who is really "guilty" of mistakes, is open to *behavioral change*.

11. **FOUR GOALS**—Dreikurs' concept of the motivating forces for misbehavior, when the child is not recognized for cooperating-as-equals. Also applicable to adolescents and adults. Four goals of attention-getting (AGM), power, revenge, and displays of inadequacy must be reinforced by movements of annoyance, provocation, deep hurt, and

hopelessness. Creative misbehaviors cannot take place without the "cooperation" (or reinforcement) of others.

12. **HUMANISTIC IDENTIFICATION**—O'Connell's term for the intrapsychic state of finding and maintaining an attitude of unconditional self-worth and similarities with all mankind.

13. **HYPERDEPENDENT**—a type of disabling relationship cherished by those with low self-esteem: a "leaning-on" orientation, hence often "frustrated and let down." Hyperdependent people are subtle tyrants. Blame is projected on the sucker who has let them down.

14. **HUMOR, SENSE OF**—ability to maintain humanistic transactions (encouraging interactions with others) under stressor conditions—without depression, paranoia, and all other kinds of blame. Implies an appreciation for such paradoxes as living in the here-and-now with a "God's eye" view, across time and space. Humor seems to be motivated by the belief "that what one is doing now is of supreme importance, yet if he died at this minute it would not matter." This ingredient completely missing in disrupting, disjunctive life styles.

Apparently the humorist is able to notice his process of life style constriction, usually following stressful situations. That is, he sees himself engaging in verbal or fantasy scenes which are discouraging (lowering self-esteem and narrowing social interest) but quickly reverses the negative nonsense process into high self esteem and wide social interest. Both wit and humor use various over- and understatements and other ploys with multiple meanings of words and situations.

15. **LOW SELF-ESTEEM**—characterized by doubt of own innate inherent significance, lack of a sense of humor, regarding feedback "hostile," time in fantasy rather than action, fear of expressing feelings directly, striving for perfection (usually through fantasy and in-action), feeling alone and isolated, leaning on others, so constantly let down and "victimized."

16. **NEGATIVE NONSENSE**—cognitive skills in inventing (inferring and deducing) hopelessness, blame, and isolation which leads to chronic problems-in-living. Implies the lack of the 3 C's theory of interdependence.

17. **OUTSIGHT**—the process of developing social interest and the ability to see the 3 C's operating in others.

18. **PSYCHOTHERAPY**—the transactional process a person enters usually in hopes of feeling better without changing his attitudes or behaviors. If therapy is successful, he learns that he can and must change attitudes and actions if he wants a happier existence.

19. **SELF-ESTEEM**—feelings of significance, worth, belonging. It is often overlooked that self-esteem is tied to a particular role. For example, one may feel "as if" he's a great person as a football player (reinforced

117

by others) but this feeling cannot cover all roles in life, especially the self-attitude. Our aim is to develop self-esteem through social interest, seen in the ability to give and ask for encouraging feedback.

20. **SOCIAL INTEREST**—concern for understanding the inner life of the other. In its extreme form, a feeling of belonging to all of life, especially mankind, past, present, and future. May lead to a cessation of negative nonsense, but does not without adequate self-esteem generate positive movements. (See Courage.)

21. **"TAKING THE WIND OUT OF THE SAILS" or "SPITTING IN THE SOUP"**—Alfred Adler's terms for the anticipation and gentle guessing at the goals of potential misbehavior. Difficult to learn, but an absolute for authentic feedback. Its use shows that you are aware of the functioning of the four goals of misbehavior as creative and even fuel for wit. You give the impression that you are "letting be" with behaviors—but you are really communicating responsibility and encouragement. For your own health you do not try to control or will what cannot be willed or controlled. By reinforcing cooperation-as-equals (how patient can or does encourage you) you are actually shaping, if you are a positively significant other, the encouragement process.

22. **THREE C's OF INTERDEPENDENCE (Constriction, Creativity, Cooperation)**—O'Connell's term for mature dependence or independence. All persons are *constricted* in that no one constantly creates his optimal self-esteem and social interest. We are all *creative* in maintaining our life style attitudes toward self and others by making the same old inferences in new and novel situations. For example, persons can always find proof to feel guilty, angry, depressed, bored, or even loving, depending upon one's goals. We all *cooperate* in reinforcing behaviors and attitudes, even though we'd like to think of ourselves as independent (when successful) or at the mercy of fate (when we fail at a task.).

23. **TRAGICOMIC PARADOX**—the beginnings of an authentic sense of humor. Person realizes that he has been living in a state of contradiction and sees both tragic and comic elements. The chief tragicomic paradox is when person's own negative nonsense has been lowering his self-esteem, while he simultaneously has demanded unconditional love from others.

24. **WIT**—the mechanisms of wit are associated with overstatements or understatements of ideas, facts, situations, and feelings. Dynamics of wit usually refer to the release of hostile or sexual repressions, according to Freud. In actuality, this mechanistic interpretation only true in discouraged and discouraging dyads. Wit can be encouraging if it helps a person to see that he is victimizing himself, but not "to blame" and can change, if he selects an encouraging environment. Frankl's technique of paradoxical intention is an example of wit, although he does not recognize its relationship to wit.

HUMANISTIC IDENTIFICATION:
A THEORY OF PERSONS (1966)

Perhaps one of the greatest needs in the field of psychotherapy is the development for future research, teaching, and tactical maneuvering, of a theory of personality change which makes sense to all participants. Too many theories, it seems, really conceptualize man as a glorified sponge or a trichotomized iceberg with hidden urges only to be evaluated by an oracular disinterested other.[15] Closure has been made too soon, and such speculations have often been incorporated dogmatically as "reality" by unwitting students of human nature. The theory about to be outlined is, like all other theoretical assumptions, merely a roadmap for future speculations, but does hopefully have to its advantage less fatalism and "closed shop" postulates than do the customary methods of regarding others.

Here man's essence is seen as his *identification*, learned in an interpersonal contact maintained by his *Eigenwelt*[12] of internalized sentences,[8] "deeper" than mere drives steered by ego mechanisms. Essentially the state of his identification (composed of the strength of his self-esteem and degree of personal involvement with humanity) is reflected in the presence or absence of double-binding actions against *himself*, as in a depressive state, or *others*, as in a paranoid condition.

The Dimensions of Phenomenological Operationalism

Adams,[1] in his attempt to free psychiatry of "non-existent verbal abstractions" posing as realities, has stated that all behavior can be ordered about two orthogonal axes of Dominance-Submission and Affection-Hostility, and traced such observations back through time to Hippocrates. Yet, it does appear that even this clarifying step overlooks the methodology of phenomenological operationalism:[3] understanding the gestalt of goal-directed attitudes and behaviors. Therefore, what is proposed here is a search for a model which conceptualizes the in-

---

Was in press with the *Journal of Existentialism* and *Existential Psychiatry* before both journals ceased publication.

terrelatedness of self-esteem and esteem for others in a reciprocal dynamic fashion.

It is assumed that one's identification is best conceived as a *process* born of the psychological need-status of the person, and the incentive values and attitudes of need-satisfiers in one's environment. In Figure 1, the horizontal continuum represents the *quality* of one's identification from narcissistic to humanistic. In other words, does a person belong to just himself, or does he feel, in the extreme, like an integral part of all mankind: past, present, and future. In theoretical steady-state the person strives to keep his quality of identification constant by his internalized and generalized sentences (his abstract evaluation of others).[8] This humanistic base can be very intense (like some "successful" mystics), or just a flat, effortless yearning due to little reinforcement reward or esteem from *others*.

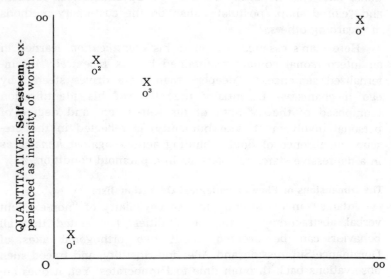

QUALITATIVE: **Social interest**, Gemeinschaftsgefühl, or humanistic identification. Inferred by observers from behavior but not an experiential state, as is self-esteem.

Fig. 1. Schematic representation of the process of identification viewed as an interaction between self-esteem and esteem for others (Gemeinschaftsgefühl). X_1 equals narcissistically withdrawn psychotic; X_2 equals the pampered one, isolated from the community; X_3 equals the "good" passive chronic patient, "loved" by the staff; X_4 equals the humanistic ideal.

The vertical or intensive aspect of identification (self-esteem) pertains to the positive or negative generalization which the person places upon himself and is concerned with the amplitude, strength, or intensity of his identification. With high self-esteem the person feels worthy in the particular quality of identification in which he operates. Self-esteem is felt by the subject, but the humanistic dimension is inferred from his behavior toward others and is usually not present in the person's awareness. Self-esteem is experienced; the quality of identification is not and is hidden from the psychotherapist who fails to see the patient in action with others. The quantity of identification or self-esteem represents the *Eigenwelt* of one's relationship to himself in feeling-tone terms. The qualitative continuum is the *Mitwelt* of man's relationship to man, extended to past and future.

In defective living, the individual strives paradoxically to maximize the vertical dimension (self-esteem) while minimizing the horizontal (social interest). Ironically, the very success of minimizing the humanistic dimension increases the *demands* for privacy, and decrease of social skills increases the dependency ultimately to extreme albeit denied *demands* for instrumental assistance.

Relevance to Psychotherapy

This schematic abstraction is an attempt to bring thinking about psychotherapy closer to life itself, from which psychotherapy is often seen as an aloof distantiation. Furthermore, it represents an urge to highlight the here-and-now struggle between the psychotherapist and patient to change the other through the communicative process. This view comes as a revolution to us—when we mature sufficiently to recognize it—but it is merely another incident of Adler rediscovered. He warned of the games people play and the dangerous, defensive, one-down psychotherapist (who could be one-up if he admitted he was one-down).[3] Years of intensive psychotherapy with institutionalized patients dragged along before I realized that although these patients may have had low self-esteem in the past and would again experience such in the cooperative community, in their patient role the esteem was relatively high, although this was never admitted. The therapist who thought only of the pathology of low self-esteem now was whipped unless he admitted this. We often think of double-binding, schizophrenic parents, but the chronic institutionalized patient is the master as well as the victim. As Van Dusen so aptly illustrated, even the double bind, like life itself, knows no dualisms.[22] The patient may allow a respecting therapist to jokingly "spit in his soup,"[7] but there are few outsightful people to enjoy solving the patient's private riddles without rancor. Such a person may request therapy, but if such doesn't concur with his personal-logic conception of therapy, he silently finds something to hate in the therapist, then forces withdrawal of the therapist through a fulmination of symptoms. Try to set up a pampering world to ameliorate the depressive's "low esteem," and he will find a personal flaw to negate the hoped-for change, since he is not perfect past, present, and future in thought, word, and deed. The same applies to the paranoid, although his assertive ire is turned subtly toward others (and denied) until the therapeutic relationship allows for present exploration of interpersonally destructive games. The premise here is that one needs to find someone else to increase his self-esteem, but the seeker's creativity often invents an unverbalized, narcissistic self-image which is secretly reinforced by his private logic. For example, the pampered or ignored patient can relate either or both of these behaviors of others to his wish for omnipotence *or* desired hopelessness. The test of the artfulness of the psychotherapist is the correct timing of a non-defensive ability to "take the wind right out of the patient's sails"[3] without giving him an excuse to scuttle the ship.

Psychological Needs

As this paper is a sketch of a possible approach to human transactions, the emphasis is upon psychological needs, admittedly a difficult and nebulous area to delineate and measure. The listed needs are those of Erich Fromm,[10] borrowed with slightly different definitions and viewed with a non-Frommian supposition that non-satisfaction of the need (through behavior and intra- or interpersonal rewards) leads to experiential tension of the subject. In brief, the human needs are those of:

relatedness: need for significant others

transcendence: the necessity of awareness beyond bodily functioning *rootedness:* the need for anchors of one's identification

personal identity: the attempt to maintain a stable continuity for identifications

frame of orientation and devotion: the need for objects of worship (material goods, personal hating or loving God, impersonal neutral God, etc.)

The Freudian basic drives of aggression and sex are assumed to be nonprimary, operating mainly in the service of identity maintenance.

One novel twist to this theory is greater emphasis placed upon significant others in one's environment. In a sense the individual is both his identification and his environment. Significant others become so possibly by the operation of secondary reinforcement:[13] they are associated with psychological drive-reduction and thereby begin to take on positive incentive values. At this point the significant other, by virtue of his enhanced value to this subject, is in a position to reward and punish actions with more striking effects. He can have a more telling influence upon the subject by his verbal and non-verbal reactions to the subject's identification (quantitative self-esteem), through such communicated generalizations as, "You are worthless," "You are wonderful," etc., beyond rewarding and punishing specific behaviors. In this manner the subject's victim's identification can be vastly altered; first the quantity of self-esteem, then the quality of narcissistic-humanistic identification by extra-therapy transactions in the real world of life. The subject, through internalized sentences or the generalizations he communicates about both himself and the environment, seeks to maintain his current identity (e.g., "I'm terrible and all others hate me."). All this is the paradigm of psychotherapy: establishing the relationship; interpreting the presence, history, and goals of the "negative nonsense" of the internalized sentences; reinforcing outsight[15] [16] or understanding of others expressed in desires and behaviors. Here is a model for psychotherapy which explains why therapy often fails when significant others with a narcissistic life style are reinforcing aberrant anti- or asocial behavior in the subject. Brainwashing, psychotherapy, child rearing, and religion[14] [15] [16] [17] are all encompassed in this theory.

Relevance to Religion

To many people the traditional concept of a transcendental God is quite dead, and there is a definite move to find an imminent God through the "gracious neighbor." [20] There is a strong movement to find a language and theory suitable to both secular humanists and representatives of various religious sects. This theory of humanistic identification has possibilities for the solution of this vexing problem. The need for an object of devotion and frame of reference acknowledges an innate urge applicable to all mankind to worship something through faith—since infinite knowledge of any object or process is always lacking.

Good works are definitely highlighted in this theory, although they are not the type that Luther and other reformers railed against. Whether one believes in good works to win the grace of God or good works as an acknowledgement of love for God, one might profit from an examination of what good works might entail as an interpersonal transaction. If one really believes Man to be the highest work and image of God, the first glimmering of good works would be a form of outsight or the Adlerian maxim to see the other through his eyes and hear through his ears.[3][15] The eventual goal, very idealistic at present, would be to develop humanistic identification in everyone. But all this means being such models ourselves and rewarding insights, outsights, and instrumental behaviors which assist isolated individuals to become humanistic neighbors. Indeed, we are our brother's keeper, responsible for being the Bishop Sheen type "Angel,"[21] the mature mentor.

One of the destroyers of America's forgotten but successful moral therapy of the nineteenth century was the belief that a developed moral sense or soul was God-given at birth.[5][6] Today there is considerable agreement that the *type* of God one envisions depends on a type of learning experience outlined in this paper.[10][16] This is another example of the move away from isolated entity-thinking to a field theory of transacting processes. Therefore, the individual, and his attitudes toward himself, others, and God, do seem to have a very great influence upon each other, although the influence of the latter upon the individual and others is a study traditionally left to theologians (or ignored completely).

Our world has always been such that virtue is seldom rewarded. We lack the social synergy[11] of encouraging man to love himself in ways which stimulate love for others. We have been victimized by another unworkable and false dichotomy: hate yourself and love others—or even worse, for our temporal existence: hate people, love God (in the canny words of Charley Brown, "I love mankind; it's people I hate."). The first admonition is an impossibility, for if one demonstrates outsight-in-action, he will usually gain some self-esteem. The second is merely religiosity: a failing of a religion which speaks of "abundant life" as a goal. In a world deficient in love an interesting circuitous route lies in the biochemical realm. Dr. Stanislav Grof, treating in-patients with heavy doses of LSD over many weeks, reports experiences and behaviors akin to humanistic identification in later stages of treatment. ". . . pleasurable experiences—mystic, religious, transcendental, esthetic . . . low self-esteem is raised . . . feel a oneness with other people."[4] Needless to say, this reaction is not forthcoming from the drugs and shocks usually found by institutional psychiatry. With present somatic methods the typical reaction is one of quiescent decrease of interpersonal (yet increase of somatic) complaints.[15] It seems a misnomer to call tranquilizers anti-psychotic. This designation is best reserved for the psychedelic possibilities of increased participation in a world of loving insight and outsight.

"Mental Illness"

In the words of Adams, "People who are perceived as being unable to understand or accept the truth, or . . . . . as being eager to bring the truth out into the open when others wish to conceal it, are the most vulnerable to being made 'mentally ill'."[2] This is one of the frequent definitions of mental illness which adds weight to the New Look of viewing the human behavioral problems as irresponsible living (dearth of insight and outsight) and treatment as an emotional education in personal existence.[17] [19] Mental illness in the extreme is illustrated by patients with narrow identification, internalized sentences, and learned behaviors; for example, a mother's pampered, "loved," 50 year-old baby with no positive interests toward others, except conforming, mother-directed actions (high self-esteem, low quality identification). Another example

125

is the victim of unstable identification where rewarding has been inconsistent and contradictory as in the double bind (low self-esteem, low quality identification). Whatever else mental illness connotes, it does at times encourage many unfruitful myths which obscure interpersonal and social variables in research and therapy.[5] In this theory true mental disease is restricted to the *negative* impairments of failing sensorimotor functions. Reactions to such objective stressors is a function of the state of identification and associated responses. The contention here, in short, is that those with the high disturbance value we label as mentally ill, are suffering from failures of identification manifested by a lack of development of outsight (and appropriate behaviors). Operationally, such distortions assume the form of *demanding* too much from others without appropriate knowledge and skills to earn such expectations from many people. In fact, they may have been rewarded for actions which were too callous of others, except pampering, isolated parent-figures.

Maturity

Maturity in a theory of humanistic identification is an ideal far removed from the vegetative blandness of adjustment. One example of efforts toward operational definition and measurement is the current research of one of my students, Richard Worthen. He regards maturity as self-direction and other-centeredness, processes which he is measuring by one's responses to anecdotes. Self-direction seems synonymous with one's assuming responsibility for one's instrumental acts or behaviors toward his goals. Taking account of the identifications of others in arriving at these decisions is conceptualized as other-centeredness, a form of outsight, consonant with one's identification.

To Worthen's formulations I have added another precious and neglected asset, Freudian humor,[9] [14] a concept which would be more at home in Adlerian theory. Such a rare attribute is the ability to understand and empathize with the self and others, plus the ability to override, with a non-hostile jest, the tragedy inherent in stressor situations which cannot be avoided. In my thinking I would also add the idea of a loving God who forgives sins when one strives to make loving transactions with human beings.[11] [20]

My students often look askance at me for such a "superstitious" rumination, but this empirical addition follows from the identificatory theory. That is, one who loves and tries to put his outsight into behavior is often communicating with people whose internalized sentences are so strongly negative as to preclude any immediate reciprocity of love. Deductions from the theory would state that we all cannot maintain a humanistic outlook for long in the face of a lack of esteem from others, in spite of Fromm's belief that mature people need others only to receive their love. How long one could maintain reality contacts in such a void is uncertain, but it does seem logical that this time span can be greatly extended by a belief in a loving God. Again there is no evidence of how long such a belief would be effective in complete social ostracism. Yet, thinking in this direction does not seem to encroach upon the theologians: domain of the *reality* of God, but rather on speculations on the psychological value of religious beliefs.

Maturity is also not seen as the absence of anxiety. It does seem to be responses to affects that are crucial in living rather than the feelings themselves. After over 15 years of close relationships with psychotics, I am realizing that my lack of their repressing and denying skills and my greater social concern renders me more susceptible to unpleasant feelings. The typical institutionalized patient's response to anxiety strenghtens his elaborate and strong avoidance skills, rendering him more inept and panicky in a responsible social world. For in the average mental hospital setting, "having something of the appealing quality of a college campus . . . one absorbs the heavy atmosphere of hundreds of people doing nothing and showing interest in nothing."[5]

Deductions

Some interesting deductions from this theory are:

One is not vulnerable or motivated toward behavioral change if behavior which satisfies psychological needs is being rewarded with esteem from others.

The individual is, in the normal course of events, responsible for his potential environmental influences, since there is no incisive demarcation between one's identification and significant others. One can, in a sense, choose his environment and indirectly his identification.

127

It is useless to attempt behavior modification unless the client, patient, victim (or other type of potential "one-downer") is under the stress of unsatisfied psychological needs. Should the therapist's needs, identification, and behavioral linkages be such that he is preoccupied mainly with himself and makes *demands* (without appropriate understanding and effort), he may actually find the patient reducing his tension and the identification will be the reverse of what is typical of therapist with patient.[18] Better for the therapist to develop the easily-said but difficult-to-practice, nondirective "letting be," than to suffer the physical and psychological tensions of untoward *demands* himself.

As long as one *demands* certain behaviors from others and these expectations are satisfied immediately and automatically by the therapist, no significant relationship is established. Reduction of tension is a necessity for the establishment of identification.

The Schema

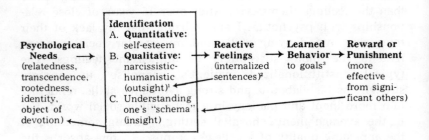

1. *Demands* on others vary from extreme with narcissistic identification to minimal with the humanistic. The latter is rewarded by giving to others in a psychological sense (assisting in psychological need-reduction), thereby receiving esteem.

2. *Frustration*, if reaction from others is less than demanded. Constancy of identification is sought through internalized sentences. Internalized sentences are also used in an effort to increase quantity of self-esteem (a favorite maneuver of the schizophrenic. He fails and tries to reconstruct reality to suit his denials and repressions). Such wishful thinking does not appreciably increase the self-esteem, but is effective in preventing transactions to increase the quality of identification.

Realistic self-esteem, it seems, must come from gaining the esteem from others.

3. *Goals* vary from power through dictatorial behavior (subtle or overt) to mature power through giving in a community of equals, and being held in esteem by many.

Summary

A theory of humanistic identification is outlined to aid in the exploration of psychological needs, learning factors, and other people in the formation of maturity. Psychotherapy and religion, in the ideal state, are regarded as education in humanism. Mental illness and health are considered obsolete and meaningless with immaturity and maturity as apt substitutes.

In brief, the theory of humanistic identification conceives of the process as conceptualized into two axes: qualitatively from narcissistic to humanistic; and quantitatively, designating amount of self-esteem. The humanistic continuum is inferred in the individual case by his behavior toward others. Self-esteem, the quantitative dimension, is experienced by the subject. One becomes a significant other by being associated with psychological tension-reduction. It is assumed that when this relationship is a positive one, the quality of identification is expanded by modeling the therapist. The latter assists the patient in developing outsight (understanding needs of others and his need for them). The patient introjects the attitudes and behaviors of the therapist, and the therapist rewards behavior which he believes is nondefensive and courageous. The therapist, as one of high incentive value to the patient, deals with patient's abstract cognitive system by eliminating inappropriate internalized sentences (negative nonsense) and increasing the patient's self-esteem by communicating, by his time and effort, esteem for the patient. Successful psychotherapy and religion, like successful living, strive to increase the quality (number of significant others) and quantity (self-esteem) of identification by exposing the patient to a mature dependency.

REFERENCES

1. Adams, H. "'Mental illness' or interpersonal behavior?" *Amer. Psychol.*, 1964, 19, 191-197.

2. Adams, J. "Deception and intrigue in so-called 'mental illness'." *J. Humanistic Psychol.*, 1964, 4, 27-38.

3. Adler, A. *Superiority and social interest.* Evanston: Northwestern University, 1964, pp. 153-154.

4. Bess, D. "LSD: The acid test." *Ramparts*, 1966, 4, No. 12, 42-50.

5. Bockoven, J. *Moral treatment in american psychiatry.* New York: Springer, 1963.

6. Dain, N., & Carlson, E. "Moral insanity in the United States, 1835-1866." *Amer. J. Psychiat.*, 1962, 118, 795-801.

7. Dreikurs, R. *Psychodynamics, Psychotherapy, and Counseling.* Chicago: Alfred Adler Institute, 1967. Rev. 1973.

8. Ellis, A. *Reason and Emotion in Psychotherapy.* New York: Lyle Stuart, 1962.

9. Freud, S. "Humor." *Int. J. Psychoanal.*, 1928, 9, 1-6.

10. Fromm, E. *The sane society.* New York: Rinehart, 1955.

11. Maslow, A. "Synergy in the society and the individual." *J. Indiv. Psychol.*, 1964, 20, 153-164.

12. May, R. "Contributions of existential psychiatry." In R. May, E. Angel, & H. Ellenberger (Eds.,) *Existence.* New York: Basic Books, 1958, pp. 61-65.

13. Mowrer, O. "Two-factor learning theory reconsidered, with special reference to secondary reinforcement and the concept of habit." *Psychoanalytic Rev.*, 1956, 63, 114-128.

14. O'Connell, W. "The adaptive functions of wit and humor." *J. abnorm. soc. Psychol.*, 1960, 61, 263-270.

15. ————. "Identification and curability of the mental hospital patient." *J. Indiv. Psychol.*, 1962, 18, 68-76.

16. ————. "Practicing christianity and humanistic identification." *J. Humanistic Psychol.*, 1964, 4, 118-129.

17. ————. "Humanistic identification: a new translation for gemeinschaftsgefühl." *J. Indiv. Psychol.*, 1965, 21, 44-47.

18. ————. "Guinness and Hawkins transactions." *Voices*, 1966, 2, 54-55.

19. ————. "Humanizing versus dehumanizing in somatotherapy and psychotherapy." *J. Indiv. Psychol.*, 1966, 22, 49-55.

20. Robinson, J. "Honest to God and after." *Dis-coveror*, 1964, 1, No., 3, 1-3.

21. Sheen, F. 'God sets many angels in our paths; often we know them not." *Syndicated Column*, January 29, 1966.

22. Van Dusen, W. "The phenomenology of a schizophrenic existence." *J. Indiv. Psychol.*, 1961, 17, 80-92.

ALFRED ADLER
A PSYCHOLOGICAL HERETIC

Psychology is being influenced today by a popular unplanned movement known as the Third Force, in sharp contrast to the influential forces of yesterday, orthodox psychoanalysis and behaviorism. If one searches hard for a father of this promising offspring, he is liable to be astounded to learn that Alfred Adler, the so-called simple and superficial psychiatrist of the Big Three of Psychoanalysis (Freud, Jung, Adler) has a most valid claim to paternity.

If existential and phenomenological psychiatry, humanistic psychotherapy, community treatment, and almost any seemingly novel and vital outlook in psychiatry have hidden connections with Adler's school of Individual Psychology, then why is that pioneer of *social* psychiatry so seldom mentioned and understood in our times? The contrast between the accolades granted to Adler and his sometime colleague and long time antagonist Sigmund Freud is a case in point to illustrate the tragedy of the heretic laboring in a period when "the time is out of joint." The psychological, spiritual, and physical differences between these two brilliant observers of human nature were so striking and foreordained to enter their theoretical views of man that one often wonders what unusual force kept them tolerably harmonious and mutually productive through the years 1902 to 1911. Both, it seems, were temporarily united by the forced isolation which followed their medical heresies: they listened to their neurotic patients seriously and thought profoundly of psychological cures in days when electricity, tonic, and vituperation were the treatments of choice for panic-prone unfortunates. But as the psychoanalytic movement conquered its rugged opposition, Freud, the aloof aristocrat in appearance and pretensions, became the rebel who sought after arbitrary power himself. The epitome of the common man, the volatile and social Adler,

---

Reprinted from: *Explorations,* 1966, 7, 19-25. P. O. Box 1254 Berkeley, CA 95701.

was more the revolutionary who wanted each man to develop the responsibility for his own decisions in the democratic tradition. When the inevitable break came between the aggressive thinkers, it was ostensibly motivated by three theoretical issues over which Adler was summarily defrocked by the Freudian clique.[1] [2] [3] Freud had been cast into a God-like role by his followers and his pronouncements were welded into dogma. Adler was denied the privilege of dialogue and after his rejection his works were never topical in polite Freudian society.

Had Adler been the type of person to delight in last laughs, he would have found the vicissitudes of orthodox psychoanalysis replete with such raw material. The dividing points of the importance of aggression; life style or ego as causal in repression; and attention to the whole character structure in symptom formation—all Adlerian contentions—were eventually slowly and silently incorporated into psychoanalysis with no apparent credit to Adler from that quarter. In later life, Freud saw psychoanalysis as part of psychology but witnessed his earlier dogmatism reflected in the incorporation of his movement by medical orthodoxy, his relentless enemy. And while Freud was living no one had the temerity to suggest to him the remarkable congruence between his equating maturity with correct sexuality and the natural law views of another foe, the Catholic Church.[4]

Freud's personality and 19th Century scientism combined to lead him to the currently unscientific and delusional belief that he was somehow in touch with ultimate reality[5] [6] instead of coping with the interplay of theoretical inferences and deductions we all take for granted today. Those who questioned Freud's ideas were therefore breaking with reality, a queer view indeed from our quantum theory frame of reference. Freud tried to find an explanation for this strange state of affairs by claiming that Adler's questioning behavior was motivated by his socialistic leanings, whereas the latter actually seemed to follow from his ultimate concern with the welfare of mankind; therefore he often chided the quietism or power seeking motivating certain socialists. Witness the contrasting reactions to arbitrary authority in Freud's note to Mussolini as "The Hero of the Culture" and Adler's "The whipped starving unloved slum child . . . becomes dictator through violence. The more intense the inferiority, the more violent the superiority . . . Mussolini's life shouts it . . . ."[2] To quote an active psychiatric

133

heretic, "psychiatry has the responsiblity to be aware of the social forces in our world and our land, seeking consciously, as well as unconsciously, to cause confusion, demoralization and mental illness in order to subvert democracy . . . . Such vigilance has been subverted far too long by the psychiatric cry of 'paranoid' ".[7] Once one is convinced that he has cornered the market on truth, all deviates are in for a rough voyage. Freud's persistent blindness toward the workings of his imagination in theory construction caused him to label all products of the imagination as pathological: religion, art, love, and so on. (Contrast this stance with Adler's comment that all concepts in time may prove to be something else.)

It seems that if a theory of personality is to carry any conviction the psychotherapist should be able to explain his own feelings and behavior by its concepts. Otherwise the error of reflexivity [8] enters in with the danger of one theory for the good guys and another for the bad, à la double standard. Adler apparently struggled to explain his own power strivings, while Freud is quoted as saying he never committed an unethical act and could not comprehend, from his theory, how he could have advanced to his stage of development.

But enough of the polemics for the present. "My analyst could lick your analyst" never solved a mystery, so we are told to look for objective scientific evidence for the differences between the two schools. And so enters the bugbear of our point in history. At present any skilled researcher can criticize and reject conclusions derived from most behavioral research on the basis that the instruments or population used did not satisfy his criteria of reliability, validity, or randomness; hence the inferences of the study could be judged to be overgeneralized. If one then resorts to utilitarian criteria such as the most good for the most people, he is faced with the human values which Freud tried to circumvent by focusing upon "originology"[9] rather than goals. If these standards are conceded to be permissible, Adler emerges brighter than ever. His group methods with personnel can then be seen as precursors of modern team approaches and extra-hospital therapies.[10] The interest of the orthodox analyst for the lower socio-economic groups and the eagerness of these people for the expensive verbal-prone therapies have never been intense, so Adler easily wins here by default.

The ultimate supposition to Freud was that man was a detached "monad" not an Adlerian social being. "Why should I love my neighbor?" asked Freud. Adler reflected that this was the psychology of the pampered child who did not realize that in the beginning the quality and quantity of self-esteem was founded upon being esteemed by others.[3] The later Adler anchored his psychotherapy upon *Gemeinschaftsgefühl* or humanistic identification.[11] He saw clearly the importance of social learning and anticipated the popular regard for psychotherapy as an education in insight and outsight.[12] Freud always leaned toward a biological fatalism, especially for homosexuals and schizophrenics. Such people were victimized by a passive constitutional libido or narcissistic neuroses, hence impossible for undergoing transference neuroses, the topic of interpretation in classic psychoanalysis. Since Freud's theories lent themselves so easily to the medical model of illness, the importance of social, economic, and political reforms was neglected, but not with Adler. His early papers were concerned with such reforms, so unusual for the physician who is characterized as preferring quick conventional symptom-removal. But when one moves away from simple organic determination he is prone to admit all types of unsavory characters and vexing questions into the high priesthood. So the inevitable happened and today in the vanguard of psychotherapy the popular techniques take the patient out of the passive, one-down position on the couch and put the psychotherapist into the *exemplar* or behavioral model spot.[13] No more "do as I say and not as I do" jokes and hypocritical double standards of "whatever you do is sick and I'm arbitrarily well." ". . . We must grudgingly admit that even as we were trying to devise, with scientific determinism, a therapy for the few, we were led to promote an ethical disease among the many. . . ."[9] Psychotherapy is, in its most viable and promising form, an education in responsible living through transactional communications in which both patient and therapist can benefit or suffer, depending on the presence or absence of authenticity or self-disclosure.[14] [15] [16] [17] Adler's tenets always were centered on mistakes rather than illness and focused beyond the individual to society itself. In contrast to materialistic, dehumanizing mentation, Adler had no penchant for analyzing the human into hidden demonological drives in which love, joy, and creativity were victims of "nothing-but" reductionism.

Adlerians are, as a rule, future-oriented and do not analyze away the life style. The latter is synonymous with a person's learned behaviors and learned attitudes, while unawareness and lack of humanistic goals lead to the so-called mental illnesses. To the typical Adlerian, an individual would not be a mere puppet of the unconscious but a non-reducible whole or life style seeking certain goals in a social context. Freedom, courage, and responsibility are not Freudian terms, since that philosophy relegated the masses to the slavery of the unconscious. In the Freudian *Weltanschauung* people are too often seen as the mere puppets of demagogues and dictators, ennobling actions really derivatives of greed, love essentially inhibited sexuality, women as crippled men, and culture regarded as always frustrating instead of potentially growth-fulfilling.[13] [18] It is no wonder that Eichmann chose such a Freudian-Manichean-medical model to rationalize his fascination for human destruction.[7]

One familiar with the little known facets of the history of psychiatry will probably know that orthodox psychoanalysis alone cannot be blamed for our sad misanthropic state and that mature societies as well as mature psychotherapists usually move through a mechanistic Alice-in-Wonderland world in which everything is really something else. Only later is the spurious depth of isolated analysis given up for the inviolability of the unique person in his surroundings. But in our democratic tradition something strange happened. Before the days of our cynical materialistic analysis and Darwinism social rationalizations combined with a peculiar defensive religiosity, our mental hospitals released over 60% of the patients never again to become wards of the state.[19] Contrast this figure with the 5% of the heyday of the authoritarian disease-model thinking we are now rapidly leaving. We are still burdened with treatment as disguised methods of silencing the subtle awkward protests of those dependent people with high nuisance value whom we are content to call patients.[20] [21] [22] [23] [24] Only when the world in a burst of Adlerian social optimism studies the psychological needs of man[24] as a science in its own right will we face our ultimate dis-ease: hopelessness and hostility inspired by negative generalizations about man by man, the truly mistaken Adlerian life styles. Adler's words have a liberal ring today when we look beyond our dehumanizing world of thing-worship and its counterpart, the custodial mental hospital. "The usual way of meeting such violence, to confine her and lock her in her room, was the wrong way. We must act differently if we wish to win this girl. It is the greatest mistake to expect an insane person to act as a normal person: Almost everyone is annoyed and irritated because the insane do not respond like ordinary beings. . ."[1]

The anathematizing of Adler by the Freudians certainly contributed to his lack of fame. But more telling factors have existed through the years. Adlerians in theory and practice are mainly interested in therapeutic activities at the expense of theory. Their founder delineated only the key concepts leaving future laborers the task of filling in the blanks. It is common knowledge that the Freudian efforts are admirably suited to the intellectual requirements of graduate studies. Years can be devoted to defining the new words added by Freud in his years of writing and to finding the new meanings given to familiar terms. The changed emphasis, meanings, and interrelationships throughout the years will also provide the graduate student with fuel for memorization. Not so with Adler, whose books have often been developed from the lecture notes taken by students, some of which have only recently been translated into English. Until the fine systematization of the Ansbachers,[1] [2] Adler was known chiefly for only two terms, the inferiority complex and the struggle for power. A schism within his own group also had an adverse effect upon his popularization. When he returned from the front during World War I, Adler was putting more weight upon the lack of social interest and the presence of defensive vanity as precipitators of problems in living and mistaken styles of life. The Nietzscheans in his midst rebelled at this debunking of power-seeking and soon split his following. Even today when Adler is mentioned, it is usually in criticism for his "will to power," the critic giving no thought to his later imperative social interest. For example, Erich Fromm,[25] who claims to be of Freudian orientation, now writes with an Adlerian spirit of his concern for biophilia and freedom as reflecting a learned character structure. But Adler is mentioned in his writings for overlooking narcissism, another instance of neglect of Adler's writings. On the other hand, Thomas Szasz, a rare revolutionary in American psychiatry, gives credit to Adler, and one can discern the Adlerian spirit of the uncommon common man echoed in Szasz's musings: "Psychiatrists perform two fundamentally different tasks in our society; they analyze the values people profess to hold and the games they like to play and they promote certain values and instruct patients in how to play certain games . . ."[22]

The real issue at stake is as old as man himself. Is man basically evil and in dire need of the dictator's leash to bring him in line? In my opinion, this is the orthodox Freudian position, which has no view of successful defense or maturity.[26] It provides more justification for dropping the Bomb or calling upon the Secret Police. Or is man capable of developing love and freedom without encroaching upon the needs of others? Take this choice and you are on the road to discovering Adler—and being called a soft-hearted do-gooder by those who are certain they are dealing with reality and not mere theories.

REFERENCES

1. Ansbacher, H. L. and Ansbacher, Rowena (Eds.) *The Individual Psychology of Alfred Adler.* (New York: Basic Books, 1956), pp. 316-317.

2. Adler, A. *Superiority and Social Interest.* (Evanston: Northwestern Univ. Press, 1964).

3. Bottome, P. *Alfred Adler: A Biography* (New York: Putman's Sons, 1946).

4. Hoffman, M. "On the Concept of Genital Primacy." *J. Nerv. Ment. Dis.,* 137, 1963, pp. 552-556.

5. Farber L. "The Therapeutic Despair." *Psychiatry,* 21, 1958, pp. 7-20.

6. Rioch, Margaret. "The Meaning of Martin Buber's 'Elements of the Interhuman' for the Practice of Psychotherapy." *Psychiatry,* 23, 1960, pp. 133-140.

7. Lehrman, N. "Psychiatry's Mission to Religion." *Reconstructionist,* 31, No. 3, 1965, pp. 7-13.

8. Oliver, W. and Landfield, A. "Reflexivity: An Unfaced Issue in Psychology," *J. Ind. Psychol.,* 18, 1962, pp. 114-124.

9. Erikson, E. *Young Man Luther* (New York: Norton, 1958), pp. 18-19.

10. O'Connell, W. "Psychotherapy for Everyman: A Look at Action Therapy." *J. Exist.* (in press).

11. O'Connell, W. "Humanistic Identification: A New Translation for Gemeinschaftsgefühl." *J. Ind. Psychol.*, 21, 1965, pp. 44-47.

12. O'Connell, W. "Practicing Christianity and Humanistic Identification." *J. Human. Psychol.*, 4, 1964, pp. 118-129.

13. Mowrer, O. *The Crisis in Psychiatry and Religion* (New York: Van Nostrand, 1961).

14. Frankl, V. *Man's Search for Meaning* (New York: Wash. Sq., 1963).

15. Glasser, W. *Reality Therapy.* (New York: Harper & Row, 1965).

16. Lederer, W. "Dragons, Delinquents, and Destiny." *Psychol. Issues*, 4, 1964, Mono. 15.

17. Shoben, E. "Personal Responsibility, Determinism, and Burden of Understanding." *Pers. & Guid. J.*, 39, 1961, pp. 342-348.

18. Lehrman, N. "Anti-therapeutic and Anti-democratic Aspects of Freudian Dynamic Psychiatry." *J. Ind. Psychol.*, 19, 1963, pp. 167-181.

19. Bockoven, J. *Moral Treatment in American Psychiatry.* (New York: Springer, 1963.)

20. Goffman, E. *Asylums.* (New York: Doubleday, 1961).

21. Haley, J. *Strategies of Psychotherapy.* (New York: Grune & Stratton, 1963).

22. Szasz. T. *The Myth of Mental Illness.* (New York: Hoeber-Harper, 1961).

23. Wertham, F. "Society and Problem Personalities: Praetorian Psychiatry." *Amer. J. Psychother.*, 17, 1963, pp. 404-416.

24. White, R. "Ego and Reality in Psychoanalytic Theory." *Psychol. Issues*, 3, 1963, Mono.11.

25. Fromm, E. *The Heart of Man.* (New York: Harper & Row, 1964).

26. Madison, P. *Freud's Concept of Repression and Defense.* (Minneapolis: Univ. Minn. Press. 1961), p. 179.

SOCIAL INTEREST IN AN OPERANT WORLD:
Interaction Between Skinnerian and Adlerian Thinking[1]

The intention of this paper is to stimulate a fruitful interaction between Skinnerian and Adlerian thinking about the nature of man and his psychological needs. To many students these two men postulated diametrically opposed premises. Already there have been some rumblings of discontent among lay people working out of Adlerian theory about the inroads of behavior modification, and a consequent fear of the specter of Skinner engulfing all the inner and outer movements of man. In the long run, such apprehensions are unwarranted for there are many unnoticed similarities between operant conditioning and Individual Psychology. The greatest gulf between the Skinnerian and Adlerian is really nothing new and alarming to the scientific world. The intellectual choice can be seen, for example, in the disparities between Lamarckian (autogenesis) and Darwinian (ectogenesis) emphases in evolutionary theory.[18] More ancient roots of the within-without dichotomy can be noted in the still viable debates between humanistic (intrinsic, behavioral) and fundamentalistic-authoritarian (extrinsic, ritualistic) religions.[13] Following the time-honored criterion of the primacy of inner or outer forces, the Adlerian can be separated from the Skinnerian by his emphasis on the creative movements of the life style, whereas the latter always points to the absolute force of external environmental forces.

My background in approaching the question of "who-is-to-train-whom?" in the schools and homes has roots in both learning theory and humanistic lines of thought. Following my

[1]Presidential Address presented at the 20th annual meeting of the American Society of Adlerian Psychology, Houston, Texas, May 26-28, 1972.

Reprinted from Voices, Vol. 9, #3, 1973.

discontent with traditional psychotherapies, especially those of a psychoanalytic variety in mental hospital treatment,[12] I explored the possibilities of classical type conditioning along with the Skinnerian operant methodology. At that time my goal was to help personnel become "significant-other" auxiliaries through secondary and primary reinforcement and stimulus generalization. I hoped that personnel who had neutral or even negative connotations for patients would become people to whom the patients would listen and with whom they would share their mistakes en route to learning more cooperative modes of interaction with other people. The end result of these efforts was action therapy,[15] [17] a type of behavior modification, because it is a here-and-now, behaviorally-oriented transaction. The action in action therapy is not in terms of life-style assessment with its early recollections and past family constellations, but focuses on *how* and *why* people lower their self-esteem and narrow their social interest at the present moment. Action therapy operates on the premise that all men are equal in their need for self-esteem. All are equal in the *constriction*, a self-induced (albeit with historical roots) lowering of self-esteem and narrowing of social interest. From prince to pauper, all humans are *creative* (not "sick") in striving to find proof for their life-style premises in novel situations. All people *cooperate* in reinforcing both useful and useless life goals of themselves and others. The goal of action therapy is for everyone (not just the psychotherapist) to guess at how the protagonist creatively constricts, and how and why others cooperate in reinforcing problem-creating behaviors. All members of an action therapy group are "wounded healers"[10] not totally free from learned constriction, yet responsible for encouraging everyone in the group at any moment. Action therapy, Adlerian in its premises that people creatively "arrange" traumata and actively look for evidence, still shares with behavior modification the conviction that all inner and outer movement is somehow reinforced by others. This premise rests on social embeddedness, taken as seriously as one can.

More important than theoretical differences is the ability of the Adlerian and Skinnerian schools to generate cooperative efforts around common problems. Bullard's[7] action program for school children with extreme problems is a prime example of such teamwork. To prepare further such efforts we shall discuss similarities between Skinner and Adler, followed by a consideration of the major differences.

COMMONALITIES

Reliance on Movement toward Goals

Both systems see in the movements of an individual toward his goal the basic psychological reality. An Adlerian will watch for verbal and nonverbal clues as to how the person creatively maintains his constrictive life-style attitudes, and cooperates in stabilizing discouragement for others. "Constriction" simply means that all persons have learned to maintain their identities through less than complete movements of self-esteem and social interest. In the words of Becker, "Character armor really refers to the whole life-style that a person assumes, in order to live and act with a certain security . . . Each person literally closes off his world, fences himself around, *in the very process of his own growth and organization.*" (author's italics) (5, P. 83)

This constriction, viewed as a universal but socially remediable waste, is one answer to the perennial question, "What do I have in common with others?" Keeping in mind two additional "C's," creativity and cooperation, prevents a search for a scapegoat and highlights human interdependence. Self- and other-blame is minimized by the premise that in every human transaction people are creative in inferring meaning into novel situations. For example, anyone well practiced in blaming self (depressive), others (paranoid), or life (psychopathic) can find evidence for his blame-orientation by selectively focusing upon behaviors as justifications for one's "reactive" dehumanized actions. One may further show his creativity by his skills in stimulating others to take actions or "cooperate" in such a way as to provide further evidence for flight or fight. As an example, Salzman[20] has noted that the paranoid's "delusions" of persecution depend upon the cooperation of others in moving against his persistent attempts to counter his low self-esteem with desperate urges of grandiosity. Everyone possesses creative power, the ability to cause or prevent change, although it is only the Adlerian who knows that power (but not always self-esteem) can be "gained" by influencing others through symptoms. The cooperation or reinforcement of others is assumed as a human necessity. The cooperative ideal is someone who reinforces others for their efforts at encouragement. He cooperates-as-an-equal rather than reinforces useless actions through movements of annoyance, provocation, hurt, or hopelessness.[8]

An operant is best defined as movement or behavior which operates upon the environment to generate consequences. This kind of movement leads to the problems of social psychology, and Skinner, in spite of his focusing upon specific responses, does see the person as moving in and responsible for his social milieu.[23] Adler noted that one can discover much useful information about a person by observing the environment he selects and how he perceives it, seeking "proof" for the premises of his life-style. "To estimate the true character of an individual we must always give full significance to the environment he has chosen or permitted for himself." (2, P. 31) Such statements strongly imply the search for "appropriate" contingencies of reinforcement, to use the language of Skinner.

Distrust of Reified Terms

Skinner is always very distrustful of conceptual inner causes, a corollary of his emphasis on movement. To quote Skinner in his disdain of abstractions as explanations, "The practice of explaining one statement in terms of the other is dangerous because it suggests we have found the cause and therefore need search no further. Such terms . . . convert what are essentially the properties of a process or relation into what appear to be things." (22, P. 31) Individual Psychology concurs, and eschews abstract concepts which cannot be anchored in movement. This particular similarity between Skinner and Adler was previously pointed out by Ansbacher (4, P. 346). An imaginary encounter between Skinner and Adler might well be highlighted by Adler's agreeing with Skinner's strong faith that personality constructs must be grounded in movement in the environment. Adler's "as if" way of looking at concepts, at abstractions, in a guessing, tentative way would certainly rule out any reification of them.

Focus on Consequences and Reinforcement

The Adlerian position, especially as exemplified by Rudolf Dreikurs,[8] focuses upon what is in reality an operant methodology, in that the behavior of the child is viewed as an

143

attempt to manipulate the environment to react with certain responses or consequences. This premise is a definition of operant conditioning as movement which operates upon the environment to generate consequences, even though Dreikurs rejects Skinnerian *behavior* modification for an Adlerian *motivation* modification. If the child is not recognized or reinforced for his movement on the useful side of life, he will move on the useless side. That is, he may resort to attention-getting, power struggles, become revenge-seeking, or search for special services, to mention Dreikurs' four goals of misbehavior. But these misbehaviors will be effective methods only if persons in the environment reinforce them and fail to reinforce cooperation-as-equals. In teaching responsibility, significant others must not reward the abstract person ("you're a perfect angel") or defend the person against noninjurious consequences of actions, but recognize efforts at solving a task which seems to be motivated by cooperation.

In psychotherapy Adler spoke of encouragement, which is in fact the same as reinforcement, as the strongest factor. In action therapy we give the person practice in receiving and giving feedback (communication of feelings, mistakes, and encouragement, without evaluating the person). Feedback in this sense is not the "touchy-feely" orientation of the encounter movement but guessing at the *why* and *how* a person actively narrows his social interest and lowers his self-esteem in the here-and-now.[15] [16] [17] Such interactions imply transactional movements and environmental consequences and so are compatible with both the Adlerian and Skinnerian ways of structuring existence.

In Skinner's view the inept therapist is one who uses non-differential reinforcement in therapy. Adlerians, I believe, would recognize the person nonverbally by stopping, looking, and listening. They would use operant reinforcement on verbal and nonverbal responses which have socially helping implications. By constantly recognizing the worth of the person nonverbally, and by reinforcing the movements of courage (active social interest), Adlerians join Skinnerians in disapproving of total unconditional positive regard (or pampering). Unfortunately, operant methodology does not understand or utilize the Adlerian method of anticipating and discussing "reactive" actions on the useless side of life.

Dissatisfaction with Autonomous Man

Skinner is dissatisfied with the concept of the autonomous man. "It is only autonomous man who has reached a dead end. Man himself may be controlled by his environment, but it is an environment which is almost wholly of his own making." (23, P. 205-206) This myth of individuality has been used for centuries to praise oneself (a form of pampering) and blame the other when he fails. Individualistic focus has led to neglect of religious, economic, political, and social factors which mold and maintain both healthy and sick life-styles.

The Adlerian approach with its emphases on social interest and encouragement likewise cannot maintain the delusion of the completely autonomous individual. Adler defined courage as active social interest. "Only the activity of an individual who plays the game, cooperates, and shares in life can be designated as courage." (3, P. 60) Operationally, courage could be defined as taking the risk of giving and asking for feedback about one's feelings as to how the other, and perhaps himself, is disrupting the potentially cooperative world in efforts to gain self-esteem.

Recently there have been a number of biographical works[19][24] citing the destructive importance of the lack of negative and positive feedback to leaders, be they dictator or president. The latter, in a desperate need for self-esteem, may select significant others whose form of encouragement is spurious. Advisers may not share feelings, guess at mistaken goals, and through such failures of communication pamper the leader. On a national level, the "love it or leave it" slogan, implies that if one does not pamper an object or person he may be an acceptable target for subsequent violence. In this case, feedback equals "hostility," and, in the popular way of looking at things, one can then respond in kind.

Subordination of Feelings

To Adler, feelings are not reasons for behavior, but are used to justify actions that the person either wittingly or unwittingly wants to transact without accepting responsibility for the consequences. "Individual Psychology is not interested in the verbal expression of feelings, but only in the intensity of a person's movement." (3, P. 283) To Skinner, feelings are mainly the result of adequacy of reinforcement, part of a pleasant-unpleasant contingency continuum. ". . . you're appealing to a

145

feeling as if it were a cause of behavior. I don't want to try to modify feelings. I want to try to modify the behavior, and the feelings will come along with it." (6, P. 12) Therefore, both schools run counter to the views of popularized psychotherapy in which release of feelings is paramount and regarded as the supreme motivation of man.[17]

Aiming at the Good of the Group

Adler with his concept of *Gemeinschaftsgefühl* believed in evolution in which the potentials of social interest would be increasingly developed. Skinner's finalistic aim also is the good of the cultural group, and he has hopes for a progression away from the individualist. "Some religions have made death more important by picturing a future existence in heaven or hell, but the individualist has a special reason to fear death; it is the prospect of personal annihilition. The individualist can find no solace in reflecting upon any contribution that will survive him. He has refused to be concerned for the survival of his culture and is not reinforced by the fact that the culture will long survive him. In the defense of his own freedom and dignity he has denied the contributions of the past and must therefore relinquish all claim upon the future." (23, P. 210) Yet, it is almost as if Skinner hoped that science or some genetic unfolding would negate narcissism and give birth to an instant democratic value system.

Favorable Disposition toward Religion

Skinner has stated that if he were a theologian he would do such things as would lead people to behave in a way which demonstrated that they believe in God. God is symbolic of positively reinforcing circumstances, while hell is a bizzare collection of adversative stimuli to Skinner.[6] Adler left interminable debates about God to theologians (as did even Thomas Acquinas at the end of his career), yet saw in the positive potentialities of religious living the goal of perfectibility of the family of man and the person in cooperative activities. Once again Skinner and Adler find themselves upon the less popular end of psychology by being favorably disposed toward religion, defined as noninstitutional potentialities for the teaching cooperative behaviors.

POINTS OF DIVERGENCE

The Issue of Creativity

The crux of the great separation is not whether we contrast the laboratory with the clinic, or specific responses with holistic situations, but rather the tremendous difference in emphasis between focusing mainly upon a creativity (Adler) or making the external environment the mover of all life (Skinner).

Adlerians are primarily concerned with man's creativity. In action therapy the focus is upon how an individual, with all his creativity in accordance with his learned life-style, continues to find evidence which leads him to narrow his social interest and to lower his self-esteem. We are all afflicted with either or both of these constricting "dis-eases." Skinner's faith that *ultimately* all human movement resolves itself through the process of external reinforcement fits well with scientistic approaches to understanding the world. Operant conditioning is a method that seems to work with animals, retardates, chronic psychotics. Unfortunately, the operant methodology is being overgeneralized into an explanation of human reality as a somewhat complicated external and eternal machine. Since Descartes the ultimate scientific ideal has been toward quantifying and controlling the world through the manipulation of variables in the *res extensa*. In our times we are testing other ways of viewing human reality, such as growth, through getting the patient to understand-the-other (social interest) rather than simply through quantifying and controlling external variables. The Adlerian emphasis on creativity and guessing at the life-style of others is part of an alternative, but less popular view of psychological science. Nineteenth Century scientism is exemplified in the world views of B. F. Skinner. It is still much with us and will be, so it seems, until we respect each life-style as a unique and precious work of art.

The Clinic Versus the Laboratory

Self-esteem and social interest are the two "depth" variables in the focus on humanistic identification.[15] [17] Both of these variables are closely anchored in human movement, subject to measurement, and so should be acceptable as variables in any theory except an extreme behaviorism. A person's demand for certain contingencies of reinforcement and, in fact,

147

his very definition of what reinforcement is in the movement of others, depends upon his evaluation of himself and the world. That is, if I were going to become a significant other to a chronic schizophrenic,[12] I would have to engage in subtle approach movements, followed by intensive association with primary reinforcers (food, drink). Perhaps through the process of time and patience I would become a significant other to him. On the other hand, someone with authentic self-esteem and social interest would see anyone as being significant merely by right of his existence. In a behaviorist's laboratory this differentiation might make no methodological difference because theoretically he would be able to control *all* of the reinforcers of the environment. Whether or not the organism is initially happy, optimistic, approaching, or sad, pessimistic, withdrawing, makes no difference in eventual outcome in such a laboratory, except for the length of training trials and numbers and amounts of reinforcement needed. The experimenter would merely create longer lab periods for the more withdrawn individual.

Historically and ideally, the Adlerian focuses upon the clinic while the Skinnerian attends to the controlled environment of the laboratory. The Adlerian hopes to train the individual to notice his untoward reactions to the world and to encourage him to do otherwise, (to become more positive) through working in situations that approach similarity to the world to which the individual will once again return.

Sense of Humor

Skinnerians emphasize behavioral control, whereas many of us are too afraid to look at our environmental dependencies. From an early age, we are trained to think we are free encapsulated "individuals" even though rewards and punishments follow us throughout life. Skinnerians have therefore been caricatured (as a way to ignore their message?) as people preoccupied with the question of control. When control is central to one's self-concerns, one is labeled an obsessive-compulsive character, the exact opposite of the humorist. To the average operant conditioner the world is one in which control is exercised by the environment. An Adlerian would hope that the individual would be able to control—through understanding and love—his own excessive demands upon the world and eventually become less arbitrary and learn how to cooperate as an equal.

Humor has generally been ignored by psychologists and references to the sense of humor are missing in Skinner's works. Yet the humorous attitude was regarded by Freud[9] as the epitome of maturity; though unfortunately such a growth concept did not fit his closed system. Adlerians, as a whole, have also ignored the sense of humor in their writings. In practice a hallmark of Adlerian psychotherapy is laughter. The therapist and the patient can laugh at mistakes. In other approaches in which the patient is viewed as an innocent, passive victim, laughter equals hostility. Humor has a logical spot in Adlerian theory,[14] for one with a sense of humor has a very well-developed social interest and an extensive self-esteem. Ideally, he is dependent upon no particular person but can ask for and give feedback to anyone in an acceptable way. The humorist is also someone who believes in multiple views of reality. He is a person who sees as many realities as there are individuals and does not demand that people agree with him or see the world the way he does. The humorist can live harmoniously in our world of paradoxes, a prime example being St. Augustine's paradox which aptly describes the activities of the humorist. According to that paradox, one should live as if whatever he did at any given moment was of extreme importance, but if he died at that time it would make no difference. Perhaps the humorist is an example of what Skinner might advocate as a method of "countercontrol." Skinner might be able to explain the working of the humorist in his own system through laborious and strained primary and secondary conditionings, stimulus generalizations, response generalizations, and various chains of coverants.[11] Any system advocating rigid environmental control has difficulty living with or explaining the humorist. He seems to be the paragon of the creativity, for it takes a humanist genius to produce humor and find reinforcement on the way to the gallows, poor in goods, and in disrepute among his peers.[14]

BASIS FOR COOPERATION

The Adlerian question is, "How do we go about cooperating as equals?" Adlerians would like to share the whole concept of social interest with Skinnerians who, if they accepted

149

it, could certainly help Adlerians in measurement, shaping, and recording. Cooperation-as-equals would mean that Adlerians would lose their phobia for specific responses which developed through the mistaken idea that specifics violate holism. It would also mean that Skinnerians would give up their quixotic stance for the glories of a moribund scientism.

A quote which follows is an example of the dangers of the blinders of scientism. "To a considerable extent an individual does appear to shape his own destiny. He is able to do something about the variables affecting him. Some degree of 'self-determination' of conduct is usually recognized in creative behavior . . . he is behaving. He controls himself precisely as he would control the behavior of anyone else—through the manipulation of variables of which his behavior is a function." Yet, Skinner continues, "his behavior in so doing is a proper object of analysis and eventually it *must* be accounted for with variables lying outside the individual himself." (22, P. 228, italics ours)

Certainly one can detect a creative self operating here which is able to manipulate variables to change himself, but this power must rest upon the reinforcements of the external world, or precise scientism is destroyed. Ultimately—no matter how circuitous and obscure the route—even the creative powers of the self must answer to external reinforcement. That is the Skinnerian act of faith.

A Skinnerian would regard the power of social interest as a genetic unfolding rewarded by the environment. Adlerians need to be more specific about what actions constitute responses of social interest. Social interest is basically defined and reinforced in interpersonal situations, and the movements of feedback are tests of one's social interest and courage (*active* social interest). Practice of these skills can take place through an understanding of the other. If the recipient becomes "deaf," violent, depressed, or shows other signs of negative nonsense, the feedback has failed. Behaviorally, courage can be shown only with another person. "There may be other people present, but, at any moment in time, only two people can be eye-to-eye." (21, P. 34) Adler, who introduced the term "human dyad" to cover such transactions,[1] seemed to be well aware that social interest, in its most developed form of courage, goes beyond feeling at home in the world or the abstract goal of *sub specie aeternitatis*. Movement is the authentic test of courage.

Try for a moment to visualize the social interest implied in the following quotation: "So far as I can see there is only one part of our emotions in life that can never be overstrained and that is social interest. If there is social interest you cannot overstrain it in such a degree that the harmony of life can be disturbed; but all other things can do so." (3, P. 167)

Is it possible, do you suppose, to have a theory of psychology which honors the courage of creative self, the reinforcing environment, the truth of social interest, and a concern for gathering evidence?

SUMMARY

The "atheoretical" operant conditioning theory of B. F. Skinner is often contrasted with the school activities of Adlerian psychologists and educators. Yet many similarities are apparent between the theories of Adler and Skinner in spite of the differences between the humanistic and the behavioristic points of view. In contrast to traditional psychoanalysis, both leaders have looked on society optimistically and on religion favorably and have been concerned with movements rather than feelings as the focus for change. Their concern has been with the individual rather than with group data, and the contributions of the person to the survival of the culture. Skinner's battle against "autonomous man" is tantamount to the Adlerian emphasis on the contribution of the family and school to the learning of cooperation. No child is isolated from the transactional learning process. Adler's maxim to "movement, the basic law of all life and consequently also of psychological life" (3, P. 52), and his "as if" stance toward internal states can also be seen as close to Skinner's system of thought.

The chief difference between Skinnerians and Adlerians appears to be in the ultimate explanation of behavioral phenomena: in terms of external variables, or of the creative self.

Both schools can learn from each other: Adlerians by defining and shaping the potential for social interest; Skinnerians by taking social interest and courage into serious consideration, and seeing creativity as a nonreductive fact of life. Preference

151

for one or the other school of psychology should rest upon the greater skill in actualizing mature persons rather than rhetoric and biases.

REFERENCES

1. Adler, A. Love is a recent invention (1937). *J. Indiv. Psychol.*, 1971, 27, 144-152.

2. Adler, A. *Problems of neurosis* (1962). New York: Harper and Row, 1964.

3. Adler, A. *Superiority and social interest.* Ed. by H. L. & Rowena R. Ansbacher, Evanston, Ill.: Northwestern Univer. Press, 1964.

4. Ansbacher, H. L. The structure of Individual Psychology. In B. B. Wolman (Ed.) *Scientific psychology.* New York: Basic Books, 1965, Pp. 340-364.

5. Becker, E. *Angel in armor.* New York: Braziller, 1969.

6. Buckley, W. *Firing line.* Columbia, S. C.: Southern Educational Communications Association, October 17, 1971.

7. Bullard, M. L. Extreme pupil behavior problems: Five years' use of special class techniques. *Indiv. Psychol.,* 1970, 26, 225.

8. Dreikurs, R. *Social equality: The challenge of today.* Chicago: Regnery, 1971.

9. Freud, S. Humor (1928). In *Collected papers.* Vol. 5. London: Hogarth, 1950, Pp. 215-221.

10. Guggenbühl-Craig, A. *Power in the helping professions.* New York: Spring, 1971.

11. Homme, L. Perspectives in psychology XXIV: Control of coverants, the operants of the mind. *Psychol. Rec.,* 1965, 15, 501-511.

12. O'Connell, W. E. Identification and curability of the mental hospital patient. *J. Indiv. Psychol.,* 1962, 18, 68-76.

13. O'Connell, W. E. Practicing Christianity and humanistic identification. *J. Human. Psychol.,* 1964, 4, 118-129.

14. O'Connell, W. E. Humor: The therapeutic impasse. *Voices,* 1969, 5(2), 25-27.

15. O'Connell, W. E. Adlerian action therapy. *Voices,* 1971, 7(2), 22-27.

16. O'Connell, W. E. Equality in encounter groups. *Indiv. Psychol.*, 1971, 8(1), 15-17.

17. O'Connell, W. E. Sensitivity training and Adlerian theory. *J. Indiv. Psychol.*, 1971, 27, 65-72.

18. O'Manique, J. Teilhard's Lamarckism. *Teilhard Rev.*, 1966, 1, 34-41.

19. Reedy, G. *The twilight of the presidency.* New York: Norton, 1970.

20. Salzman, L. Paranoid state—theory and therapy. *Arch. Gen. Psychiat.*, 1960, 2, 679-793.

21. Satir, V. *Peoplemaking.* Palo Alto: Science and Behavior Books, 1972.

22. Skinner, B. F. *Science and human behavior.* New York: MacMillan, 1953.

23. Skinner, B. F. *Beyond freedom and dignity.* New York: Knopf, 1971.

24. Speer, A. *Inside the Third Reich.* New York: MacMillan, 1970.

SENSITIVITY TRAINING AND ADLERIAN THEORY[1]

This paper is a beginning attempt to plot an Adlerian position and course with respect to the burgeoning group phenomena of the last few years. To clarify our terms at the outset, let us state that sensitivity training will denote the entire field of encounter and similar therapy groups. This will include the human relations laboratory groups which are usually differentiated from the short-term encounter groups by more carefully constructed instruments and exercises to identify crucial elements of group life, rather than reliance solely on the expertise of group leaders.[3] In the laboratory groups leadership may emerge from the interplay of the individual life styles within the group (D-groups, for developmental), or leaders may be engaged as "trainers" or facilitators who catalyze the group activities by nonverbal techniques and here-and-now interpretations (T-groups, for trainer-led).

These differences in composition and task of the groups are of minor significance, however, compared to the difference in their purpose. The thesis of this paper is, specifically, that the real and far-reaching distinction between groups is whether they are implicitly motivated by goals of release-of-drives or of learning-to-be-human.

Merits of Sensitivity Training in General

No search-and-destroy attack on the sensitivity-encounter group movement is herein intended. Any phenomenon labeled by ultrareactionary individuals as part of "the conspiratorial Left,"[2] and "the devil's three-pronged fork—sex, drugs, and

---

[1]Presented in part at Divisions 24 & 29 (Philosophical Psychology & Psychotherapy) Symposium, "Adlerian Principles in Modern Psychotherapy," commemorating the Centennial of Alfred Adler's birth, at the 78th Annual Convention, American Psychological Association, Miami Beach, September 14, 1970.

Reprinted from Journal of Individual Psychology, Vol. 27,65-72, May 1971.

sensitivity training"[6] can't be all wrong. Extreme resistances to the encounter movement often serve as a vehicle for displaced and projected urges, for some of its most vocal critics have read little about such groups and have experienced even less.[7] In our fragmented and dehumanized world of obsessive-compulsive hyperindividuality, any skin-stretching to include concern for others as equals will run afoul of authoritarian fears and dictates.

The social movement of which sensitivity training is a part is a rebellion against the cultural preoccupation with abstract, analytical, and there-and-then modes of conceptualizing man. In this sense, the movement's here-and-now focus has much in common with Adlerian theory. The leaderless developmental groups (D-groups) and even the trainer-led groups (T-groups) have a democratic potentiality for mutual respect so foreign to orthodox psychoanalytic theory. There is an air of optimism in the approach of the human relations laboratory and the therapeutic methods of Individual Psychology.

It may be that more tolerance and understanding for therapeutic innovations would follow from viewing these efforts with a sense of historical time.[9] From the days of the early Greeks there has been a continuing, albeit relatively faint, puzzlement about man's growth-inspiring actions.[10] [16] Philia, eros, and agape, three traditional types of love, can be considered nodal points on a continuum of positive approach behaviors. As such they correspond to various strategies and goals of 20th century psychotherapy. Philia, or friendship, is still the initial subgoal of most types of individual and group psychotherapy; a multilateral groping for friendship or relatedness is the hallmark of the entire group movement. Eros, or the drive toward interpersonal union, is one aim of the sensitivity or encounter movement, which seeks to realize it primarily on the nonverbal level of communication. Agape, or the selfless brotherly concern for others, is the aim of Adlerian groups, who seek to realize it through understanding on the cognitive level.

"Drive" Release Groups

Essential points separate the Adlerian, hoping to promote the spirit of agape from the "pseudospontaneity of the turner-onners,"[14] the instant-eros bunch. An Adlerian would operate

155

out of a theory of the life style and be subject to the label of "intellectual" by those who foster a dualism between thought and feeling. An Adlerian, of course, believes that feeling is a reaction to one's thoughts, all in the service of life-style goals. The popularized "Bob and Carol and Ted and Alice" type of trainer appears to be almost anti-intellectual, seeing thought and feeling as separate domains and opting for the latter. Meaning is sought-after through catharsis in a release of emotions.[11] [12]

Implicit encounter group assumptions, more characteristic of Esalen than Bethel, seem to be based on a Lockean view of man: the individual being shaped by exposure to external forces.[3] An Adlerian with a more pronounced Liebnitzean bent will see the active individual creating wily maneuvers in accordance with his life style, to gain such ends as approval, intellectual and moral superiority, dependency, control, and abuse. Therefore the prime therapeutic aim is not release of repressed love and hate, but expanding self-esteem simultaneously with social interest.

Popularized sensitivity training in practice is often a quickie-type "psychoanalysis," using social "objects" to gain release of hidden positive and negative drives. This type of trainer may seek an immediate (almost magic) solution to problems. His here-and-now emphasis seldom acknowledges purposes and gains of the participant's arbitrary demands upon others. Too little emphasis is placed on understanding the life of the other (as in role reversal) and practicing the giving and receiving of feedback in a democratic manner.

In a sense one's body can be considered an inferior organ, for it is too often the focus of excessive attention. The poorly-led here-and-now sensitivity group reinforces the neurotic behavior of the self-centered person by existing mainly to have him experience his own sensations, talk about them, and attack others, verbally or physically in a fit of "honesty." Real honesty can prosper only in a group of equals in the mutuality of feedback without demands.

If the leader facilitates the democratic ethos, a person can learn a great deal about his arbitrary demands and untoward reactions. Unfortunately, encounter groups have often been directed toward cathartic-touch-and-tell only. In the desperate effort to transcend our culturally conditioned skin-tight identities, groups have failed to examine their premises and demanded instant ecstasy and nirvana by crying, touching, wrestling, and other regressive actions. There is often an unverbalized contest for power in the struggle to be the greatest weeper, toucher, or confessor. They "strive for spontaneity" and a feeling of "down-loose rather than uptight."[17] According to Ryckoff[15], culmination of "our terrible need really to know each other" will be "a mutual Proctoscopy group . . . comfortably arranged around the swimming pool in the end-chest position, peering into each others' colons" (p. 206).

Human relations laboratories well-grounded in democratic principles do not violate human dignity as do those dominated by hippiephrenic *demands*.

Adlerian Sense-Ability Training

All behavior is purposive to Adlerians, and therefore, "telling it like it is" is also closely connected to goals. The decisive factor is whether the goal is imbued with social interest or not, i.e., whether it is a goal of cooperation, or a less mature goal of attention, power, revenge, or the hidden demands for special service. It is the goals of here-and-now behavior that are examined by Adlerians. For encounter groups of other orientations it is extremely rare to advance beyond descriptive labels. For example, a participant may be given feedback that others are disturbed because he is "over-reacting." No effort is then made to examine the person's self-esteem, social interest, and the hidden goals of his "over-reacting." When Adlerian methodology uses action techniques the focus is upon insight and outsight into the purposes of behavior. Outsight is the learned ability to see, hear, and feel along with others. This social process, the basic element of warm relationships, prevents the reactive dis-ease of arbitrary demands. Outsight is as important as insight and neither concept is divorced from the other. Professed love or understanding is not accepted on the verbal level only ("trust only movement"). Social change is demonstrated by practicing new behaviors and outsights and decreasing hidden and rationalized arbitrary demands.

Social interest is not synonymous with social conformity but connotes a feeling of intimate belonging to the full spectrum of humanity: past, present, and future. With such a life style the person does not suffer from alienation and loneliness, the hallmark of mental disturbances. When social interest is examined and tried, after all other diversions fail, the royal road to the rarest human virtue, agape, will be found. In our pre-Christian times agape still remains untried. Agape, selfless love, is the way to superiority without distancing from others, hiding one's feelings, and flogging the self for spurious self-esteem. Agape is to put one's self in the other's situation. Encouraging the other, in this ideal state, would be as natural as "breathing and the upright gait,"[1] because there would be no neurotic need to elevate the self by depreciating others. One can learn, by receiving encouragement and well-intentioned feedback, the extent and damage of one's arbitrary demands. Then the search for a modicum of puny esteem (all the individual believes he can get) through attention-getting, power striving, revenge struggles, or a display of inadequacy is no longer pressing. In democratic groups a loving atmosphere is engendered by "letting-be."

> To illustrate: In some sensitivity groups the silent withdrawn individual might be told suddenly to try to break into the group, the other members linking hands to keep him out. This nonverbal exercise would perhaps take place with little ensuing comment on the purpose of the withdrawal or the underlying pathology of self-esteem and social interest. In the Adlerian sense-ability training, the silent one would not be forced to do anything. The other participants might talk about their feelings about his silence, its presumed goals, what the silent one selectively perceives and tells himself to create and maintain his silence, and how he actively rejects his own potential and that of others. If his peers demand activity, that becomes their problem—also to be shared and studied. In Action Therapy (Adlerian psychodrama techniques), each participant can mirror another's explicit and implicit life style, i.e., his behavior and his cognitive selectivities, but only with his permission. One asks his permission, and if he refuses, one may openly reflect on this, but one does not see oneself as an omnipotent or an isolated judge. For example one may say, "My guess is that Joe is trying so hard to be perfect that he's afraid he'll fail if he says anything. I wish I could help him and the group, but if he won't now share, that's his decision. What do you think?"

The person then learns the logical consequences of his choices, no longer disguised as necessary and externally conditioned actions. Such a group does not exist for the shock value of stimulating and creating unlikely situations. There is more

158

to be examined in the fears and demands of daily existence without contrived disrobing and physical attacks. Regressive behavior can be fun, but social interest grows from incorporating a democratic theory and practice of understanding the other.

The Adlerian system works in a social-learning frame of reference, dealing with the depth factors of "why" and "how" a person maintains low self-esteem and low social interest, with the goal of raising both interdependently. The therapist aims at becoming a significant other to the patient through verbal and nonverbal expressions of belonging and worth. It is assumed that the therapist already has a well-developed sense of philia, so the task is a unilateral bond of friendship, patient to therapist.

According to the Beechers,[4] "One of the more pathetic or amusing levels of eros friendship amounts to mutual baby sitting of one adult by another" (p. 103). "Agape . . . is entirely nonpossessive and demands nothing for itself. It does not judge, discriminate, evaluate" (p. 93).

The well-functioning Adlerian psychotherapist, no matter what the label of his activity, personifies this agape-in-action. Ideally, he shows agape toward all, for this behavior is synonymous with social interest. But the movements of agape are not those of the touch-and-tell sensitivity groups. Agape is demandless love, akin to equality.[5] Agape (and social interest) sees the self and others as of incomparable worth and always able to make decisions. The Adlerian is open to give and receive feedback. He guesses at the reaction of the person with whom he is about to be open and authentic. Since he is not dependent upon this person (the eros-motive is not operating), he can risk honesty. Even when a patient becomes so actively or passively violent that verbal dialogue of psychotherapy is precluded, agape is still viable as long as the therapist does not show in verbal or motoric behavior that he is labeling the patient eternally hopeless and helpless. The Adlerian does not forget that the world turns on the eros-motive and teaches his client that if he wants to be esteemed by his agape-less friends, he'd do well to be prepared to confirm them in the way that they unwittingly demand.

Laboratory group methods using the Adlerian approach offer an immediate here-and-now interpersonal diagnosis, shared by all, and not divorced from treatment. For example, the participant feels and inadvertently shows his anxiety (and ways of dealing with such) when faced with the culturally atypical task of merely looking at another face. In well-conducted democratic groups the participant can experience the frustrations of not being able to use habitual ways of evaluating and devaluating self and others to gain self-esteem. He can experience the beauty and awe of coming "back to his senses," untethered by the need for "negative nonsense."

The oft-repeated right-wing claim that the essence of sensitivity training is a substituting of the will and judgment of the group for that of the individual has not been shown in research on democratic human relations laboratories.[13] In fact, the opposite has been true. The patient's self-esteem has increased and he has become less dependent on the group.

Summary

The popular yet amorphous movement called sensitivity and encounter groups has superficial similarities with the Adlerian approach, more generally so, when the innovative groups have democratic leaders and atmospheres. While the usual sensitivity trainer and the Adlerian therapist share optimism, a distrust of autocratic depersonalization, and the aim to extend interpersonal relatedness, in practice their implicit assumptions and methodologies differ strikingly. Whereas release-of-drives is primarily the goal of many encounter groups, practice and growth of self-acceptance in a harmonious and democratic understanding of and interaction with others is the goal of Adlerian-oriented groups. Encouragement and feedback, based on the leader's offer of friendship, in an atmosphere of mutual respect as well as honesty, minimizes acting-out for narrow self-centered needs and the overwhelming of the person by power-driven group participants. Giving and receiving feedback with psychodramatic techniques is practicing courage, and overcomes the habitual distancing from others in the service of faulty self-esteem. The individual is given the chance to see himself as others do, and is encouraged to choose between offered alternatives.

A socio-historical approach to the sensitivity-encounter movement would elicit more tolerance and understanding. It appears as a reaction to our age of obsessive-compulsive hyperindividuality, and like all compensatory movements, often overshoots its mark. Philosophically, its roots lie in Lockean tradition, overemphasizing the power of external agents in precipitating change. Although all groups are seeking philia, some form of friendship, each in its own way, sensitivity for instant relatedness which all too quickly fades in "postlab depressions," the encounter movement fails to tap the secret of agape: the demandless concern for the other. The Adlerian group expresses agape in its endeavor to understand the life style of the other and enables him to modify it.

REFERENCES

1. Adler, A. *Social interest: A challenge to mankind* (1938). New York: Capricorn, 1964.

2 Allen, G. Hate therapy: Sensitivity training for "planned change." *Amer. Opinion*, 1968, II, 73-86.

3. Allport, G. W. *Becoming.* New Haven: Yale Univer. Press, 1955.

4. Beecher, W., & Beecher, Marguerite. *Beyond success and failure.* New York: Julian, 1966.

5. Dreikurs, R. *Equality: The challenge of our times.* Chicago: Alfred Adler Institute, 1961.

6. Effenberger, D. Wanderer forum speakers criticize "heretical" textbooks. *Texas Catholic Herald*, July 10, 1970. I.

7. Greeley, A. Sensitivity training violates man's soul. *Texas Catholic Herald*, August 22, 1969, 4.

8. Hanson, P., Rothaus, T., O'Connell, W. E., & Wiggins, G. Training patients for effective participation in back-home groups. *Amer. J. Psychiat.*, 1969, 126, 857-862.

9. Masserman, J. Humanitarian psychiatry. *Bull. N. Y. Acad. Med.*, 1963, 39, 533-544.

10. Nygren, A. *Agape and eros.* New York: Macmillan, 1933.

11. O'Connell, W. E. The equal collaborator. *Indiv. Psychol. News Letter,* 1969, 19, 25-26.

12. O'Connell, W. E. Democracy in human relations. *Desert Call,* 1970, 5(2), 8-9.

13. O'Connell, W., & Hanson, P. The protagonist in human relations training. *Group Psychother. Psychodrama,* 1970, 23, 45-55.

14. Perls, F. I am what I am—no instant joy. *Existent. Psychiat.,* 1969, 7(26-27), 5-7.

15. Ryckoff, I. Encounter: Over-the-counter. *Rev. Existent. Psychol. Psychiat.,* 1969, 9(2-3), 198-207.

16. Tharp, L. Mowrer's integrity therapy: A psychological and a Protestant theological critique. *Insight,* 1967, 5(4), 31-44.

17. Woestendiek, J. Getting in touch. *Texas Sunday Mag.,* June 14, 1970.

A CRITICISM OF LOGOTHERAPY

Who Dares be Critical of the Brave?

"A criticism of Logotherapy" is centered upon the theoretical differences between Alfred Adler and his former colleague, Viktor Frankl, from the point of view of a psychologist whose clinical beliefs have been influenced by both leaders. Such a confrontation cannot be honestly avoided by one with an Adlerian orientation, for Frankl treats Adlerian psychology with paradoxical praise and disdain. He has, at times, credited Adler with pioneering existential psychiatry and discovering the importance of social factors. Yet he regards his own contributions to psychiatry as sufficient to warrant the establishment of a "Third Viennese School of Psychotherapy."

This critical analysis of the views of Viktor Frankl is from the biased stance of one who has faith, through experience, in the basic premises of Adlerian or Individual Psychology. The main portion of the paper is an abridgment of the ideas set forth at the Alfred Adler Centennial Meeting (1970, New York City), later published by the *Journal of Religion and Health* (O'Connell, 1972). The last section touches upon some of my thoughts presented at the 1973 Annual Meeting of the American Society of Adlerian Psychology (O'Connell, W., Chorens, J., Wiggins, G., Hiner, D., 1973).

My earlier evaluation of the works of Viktor Frankl followed one of my courses in Psychology and Religion in which I assigned all of Frankl's books to the class. It was not long before I was asked why I allowed myself to be labeled as an Adlerian since Viktor Frankl communicated in his books in no uncertain terms that his Third Viennese School had "overarched" the second school, that of his unacknowledged mentor, Alfred Adler. In 1970 I believed Frankl completely wrong on this contention, and three years later, after seeing little inclination for creative theoretical and experimental movement in

An extended version of *Frankl Adler & Spirituality Journal of Religion and Health*, 1972, 11, 134-138.

logotherapy, I am more pessimistic of its further contributions to humanistic psychotherapy.

The Overarching Fantasy

There is little doubt that Frankl has, by his personal actions, re-emphasized in our times the necessity of a psychology of courage and spirituality. It is likewise important to emphasize that Frankl's existential analysis can flourish only by misinterpreting the meaning and intent of Adlerian efforts.

Personally, I have little doubt "that Viktor E. Frankl is one of the kindest and bravest men who ever was a pupil of Alfred Adler" (Birnbaum, 1961). Beyond this character assessment there is considerable danger for the Individual (or Adlerian) psychologist that students and clergy will take seriously Frankl's contention that Adlerian psychology is "not nullified by logotherapy but rather overarched by it" (Frankl, 1969). Yet there is the possibility that by restricting his theory to a joyless resignation to a feudal social system, Frankl has introduced a destructive blind spot into his system. Even so, Adlerians had best develop self-esteem and social interest sufficient to give feedback to Frankl, rather than a mere irresponsible elation over being "good enough" to be mentioned by him.

It may be sufficient to generate an enlivening and friendly disputation by stating that Frankl has been unfair to the Adlerian movement by his misinterpretation of: (a) the chief motive of the Adlerian approach as a simple "will to power," (b) social interest as devoid of socio-temporal connotations, (c) spirituality as different from social interest, (d) logotherapy (and humor) as something new and novel in psychotherapy. His system seems further limited by a professional fixation and a fascination with concepts that lack definition and operational identification. For example, "once the existential vacuum has eventuated into noogenic neurosis, it goes without saying that its treatment is reserved to the medical profession" (Frankl, 1969). Time is running out for the Divine-Right (or "goes-without-saying") policy in the 1970's.

A very limited summary of these points follows:

1. *Will to power.* "Adler organized his own idea in terms of an extended conception of *power*. The emphasis on power does not mean an emphasis upon aggression; rather it relates to fulfillment of one's individuality and one's milieu" (Murphy,

1970). How and why Frankl could ever have interpreted Adler's "power" as crass force, apart from "meaning" or the ideal of expanded self-esteem and social interest, is a mystery. Someone with more knowledge of the times and persons should answer this.

2. *Social interest.* "Social interest to the Adlerian is not synonymous with social conformity but connotes a feeling of intimate belonging to the full spectrum of mankind, past, present, and future" (O'Connell, 1967).

It seems that Frankl, quite paradoxically since he seems to be of mystical bent, has taken all the mystery out of *gemeinschaftsgefühl* by an overly literal interpretation. Even worse, he ascribes a "there-and-then" environmental stance to the tenets of Individual Psychology. So in Frankl's thinking, an Adlerian psychotherapist will always be victimized by the patients' subtle ploys. In his mind, Adlerian theory is for the adolescent. The therapist of that persuasion generates excessive guilt for parents and directs patients toward status needs that are self-defeating (Ungersma, 1968). In truth, Adlerians have always seen guilt feelings as ways of dominating others and status needs as reflecting self-fulfilling constrictions in self-esteem and social interest. Frankl, without doubt, experienced the worst behavior of man to man. Yet he benefited and benefited the world through his response to the objectively miserable conditions. It is true that this priceless empathic process is not an automatic, mechanistic one. One cannot demand to survive and become influential. But an abysmal waste of human potentialities does not invalidate the principle of growth through commitment to humanity.

3. *Spirituality.* In spite of the fact that Frankl claims no theological meaning for his "spirituality," clergy are drawn to existential analysis by the term. Frankl's spirituality seems to be Adler's social interest in disguise. ". . . the spiritual is 'with' (Bei-sein) other objects and persons in the world" (Tweedie, 1961). It is a striving for completion, through enhancing social interest, germane to later Adlerian thought. Frankl's spirituality leads, in his thoughts, to self-transcendence and responsibility. But in a more respectable, scientific system of processes and forces (rather than entities), one fulfills one's self, probably only in temporary peak experiences, by maximizing self-esteem (as a person, not a role) and social interest. But we do not

165

leave the self or the milieu no matter how hard we try. Even creativity or spirituality has its limits. Frankl's spirituality is in reality a calling attention to the natural (interpersonal) ground of spirituality. One's view of God reflects the more basic attitudes toward self and others. A hating person can't create a loving God. Frankl's spirituality being one-sided does not show how such pre-Reformation theological concepts of *anologia entis* and good works (toward persons rather than institutions) can raise self-esteem and social interest for one on the crust of this earth (O'Connell, 1973).

4. *Psychotherapy.* Logotherapy offers no advances beyond traditional Adlerian psychotherapy. Its new descriptive vocabulary fails where it is most needed: To focus upon the variables involved in the process of identification. What are the influences of life styles—and their hidden goals—upon each other that lead to change of attitude and behavior? Frankl is not drawn to such questions because he does not view life as a creative process in which man is responsible for his auto-evolution (e.g., Adler, Teilhard de Chardin). Living, to Frankl, is finding the "true" meaning already "out there." Hitler's conscience, for example, is "there," but suppressed. Life seems much simpler in such a system, but where is the person and his development? Logotherapy attempts to have the patient re-enact, to the point of caricature, what he fears most. Then one encourages the patient to focus his energy outward to his social milieu and toward the future. When he states, "It is a peculiarity of man that he can only live by looking toward the future—*sub specie aeternitatis*" (Frankl, 1969), Frankl is giving a definition of *gemeinschaftsgefühl* or social interest, under his rubric of "spirituality" or "noetic."

It may be that the practice of overstating and understating a patient's demands, in an atmosphere of mutual respect and equality, is the hallmark of the outstanding therapist. The same exaggeration is a necessary technique of wit and humor. Frankl should be given credit for his emphasis upon the maturity of humor. But again there is the inherent belief that one simply puts on humor as he does a new pair of gloves. It just isn't that simple: True humor grows from a well-developed self-esteem and social interest (Worthen & O'Connell, 1969). It does not grow until the patient stops searching for and receiving esteem through subtle self-punishment, distancing from others, and harboring the hyperambition of one who lacks courage to make mistakes. Here again Frankl misses the perspective of patient's learning and therapists' modeling and reinforcement.

Over 20 years ago, Birnbaum (1961) showed a difference between Frankl and Adler in their responses to the questions of patients. The former responded to existential-psychological questions with existential-philosophical answers, while Adler remained psychological throughout. For example, to the query, "Why should I love my neighbor?" Adler would, I am told, respond "I cannot answer that question, but I can tell you why you ask it." Frankl, on the other hand, would give philosophical (or psychological) reasons as why, in general, all men should love. One therefore can see Frankl as being the orthodox tutor: he who lectures to one person. In contrast, Adler wanted the person to discover the demands, goals, rationalizations, and frustrations of his unique life style in interaction with others. Compare Frankl's exhortations to patients to behave differently in paradoxical intention (Frankl, 1960) with Adler's indirect treatment method (Adler, 1964). Adler's contribution was to expose the patient to situations that highlighted for him the way he ordinarily avoided contributing to mutual solutions of problems. With Adler, the patient would be given only simple "hackneyed" advice but could infer the enervating effect of his life style by becoming aware of his subtle refusal to follow socially harmonious suggestions. In short, the authentic Individual psychologist would be much more impressed, than would the existential analysts, with the terrible beauty of patients' life style. The Adlerian would admire the patient's ability to learn and relearn in an environment that, rather than reward actions of low social interest, would stimulate learning from immediate actions.

Teaching Courage

Frankl's survival under a regime in which a dearth of extensive social interest was esteemed is a classic epic tale, it is true. Yet the general tenor of his psychiatric thought seems too charismatic, conducive to medical expansionism, and not at all concerned with the human needs and movements which precipitate the growth of communal feelings. Frankl, it seems, has become an heroic figure because he was able to experience, survive, and report clearly on the most glaring dangers of our times: unchecked egotism. His skills have included giving the appearance of building upon Freudian psychiatry, while remaining a crypto-Adlerian; being regarded as religiously oriented when he cannot tell how religious views can benefit self-esteem and social interest; and appearing interested in expanding the lay movements when, in fact, he champions the exclusive right of the medical man if the latter can read "symptomatology" into complaints. In reality Frankl seems to be of Adlerian heritage in his belief in human creativity rather than rigid psychic determinism, his emphasis upon the future rather than the past, and by his wholehearted focus on purposes and goals rather than on the enervating effects on assumed psychic traumata. He went beyond the Adlerian thinking of his day when he so aptly described tragic aspects of existence, not easily recognized in the writings of Adler. Yet Frankl seems to be mired in tragedy and in telling the world about his experiences of almost a generation ago. He has not been able to formulate for others the experiences necessary to actualize the creative and experiential values of life. Joy and play; the values of rebellious and revolutionary thinking for the evolution of the world; the uses of humor other than under the objective stress of the gallows—all of these areas are still foreign to existential analysis.

Frankl, like Freud, seems incapable of incorporating the "discovery" of humor as the epitome of maturity into his psychiatric system. My research and clinical experience with humor suggests that only persons with high self-esteem as-a-person (not merely the feeling of significance stemming from a narrow social role); wide experiences of social interest (finding similarities with others); a love for paradoxes (not certainties); and acceptance of as many realities as people, are skilled in humor. Freud noted 45 years ago that there are two types of humor, self-directed and other-directed. As illustrated by the psychotherapeutic dyad, other-directed humor might be the therapist relating to the patient. He is not hyperdependent or competitive (passively or actively) with the patient and can model the behavior he hopes the patient will emulate. In other words, the therapist can give time-space perspective to the patient's problems. How the patient ever learns this skill neither Frankl nor Freud could tell us. Frankl moves autocratically by suggesting that the patient overreacts to symptoms. Perhaps if the patient is in a power struggle with the therapist, he will then do the opposite and slowly give up his symptoms (e.g.,

"He tells me to faint well, but I'm only worthwhile if I can beat him. Therefore I'll give it all up and not do as he demands."). If the patient is close to his therapist in a positive sense, the latter will teach courage by modeling (example) and reinforcement (social approval), but in no way can lasting humor (as an attitude toward existence) be taught directly, especially by autocratic suggestion. In my work I find that genuine (self-directed) humor is an indirect effect of other attitudes (as Frankl taught us about happiness, sex, and sleep). Appreciation for the tragicomic paradox signals the beginnings of an authentic sense of humor. The incipient humorist realizes that he has been living in a state of contradiction and sees simultaneously both tragic and comic elements of this paradox. The chief tragicomic paradox occurs when one realizes how he has lowered his own self-esteem through self-induced "negative nonsense" and just as unknowingly has demanded unconditional love from others. For this creative act to occur, as a rule, the therapist must model and reinforce it through his own self-directed humor. The therapist's other-directed humor, toward the patient, will go awry unless a positive nonpampering and nonautocratic relationship has been established and maintained.

Frankl's abstract (nonprocess) approach to life as mere discovery rather than continuous growth does not concern itself with relationships. Therefore rather than teach psychiatric discoveries to people, the latter are overawed by the magic of one who claims to talk in facile abstractions about "true" conscience and reality. A lesson in contrasts can be seen in the difference between Frankl and Adler in their movements toward patients with insomnia. Frankl would use paradoxical intention to tell the patient to stay awake. (How wonderful, though, to find a doctor like Frankl who will not prescribe a pill for sleep, then complain about the drug problems of society!) Adler, even though he didn't write about humor, used it more adroitly in suggesting the patient think of helping others as he stayed awake. Eventually the patient was told to merely *think* of helping the therapist in sleepless periods—and later reported immediate sleep. In neither case, I assume, would Frankl or Adler reinforce patients' useless goals: Insomnia for the purpose of attention, to get power or revenge, or to prove total disability. Such maneuvers would indicate humorless therapists making humorless patients. But for all the credit

Frankl gives to humor as a descriptive attitudinal value, he tells nothing about its experiential creative beginnings.

The world still awaits an optimistic school of psychiatry which can teach, through didactic-experiential methods, the elements of encouragement. The importance of stopping, looking, and listening, sharing creative constrictions, giving and asking for basic and advanced feedback, and working toward a sense of humor in human dyads is still neglected in safe and easy search for "objective" sources for psychopathology. Frankl for all his attempts to sound hopeful, got lost in abstract universals and never became committed to teaching of the values and movements of courage (active social interest), *specie aeternitatis.* His bravery was forever ennobling, his courage—in the Adlerian sense—has not yet bloomed.

REFERENCES

1. Adler, A. (1929). *Problems of neurosis.* New York: Harper and Row, 1964.

2. Birnbaum, F. (1947). Frankl's existential psychology from the viewpoint of individual psychology. *Journal of Individual Psychology,* 1961, 17, 162-166.

3. Frankl, V. E. *Man's search for meaning.* New York: Washington Square Press, 1959.

4. Frankl, V. E. Paradoxical intention: A logotherapy technique. *American Journal of Psychotherapy,* 1960, 14, 520-535.

5. Frankl, V. E. *The will to meaning: Foundations and applications of logotherapy.* New York: World Publishing Co., 1969.

6. Murphy, G. Fulfillment of one's individuality and milieu. *Journal of Individual Psychology,* 1970, 26, 14-15.

7. O'Connell, W. E. Individual psychology. In *New Catholic Encyclopedia.* New York: McGraw-Hill, 1967, 472-474.

8. O'Connell, W. E. Frankl, Adler, and spirituality. *Journal of Religion and Health,* 1972, 2, 134-138.

9. O'Connell, W. E. Inductive faith: The confluence of religion and humanistic psychology. *Desert Call,* 1973, 8 (1), 14-16.

10. O'Connell, W. E., Chorens, J., Wiggins, G. and Hiner, D. Natural high therapy: For research and treatment on a Methodone-maintenance program. *Newsletter for Research in Mental Health and Behavioral Science,* 1973, 15, (2) 19-21.

11. Tweedie, D. F. *Logotherapy and the Christian faith.* Grand Rapids, Mich: Baker Books, 1961.

12. Ungersma, A. *The search for meaning: A new approach in psychotherapy.* Philadelphia: Westminister Press, 1968.

13. Worthen, R., and O'Connell, W. E. Social interest and humor. *International Journal of Social Psychiatry,* 1969, 15, 179-188.

THE ADLERIAN-JUNGIAN SOUNDS
OF SILENCE (1974)

Each of us can carry the torch of knowledge but a part of the way, until another takes it from him. Could we but accept this in an impersonal way—could we but grasp the fact that we are not the personal creators of our truths, but only their exponents who thus make articulate the psychic needs of our day—then much of the poison and bitterness might be spared and we should be able to perceive the profound and super-personal continuity of the human mind . . . (Jung, 1933, pps. 46-47).

Stone Walls Good Neighbors Make

Although the Chamber of Commerce is unaware of the honor, Houston is probably the only city in the world to house on one street societies dedicated to the growth of Adlerian and Jungian psychologies. This proximity has not in the least contributed to the growth of *social interest* or *individuation* of their respective memberships. The key to this dilemma can be found in the two preceding concepts which have separated the two schools. Traditionally the Adlerian movement (in spite of misinterpretations of the label "individual psychology") has had its criteria of maturity in interpersonal actions. That is, the individual finds his temporal salvation or mental health in dyadic transactions which precipitate growth of others, hence, the Adlerian emphasis on social interest, communal feelings, *Gemeinschaftsgefühl*, humanistic identification (O'Connell, 1965)—or however we choose to describe this not-yet-understood process of interpersonal transcendence. As the psychiatrist-in-the-street sees it, Jungians select "depth" rather than the "width" of a temporal social context. Their inner space travel knows no rival, going beyond the Freudian personal unconscious into a collective one. This life-long inner journey gave birth to the aphorism that the only way to terminate a Jungian analysis is through the death of the analyst.

172

According to Ellenberger ". . . Contrary to common assumption, neither Adler nor Jung is a 'psychoanalytic deviant', . . . both had their own ideas before meeting Freud, collaborated with him while keeping their independence, and after leaving him, developed systems that were basically different from psychoanalysis and also basically different from each other" (1970, p. 571). One specious differentiation has a Jungian self-actualization as an individuation process which transcends the primitive collective unconscious; Adlerian self-actualization takes place socially, with others, on the crust of this poor earth. Unfortunately both Jung and Adler, leaving Freudian reductionistic materialism, never discussed their common hopeful, optimistic humanism. The mutual impressions they retained were probably of the Adler and Jung of 1910 and do not truly apply to the individual and analytic psychologist of 1974. Although dialogue was absent, contributions were informally exchanged. Adler used the Jungian complex to describe the motives of felt personal inferiority (inferiority complex). Jung appears to have appropriated the concept of compensation from Adler. Jung credited Adlerian psychology as practical and intuitive (*Menschenkenntnis*). "The Adlerian school, with its educational intent, begins at the very point where Freud leaves off, and this helps the patient who has learned to see into himself, to find the way to normal life." (Jung, 1933, p. 45).

In short, Adler and Jung, both of whom broke with Freud before World War I, seem to have been creative in different directions, relating to different types of persons. Jungians turn within, attract people over 35 years of age, for what seems to the individual psychologist to be an interminable length of treatment time. Adlerians move outward, attuned to social factors, hoping to influence change by winning the cooperation of parents and teachers in an effort to teach social responsibility. Historically the Jungian school of analytic psychology can be classified as a prime example of the ethos of romanticism: isolated man bravely struggling to subdue and tame, dark, irrational drives. On the other hand, the Adlerian movement can be regarded as an offspring of the age of enlightenment: The man of reason constructing his utopia through cooperation-as-equals with others (Ellenberger, 1970). The tragic caricature of romanticism is seen in the ravages of the elite, rationalizing the suffering of other persons as being unimportant in the grand-scheme-of-things. Institutionalized religion and psychiatry are certainly no strangers to this dehumanizing, autocratic life style.

Growth as Transcendence

The question in all existential humanistic growth theories, of which the Jungians and Adlerians are the most time-honored examples, is not whether there is transcendence operating, but on what level and with what psychological assistance from significant dyads (traditionally the psychotherapist). Jungians go beyond the here-and-now to inner symbols, guided mainly by the therapist; Adlerians go outward into a multi-dyadic world, getting by "with the help of . . . friends".

Unfortunately Adlerians have not yet been able to sell (or perhaps even spell out in movement) the meaning of social interest for public consumption. Yet it is a term with latent revolutionary meaning. Incorporating the feeling of being at home with humanity, past, present and future, with the courage to be imperfect, moves one away from mere preoccupation with the present social order. Yet one crypto-Adlerian psychiatrist, Viktor Frankl, misconstrued Adlerian social interest and thought of the force entirely in here-and-now terms. To bring back the spirit of Adler he added a "spiritual" dimension which seems to be entirely the naturalistic phase of an authentic, loving religion—or humanistic indentification (O'Connell, 1972).

As a tribute to Jung upon his death, Farau (1961) wrote of Jung's "transcendental courage," the willingness to go beyond positivistic and materialistic causes. Farau himself expressed this courage of transcendence in his interpretations of *gemeinschaftsgefühl* which went beyond the immediate social environment (Farau, 1972). To a growth-motivated Adlerian, Jung's critique of Adlerian psychology, printed 40 years ago, does not ring true: "the type to whom the Adlerian psychology applies, . . . an unsuccessful person with an infantile need for self-assertion" (Jung, 1933, p. 59). In reality the boundary between the Jungian and Adlerian school is becoming more fuzzy and nebulous. The Jungian approach to the understanding of our shared humanity must have a more powerful pull for the modern Adlerian psychologist, especially if he finds himself, as most do, in the camp of the growth motivation rather than deficit motivation thinkers (Ansbacher, 1970).

The Road to Mutuality

Jung, like Frankl, appears to have seriously misconstrued the views of a later Adler on the concept of social interest. Frankl saw social interest too literally in terms of a here-and-now social acceptance, hence his urge to postulate a nontheistic spirituality, really akin to Adler's social interest or communal feeling. Jung regarded social interest too mechanistically in terms of simple social criteria. To him, social interest meant a "social contribution" which most persons apparently blundered into by the age of 35. Jung did not look at self-esteem and social interest as lifelong processes (not end-states) which are cognitively controlled, even to the extent of unwittingly deciding what movement of self and others is behaviorally reinforcing. (O'Connell, 1973b). In the 1970's Adlerian psychology (especially as represented by my *transcendental humanism)* is a growth psychology, not simply a methodology for molding average persons from psychopathological individuals. A premise of this growth psychology is that all people are constricted in the sense that we have learned to obtain power (influence) through self-and-other-directed negative nonsense which narrows the possibility of human creativity and happiness. In this sociohistorical age we realize that we do not know enough about the meaning and movements of love and encouragement to assume, as Jung did in the early years of the century, that one external movement ("social contribution") gained a person the *possession* of social interest. Social interest is not usually an all-or-nothing possession of an individual. Extreme social interest, though, cannot be equated with anything so nebulous and mechanical as a one-time "social contribution."

In spite of the disparity in the meaning of social maturity, the cooperative Adlerian would find a tremendous pull toward the formulations of Jung. His emphasis on experience, future orientation, and social awareness is a case in point. In my own case I find Jung a fellow pilgrim from our mutual background of years laboring with chronic schizophrenics, and viewing that dis-ease as a psychosomatic effect rather than from a purely somatogenic cause. In a book on Teilhard de Chardin,

175

Jung is seen as an ally whose view of science concurred with that of Teilhard (Towers, 1965). Ironically the same emphasis on immanent purposes rather than solely in terms of a reductive analysis into material and efficient causes was characteristic of Adlerian as well as Jungian and Teilhardian thought. Jung realized the value of an instrumental, experiential, as contrasted with an institutional, religion. Some Jungians half-jokingly refer to the "Wise Old Man of Küsnacht" as a reincarnation of Meister Eckhart, the 13th century theologian who knew that regarding oneself as harboring an uncreated part of God would work wonders for self-esteem and social interest (O'Connell, 1973b). The humanity of Jung shines through in his concepts of psychotherapy as a dyadic growth transaction for both healer and patient, and his rejection of transference maneuvers, considered by him as regressive rather than therapeutic.

In summary, the prediction is being made that by the end of the century the hopeful and optimistic existential-humanistic theories will be united, through an open authentic dialogue around their goals and shadow sides. Essentially the union will be that of two poles; an answer to the psychic energy crisis from tapping the resources of the inner universe (Jungian) and the harnessing of the outer catalysts (Adlerian) for humanistic indentififification (or *gemeinschaftsgefühl*). A harbinger of this ideal is the optimistic hyperphysics of Teilhard de Chardin in which the growth of the person (self-esteem) is complementary with the growth of the environment (one's courage stimulates social interest in others): the ultimate is a synergy of an open rather than closed (e.g., Freudian) system of universal growth. The inner road will no longer be viewed as antagonistic to the outer. The focus of what once was Adlerian psychology will then be simply a part of the whole, the concern with environmental sources of growth.

Above all Adler and Jung were the pioneers of a truly humanistic psychology in which a man's life style is, to borrow Jung's expression, more than an appendage of his genitals. Their humanistic faith would prevent them from entering into this era's common collusion with patients: that feelings can change through chemical intervention without a causative change in a person's inner and outer behaviors—not bad models to emulate, humanistically speaking.

REFERENCES

1. Ansbacher, H. Alfred Adler and Humanistic Psychology, *Journal of Humanistic Psychology*, 1971, 11, 53-63.

2. Ellenberger, H. *The Discovery of the Unconscious*. N. Y.: Basic Books, 1970.

3. Farau, A. C. G. Jung: An Adlerian appreciation. *Journal of Individual Psychology*. 1961, 17, 135-141.

4. Farau, A. The Legacy of Alfred Adler. *Pirquet Bulletin of Clinical Medicine*, 1972, 20, 7-12.

5. Jung, C. *Modern Man in Search of a Soul*. N. Y.: Harcourt, Brace, & World, 1933.

6. O'Connell, W. Humanistic identification, a new translation for gemeinschaftsgefühl. *Journal of Individual Psychology*, 1965, 21, 44-47.

7. O'Connell, W. Frankl, Adler, and spirituality. *Journal of Religion and Health*, 1972, 11, 134-138.

8. O'Connell, W. Inductive faith: the confluence of humanistic psychology and religion. *Desert Call*, 1973, 8 (1), 14-16 a.

9. O'Connell, W. Social interest in an operant world: the interaction between operant and existential-humanistic thinking. *Voices: The Art and Science of Psychotherapy*, 1973, 9 (3), 42-49 b.

10. Towers, B. Jung and Teilhard. In Braybrooke, N. (Ed.) *Teilhard de Chardin: Pilgrim of the Future*. London: Darton, Longman, & Todd, 1965, 79-87.

HUMOR:
THE THERAPEUTIC IMPASSE

Of all the accusations from his fellows denied by man, the two most stinging are, "You have no sense of humor!" and "You have no courage!" In the event such direct confrontations are absent, many people kill time by searching for "latent" meanings with this flavor. The "victim's" usual reaction to such candid indictments is BLAME, the time-honored scapegoating which, in my opinion at least, derails movements to define, measure, and PRACTICE love. The prime negative over-generalization is, "I am now and forever worthless." The more symptomatic or secondary derivatives of negative non-sense[2] are, "They (substitute any group of your choice) are not fit to live happily." Then follows the chronic search for evidence, and the refusal to be confused by the phenomenological facts of the others' experience. All manner of radii of action are reactively possible to those authentic sins against mankind, depending upon the strength of the con-clusion to the mistaken certainty (e.g., "therefore they must be avoided . . . ridiculed . . . discouraged . . . destroyed . . . " *ad nauseum*). The *perceived* reward or punishment of the environ-ment to such behavior is crucial, but here we should give man his due. He is not the passive victim the "litany of the pro's" would like us to believe. Even the "hopeless," chronic schizophrenic shows his creativity in so construing events to mean, "I am the greatest martyr . . . magician, etc." and find-ing plausible reward from others for his crazy behavior.

Now enters the gallant psychotherapist, a veritable Babe-in-the-Woods unless he is a stroker and spitter,[8] well-versed in the humor and comedies of life. By "letting-be," reflecting feelings, giving time and attention, he allows himself to be elevated to the status of a friendly significant-other by the patient, the lat-ter now being as one-down and vulnerable as we all are when we need *a particular* other. Now he uses Socratic questioning to highlight the patient's demands which follow from the negative over-generalizations (frights, fights, and flights). He "spits" by pointing out in a paradoxical manner (e.g., a reactive smile) the "victim's" eventually self-defeating responses to cognitive garbage. The patient's "repressed" decisions and distortions of anxiety by his endless private acts of Bad Faith are re-enacted (e.g., by mirroring him in Action Therapy).[6] [7] Feelings of unique but shared selfhood grow with awareness of the "I" of decisions and responsibilities (personal promises, errors, active alternatives).

Now the tutoring in courage-humor in the Freudian sense:[4] Humor—the jesting nonhostile response to inevitable existential stressors—does not grow from the "removing the accent from his own ego and transferring it onto his superego."[3] In the real world it grows from a healthy identification with the therapist's methods of coping with potential stressors. But the therapist's dilemmas must be seen by the patient and his methods of coping, attractive. Identification with the therapist's *person* is not fostered (e.g., the pathological caricature of sameness of dress, manner, and appearance). The rewarded modeling is of the therapist's evaluation of anxiety as a self-inflicted narrowness of outlook, and not a reason for behavior. ("When I feel tension I decide to . . . " instead of, "anxiety and depression force me to . . . ")

Now the therapist can laugh at the patients' mistakes. The therapist does not need the patients' subtle adoration, does not identify with them, therefore can see them in the perspective of time, space, and the hidden, undeveloped consciousness of choice. Have you ever laughed at a patient's intense, incongruous expenditure of energy, his avoidances of failure while he punishes himself with negative over-generalizations which maintain his failure-identity? Why haven't you? You can't, because you don't want to inform him he's a failure? But he does that and must be made aware of it; you still accept the *person* empathically. You see him as a helpless victim of dark inner forces? You've been reading science fiction alone in your office too much. You see your mistakes in him and lack the courage to admit imperfections? Now that's more like it! It may be that when the therapist laughs at the patients' over-and-under-reactions to life tasks, he is testing the patients' extent of outsight or humanistic identification.[5] In other words, what is the condition of the patient's current self-esteem and extent of identification? Does the patient still demand that the therapist treat him with unconditional love (pampering) or can he start to see the humanity of the other? At the same time as the demand-state of the patient is being diagnosed, valuable practice in relating to the "villains" of the real world is taking place. What do you do when someone laughs at you? Can you change him? . . . How? . . . Why bother? . . .

All of this atypical behavior on the therapist's part is based upon the assumption that the patient's disease stems from a lack of humanistic identification .* In other words, self-esteem is low and the extent of authentic non-demanding but concerned relationships nil. Stroking, the "letting-be" and nonverbal praise, solidifies the face-to-face relationship, as a fulcrum for later maneuvers. Spitting, interrupting, and not rewarding compulsive, crude one-upmanship and the progressively defeating tactics of the patient, is for the purpose of showing even the passive person how actively he works against increasing his esteem. After this, the patient cuts the cord, with laughter of his own. Hopefully, he ventures into the real world to esteem himself and all others on a cooperatively high level, "hating mistakes, but loving the sinner."

The true sense of humor flourishes in those who are, in the Teilhardian sense, "faithful to the earth,"[9] and who grow by not *demanding* growth, whose goal is a silent hopeful "building the earth." Humor is the *indirect* result of humanistic identification: a hopeful, humanistic relatedness to life, anchored to a sense of purposeful historicity. This· precious perspective is

---

*In this system, identification with another takes place when "one" under tension of unfulfilled psychological needs for positive worth and belonging finds the "other" whose behavior reduces these needs. While we all need others, the state of that need varies from the one with a high degree of worth and great extent of empathy to the opposite, the regressed psychotic. In addition to the self-esteem and extent of empathy, the demand-state of the need-reducer is an important variable, but is not discussed here. The denial of psychological needs also works against identification, for one who DEMANDS the need-satisfaction does not experience the importance of the other. The mature one (humanistic identification) needs no particular one, just "everyman" to relate to through *giving.* His counterpart, the "sick" one, interacts to only a select few by *demanding;* hence he has almost no degrees of freedom to relate to his fellows and become humanized.

echoed in the timeless precepts of St. Augustine to regard one's behavior to be of the greatest importance yet of no worth. Again it's heard in his socially hedonistic goal[2] to love each person as though you had love for him alone, and to love all as though all were one. What a wonderful operational defintion of *gemeinschaftsgefühl!*[5]

Our Dark Ages of Quietment (i.e., treatment equals silencing) has no use for such non-Aristotelian logic—it "makes" one "anxious." So for a loving taste of the courage-humor fruit, our youth head for the easy but eventually crippling, craving for drugs. Others look for "the Eastern guru"—and identify with the bearded garb or the passivity of behavior, rather than courage-humor. At home we have this quotation from Dick Gregory: "Humor can no more find the solution to race problems than it can cure cancer."[1] In truth there is no such "thing" as humor. It cannot be purchased, legislated, or taken away. It is a rare product of the effort to see with the eyes and hear with the ears of the other, across time and space, using "positive sense," not negative nonsense.

Awareness of the interpersonal potentiality for creating an active, nondemanding, insightful-outsightful person is not yet upon us, so neither is humor. The unmet need is more frightening than the hydrogen bomb. Isn't it?

REFERENCES

1. Davis, Patricia. Humor: Can it Keep the Ghetto Cool? *Houston Post Spotlight,* April 4, 1968, 31.

2. Ellis, A. *Reason and Emotion in Psychotherapy,* N. Y.: Lyle Stuart, 1962.

3. Freud, S. Humor, *International Journal of Psychoanalysis, 1928, 1* 1-6.

4. O'Connell, W. The Adaptive Functions of Wit and Humor. *Journal of Abnormal and Social Psychology,* 1960, 61, 263-270.

5. O'Connell, W. Humanistic Identification, A New Translation for Gemeinschaftsgefühl. *Journal of Individual Psychology,* 1965, 21, 44-47.

6. O'Connell, W. Psychotherapy for Everyman: A Look at Action Therapy. *Journal of Existentialism,* 1966, 7, #25, 85-91.

7. O'Connell, W. Psychodrama: Involving the Audience. *Rational Living,* 1967, 2, #1, 22-25.

8. O'Connell, W. Spitting and Stroking. *The Individual Psychologist,* 1967, 5, #1, 29-31.

9. Teilhard de Chardin, D. *The Future of Man.* N. Y.: Harper and Row, 1964.

THE HUMOROUS ATTITUDE: RESEARCH AND CLINICAL BEGINNINGS (1970)

In truth there is no such "thing" as humor. It cannot be purchased, legislated or taken away. It is a rare product of the effort to see with the eyes and hear with the ears of the other, across time and space, using "positive sense," not negative nonsense (O'Connell, 1969e, p. 27).

. . . when the patient has decided to become schizophrenic or melancholic, a great tension has to work and create an insanity as an artistic creation (Adler, 1964b, p. 234).

Introduction

The sense of humor is universally recognized as a priceless asset. People will fight and die to deny the truth that they really have no sense of humor. Analytically and pathologically-oriented disciples of psychology and psychiatry pay lip service only to humor, in an abstract way, but fail to give time and effort to the study of its functions and growth.

The purpose of this paper is to look at the humorist as he was briefly but emphatically described by Freud (1938, 1950). For unexplained reasons the significance of these works for a psychology of maturity has been lost. In brief, we are left with the outline of Freud's epitome of maturity: a man who is about to be executed who shows no hatred or self-pity and leaves life with a jest. Why did he do this? Does such action have meaning for our lives? And what is a jest anyway? In contrast to this humorist, Freud regarded the wit as a person more like you and me. That is, someone who was angry but lacked the courage to verbalize this emotion directly and turned to subtle modes of communication for a safer sneak attack. Although the motives of the wit and humorist differed drastically, the same techniques of playing-with-words were shared in common.

Defining the concept in interpersonal terms is difficult enough; placing the techniques of humor within psychotherapeutic maneuvering is nearly impossible. Freud eulogized the appreciation and creation of humor. He described the movements of the humorist who regards the self and others, as a loving parent smiles at the naive efforts of the child. Freud focused upon the extreme case of gallows humor, then quickly dropped the subject. He may have left the field for two reasons. First, the humorist denied "reality," and sublimation of the drives to reality was the healthy motive in Freud's system. Then the humorist's personality structure was blessed with a benign superego, another paradox in a theory of supposedly prohibitive superegos and frustrating cultures (O'Connell, 1969e).

Freud's inability to fit the puzzling yet captivating humorist into his closed system probably partly accounts for the aversion to humor in personality theory. The innovative researchers on the double bind concept have shown interest in "humor" in communications (Bateson, Jackson, Haley, Weakland, 1956). Unfortunately, this group of communication analysts harbors traditional blindness to wit and humor differences. In their studies of paradoxical messages they have really centered upon the techniques of wit under the guise of humor and have overlooked the motivational facets of both wit and humor. In any event, the topic of humor as defined by Freud is still unexplored territory. Yet, it may be that 100 years from today the sense of humor—or the humorous attitude—will be the most important subject in the classroom and the one sign of psychotherapeutic success.

What follows is a summary of this author's research efforts, the only concerted attempt to make relevant Freud's seminal ideas on humor. The following section is concerned with the movements, both phenomenological and behavioral, that characterize the humorist in the lengthy periods when his humor is latent. The last section pertains to techniques of psychotherapists who do "crazy" (or atypical) things conducive to the development of the humorous attitude with patients who cannot smile and contribute at the same time.

Humor Research

In Freud's theory, humor (his conception of psychological maturity) was denoted more by specific behavior rather than abstract terms. That is, the chief example was the person who under unavoidable objective stressors did not display emotional decompensation and hostile regression but faced those stressors with nonhostile jests. Resignation was used by Freud to describe the behavior of one who faced the same type of stressors but with a calm fatalism (Freud, 1950). Such behavior was regarded as nonpathological, yet was not remotely as mature as humor. Throughout his years of practice, Freud, and psychiatric theorists in general, have been undecided about the pathology of wit. In his early work Freud saw wit as part of the neuroses, while later he regarded it as a release mechanism of the healthy (Freud, 1947). In general, wit has been characterized as a subtle derivative of hostile and sexual repressions. Impulses outflank the censor when the latter is caught flat-footed by the hidden multiple meanings of wit mechanisms. Nonsense wit, like humor, was not connected with any repressed drive, but simply a use of verbal techniques for infantile, aimless play. Freud's contention that the appreciation as well as the production of wit and humor mirrored similar psychological states and made initial psychological testing and research more feasible, allowing for the development of paper-pencil tests. The prototype of psychometric humor appreciation is the preference for nonhostile jesting in anecdotes describing inescapable stress situations, instead of selecting hostile or resigned responses.

In the first research study of psychoanalytic humor, humor appreciation was discovered to be a rather stable personality trait associated with maturity as defined by a self-report test of self-ideal discrepancies (O'Connell, 1960). Humor did not appear to be affected by situational stressors and there were no sex differences except when hostile themes appeared in the humorist's retorts (O'Connell, 1962). In all studies, humor appreciation has differed from resignation and hostile wit appreciation, and there seems to be more types of humor than the gallows example specifically mentioned by Freud (O'Connell, 1964, 1964b). Community leaders are the highest in humor appreciation, while hospitalized schizophrenics are quite low (Worthen & O'Connell, 1969). Humor does not correlate with pathology scales or even maturity scales of traditional psychological tests (O'Connell, 1969b). In general, low-humor response is related to repressive life styles (O'Connell & Cowgill, 1970; O'Connell & Peterson, 1964). Appreciation for humor, especially for gallows or death variety, is negatively associated with anxiety about death and especially the fear of one's own physical dissolution (O'Connell, 1968b; O'Connell & Covert, 1967). The liking of humor does not seem inherently related to the impairment of abstract cognitive abilities (O'Connell, 1968a) but rather with the growth of a nonblaming creative orientation to life.

The creation of humor is a rarer ability than its mere appreciation (O'Connell, 1969a). It varies directly with the production of hostile wit and is not significantly correlated with the traditional nonreactive and impunitive orientation to frustration. The creator of humor appears quite different from the one who simply likes the reaction, although both types appear to be creative and productive persons. The producer of humor is probably a more socially creative type of individual than the more inactive variety of humorist (O'Connell, 1969c). Humor creation is seen more vividly in the authentic and prominent group leader (O'Connell, Rothaus, Hanson, & Moyer, 1969). This kind of a person differs drastically in his behavior from the hostile wit and resignation appreciator and the producer of sarcastic wit. The latter, while active, is not the popular productive leader, as is the humorist. He is too hostile, striving for individual attention, rather than group social goals.

Resignation and hostile wit appreciation have been strongly associated with psychopathological states. If stressors are added in terms of insult in the environment or death themes in the jest, the appreciation by the emotionally disturbed lowers strikingly (O'Connell, 1960, 1968b). Length of hospitalization seems to have an affect upon wit appreciation, nonsense wit becoming more preferable to patients than hostile wit (O'Connell, 1968a). Hostile wit seems to have more cultural support for males than females, the latter resorting more to the nonsense variety (O'Connell, 1960, 1964a). This sexual difference is not innate, for if males become the object of hostile wit, the traditional preference for hostile wit disappears. (O'Connell, 1969b). This wit reaction is affected by the variables of personality, sex, and stressors to a much greater degree than is humor (which seems to vary principally with a type of maturity) and has less relevance for prognosis and change research.

The Existential Humorist

The term "existential paradoxes" is introduced to connote the multiple realities of an authentic existence. Twentieth century Western Man is generally not aware that the realities of Mr. X may be different from those of Mr. Y because each has a different life style based upon differing premises about the self and others. On the other hand, Mr. X's own existence has been so thoroughly and uniformly fragmented that he is unaware that the world might move smoother and faster without rigid dualities of self-other, superior-inferior, sick-well, patient-doctor, divine-human, soul-body, psyche-soma, spiritual-material, responsible-irresponsible, etc., which are now synonymous with his very existence. As Hardin (1961) so aptly noted the purely physical scientist, and people who unwittingly emulate his faith, believe in one reality only, the Class I truth ("those truths that are unaltered by the saying of them"). Such an ethos of one reality (perhaps an underlying "organic" one) characterizes the medical model as it is uncritically used in the market place. And we psychotherapists are historical accidents, still unhappily using the terminology and trappings of an objective and disinterested medical model while awaiting a more secure style for relating.

It is my contention that the humorist is the rarest of all humans because he is not dependent upon such inflexible views of reality foisted on us from birth. Growing out of this kind of a world, the profession of psychotherapy also produces persons like me and you who are agitated by nondualistic thinking and feeling as if there are as many realities as there are people. Formal logic and natural science are relatively free from the influence of time and person. Institutional and descriptive psychiatry are very often heirs to natural science logic. Holders of such "reality" see a simplified world of diagnosis and prognosis, doctor and patient: one forever treating the other in rigid complementary style. There are no paradoxes since oneself is well anchored and dualistically separated from otherselves. Therefore, humorous reactions are exceedingly rare when there is no spark to leap between the paradoxical poles.

In contrast to the victim of the double bind who is trapped and suffering, the humorist is at home in multiple and nondualistic realities. The individual in the double bind is hyperdependent. He is confused by the conflicting incongruous messages of verbalizations and their interminable nonverbal qualifiers. Unlike the victim of the double bind, the humorist—in the ideal and well developed state—feels himself to be of unique personal worth. His *self-esteem* is high and his *social interest* extensive. The model humorist can readily identify with others, so he does not place inordinate and hidden demands on them. He is St. Augustine's paradox personified: one who lives as if what he does is extremely important for the world, but if he died that moment it would not matter (O'Connell, 1969e). And lastly, the humorist moves well in the world of existential paradoxes. He can deftly move into a fluid unstructured world which nurtures innumerable simultaneous realities. He may even move outside of space and time and perceive his own paradoxical insignificance and significance, yet quickly return to his own task of aiding in the development of humanity. It is interesting to note that the best example of gallows humor, Thomas More (O'Connell, 1966), didn't fully arrive at his humorous orientation until he became skilled at switching frames of references (or paradoxes). As he trained himself to transcend time and space—without ever leaving the crust of this poor world—he became a humorist. Note that he did not become impaled on dualistic extremes (mystical-mundane) but could move rapidly through perspectives of time and person. (Parenthetically, More's ability to experience perspectives of others might have been enhanced by his use of "psychodrama," a 16th century precursor of J. L. Moreno.) More's remarks to his prosecutors were almost verbatim the words Freud attributed to the humorist's superego, almost 400 years later. "Look here! This is all that this seemingly dangerous world amounts to. Child's play—the very thing to jest about (Freud, 1950, p. 220)."

All that has now been stated about the humorist conforms to Freud's ideal, the gallows humorist. But psychologists cannot study people who have been executed. If the emphasis were less on extremely severe existential stressors and more on overcoming life style failures as hallmarks of humor, the humorist would be less rare and more alive. The change in criteria for humor from facing death to developing more open feedback would surely make the humorist more available for study. Stressors can be operating in bed as well as on the gallows.

Tutoring in Humor: The Crazy Therapist

The humorist could not maintain his flexibility in moving across many frames of references without adequate self-esteem and social interest. He avoids the pitfalls of Hardin's Class II and III truths. Class II truths, which become so by being said include such inner actions as "Negative Nonsense" (Ellis, 1962). One can victimize oneself by making negative overgeneralizations about himself and others, unwittingly keeping self-esteem low. Class III truths, those rendered false by being stated (e.g., "I am humble and loving") can be avoided by receiving functional esteem through feedback only. We laugh at—or hospitalize—the braggart but do not believe this Class III violator. One with extensive social interest has trained himself to empathize with others and not disturb with arbitrary

188

narcissistic demands. The humorist is involved in giving and receiving feedback (O'Connell, 1970), but is an outsider in his cognitive structuring of reality, since he eschews rigid dualisms and can move rapidly between them. Also fracturing the popular view of reality is the humorist's knowledge that reality differs from person to person, beyond the accepted conventions of time, place, and person. This state of flexibility in reality testing follows from acceptance of the existential paradox. Mild tensions are engendered in switching frames of references which, with the humorist or wise psychotherapist, are dissipated in pleasurable smiles or easy laughter.

Any method which increases the patient's self-esteem, social interest, and enjoyment of existential paradoxes is teaching him at least the rudiments of the humorous attitude. Directive or action techniques readily highlight such a patient's verbal desire to be cured along side his incessant devaluation of self and others. (Is he a victim or a perpetrator?) Unusual, "crazy" ploys by therapists also loosen the patient's desperate hold on a one-reality, dualistic world. A fourth benefit of the jesting, yet serious approach, is that in the absence of a rigidly autocratic doctor-patient relationship, the therapist is sometimes the "patient." He can be open and model (serious?) humor when he is faced with (or self-creates?) his stressful world. (Even the most skilled therapist has some demands or expectations which are frustrated.)

Crazy, productive therapists that I have observed have all used the most time-honored technique of them all: Socratic irony. With this tactic the therapist does not trap himself by assuming all the answers, *à la* the omnipotent one. He rather makes a pretense of ignorance and of willingness to learn from another in order to make the other's false conceptions clear by adroit questioning. (Is he wise man, fool, or both simultaneously?)

There are psychotherapists who report techniques which lend themselves to teaching the humorous attitude toward life's tasks. All of these authors noted that their techniques should take place in a humorous atmosphere or at least in situations where the patient is treated with kindness and respect. To anyone who is at least temporarily outside the rigidly compartmentalized split worlds, the therapists' techniques seem humorous. I laughed over Adler's interaction with patients although they contained no reference to humor. Adler himself referred indirectly to existential paradoxes when he said everything could also be something else. In a sense the patient could act as a victim of a mysterious disease, but he also could behave as if he were actually perpetuating his own dis-ease by unwittingly destroying his own self-esteem and social interest in the service of a meager life style. Patients often behave like doctors "are supposed to" and doctors like patients. Therapy is like serious treatment and yet often similar to play. The therapist hopes to help the patient reduce his anxiety level, but he also stimulates tension by his tutoring efforts. Everything-can-be-something-else. Sudden switches in basic perceptions precipitate tension—which laughter reduces. For those who believe they have discovered reality rather than merely constructed a theory to describe it, alternative explanations are forbidden and blocked from consciousness. "Crazy" therapists, whose concepts fluctuate in meaning, are misunderstood by "one-reality" folk. Their movements are therefore considered anything but funny.

Adler's approach, like that of any mature therapist, was not to quash the patient by overwhelming the symptom (along with the patient) with electricity, chemicals, cutting, or commands. Adler manipulated the patient into a therapeutic trap. Symptoms were encouraged but switched into socially useful movements. Patient was faced with the paradox of keeping a symptom which had now lost its useless value—or giving it up entirely.

Humorous devices teach humor through over—and under-reactions. They show the patient how he actively reduces self-esteem and social interest, while stimulating social development. The patient is also tutored in experiencing "wonderland": that things are not always—despite his most earnest wish—what he feels them to be. Imagine the wily Adler and tricky patient, both trying to teach the other something; Adler toward a healthy flexibility and the patient toward a deterministic disease analogy.

To return to the indirect method of treatment: I recommend it especially in melancholia. After establishing a sympathetic relation I give suggestions for a change of conduct in two stages. In the first stage my suggestion is "Only do what is agreeable to you." The patient usually answers, "Nothing is agreeable." "Then at least," I respond, "do not exert yourself to do what is disagreeable." The patient, who has usually been exhorted to do various uncongenial things to remedy his condition, finds a rather flattering novelty in my advice, and may improve in behavior. Later I insinuate the second rule of conduct, saying that "it is much more difficult and I do not know if you can follow it." After saying this I am silent, and look doubtfully at the patient. In this way I excite his curiosity and ensure his attention, and then proceed, "If you could follow this second rule you would be cured in fourteen days. It is—to consider from time to time how you can give another person pleasure. It would very soon enable you to sleep and would chase away all your sad thoughts. You feel yourself to be useful and worth while."

I receive various replies to my suggestion, but every patient thinks it is too difficult to act upon. If the answer is, "How can I give pleasure to others when I have none myself?" I relieve the prospect by saying, "Then you will need four weeks." The more transparent response, "Who gives *me* pleasure?" I encounter with what is probably the strongest move in the game, by saying, "Perhaps you had better train yourself a little thus: do not actually *do* anything to please anyone else, but just think out how you *could* do it."

Melancholy subjects who reply, "Oh, that is quite easy; it is what I have always done," are to be suspected of dispensing favours in order to get the upper hand of others. To them I say, "Do you think the people you favoured were really pleased by it?" I sometimes give in, admitting that it is too difficult at present because the patient needs practice and training, by which compromise I carry a milder measure in terms:—"Remember all the ideas you have in the night, and give me pleasure by telling them to *me* the next day."

The next day such a patient quite probably replies, "I slept all night," when asked for his midnight reflections, even though he had not previously slept for many days! (Adler, 1964a, Pp. 25-27)

In another case we see the same overriding of the healthy-sick dualism, with Adler again paradoxically wedding a symptom of "sickness" to healthful social interest.

His activity during the night can be used in the treatment of the sufferer from sleeplessness. When such a person complains about his sleeplessness, he usually maintains that he is lost because without sleep he cannot go on any longer. If you tell him that it does not matter, that you yourself do not sleep more, and that others you know do not sleep much more either, the patient will become angry. But if you are kind and do not ridicule him, you can make an impression on him, Tell him, "You can use the time in which you cannot sleep to help in our treatment. You can collect all the thoughts you have during this time and remember them and tell me tomorrow, and then we can make use of your sleeplessness."

It will be a new experience for him to use his sleeplessness in a constructive way. Sometimes he cannot maintain his sleeplessness if it can be used for a good cause. He can remain sleepless only if he regards it as a disturbance. In either case, if he remembers his thoughts or if he now falls asleep, he may be able to recognize the purpose of sleep or sleeplessness. He may even understand that his sleeplessness has not played the role which he believed it did. (Adler, 1964b, p. 237).

As in all these examples reported, the patient is approved for achieving the symptom ("as if" he created it) and it is put to use to benefit others (a healthy sign of sickness). These are the sudden ploys of the flexible therapist who does not believe in his public image. He doesn't limit himself to nondirective moves and "How does that make you feel?" followed by "Why do you feel that way?"

A good example of audience reactions to paradoxical behaviors is the case of Harold Greenwald (1968). In a workshop presentation filmed for professional distribution, Greenwald interviewed two females, one who said she wanted to give up crying while the second desired to be able to express anger at the weak, as exemplified by her co-patient. By convincing the weeper that she was always in control by her "involuntary" symptoms and demonstrating such in the here-and-now interactions, both girls learned that the helpless patient may paradoxically be simultaneously strong. With the girl who wanted to develop anger, Greenwald demonstrated that this impossiblity was really quite easy, for she erupted at the therapist who told her never to anger. Greenwald controlled the level of laughter by his frequent over—and understatements, and by committing the Type III self-reflexive error, the "truth" of which is negated by the statement itself (e.g., "I am a wonderful therapist.").[1] The audience generally reacted to the uncovering of alternative (paradoxical) perceptions of reality with laughter, but there was always the vocal minority which believed Greenwald didn't understand and love these patients. Such is the price for making the familiar appear unorthodox.

Viktor Frankl (1959) regards the sense of humor as part of man's capacity for self-detachment. In his logotherapy a patient is told to engage in negative practice and intensify his symptom (e.g., "Faint a number of times right now."). Frankl uses the overstatement (or hyperbole), which makes the symptom into a caricature. To Frankl, logotherapy, practiced with rapport and humor, precipitates self-detachment. The latter may follow though from other explanations. When the patient is in a power struggle with the therapist, he may practice negative obedience. That is, if the therapist commands the symptom, the patient does otherwise. On the other hand, if the patient identifies with the therapist he may sense how he inadvertently brings about his symptoms by getting himself into a frenzy of self-devaluations. At the times when I used the technique of logotherapy I found that patients cannot produce their symptoms unless they are in a state of tension from trying to hide their problems in aiming for perfection. The symptoms result from unsuccessful efforts to overcompensate for the self-created inferiorities produced by "skills" in negative nonsense. A crazy paradox!

Like Adler, Don Jackson (1956) was not content with merely caricaturizing the symptom, but wanted to control its expression toward the useful side of life. He encouraged paranoids to become even more watchful and acted as their ally in this unusual behavior. Yet, he was also teaching the patient to see foibles, pathos, stupidities, by searching for other-centered realities.

Shulman (1962) used a Midas-technique also following the techniques of wit and humor. His groups learned to interpret hidden goals through the use of early recollections. Like all the above methods, the Midas-technique was used against a paradoxical background of both play and treatment. For uncooperative members the group satiated the culprits (or sick ones) with excessive attention, power, or special service. Again patients progressed by giving up symptoms they previously felt powerless toward. The interpretations were accepted when they were delivered in exaggerated forms.

The tools of the humorist are useful in Action Therapy. Directors' worst moments are always when they think with one-reality, Class I logic, and demand "well" behavior from "sick" persons. Valuable Action Therapy sessions have produced laughter and understanding of a multi-reality world in which people make themselves sick "crazily" in hopes of feeling better about themselves. All psychodramatic actions highlight the dictum that reality is not whatever you demand it to be. Doctor-patient, play-therapy, superior-inferior, there and then-here and now, strength-weakness, and passive-active switch rapidly just as they do when one looks for paradoxes. In Action Therapy doctors play patients and show how "passive" patients actively practice self-pathology. Sickness becomes creative skill ("patients must work to behave crazily"). All excuses to avoid commitment to treatment are welcomed: "I'm too nervous": "Good we need nervousness for the next scene. Try to do a good job of it." "I've solved all my problems": "Excellent, you can contribute by showing us how you did this." "It's not real": "No, just enjoy yourself learning how to play." "I'm no actor": "Yes, you are. You're a bad one."

Jay Haley has written at least four papers which are classic examples of describing psychotherapy in a witty and humorous manner. In psychotherapy itself he redefines the symptom into cooperation and makes the continuation of symptoms so difficult and painful that the patient will choose health. In one he writes of a fictitious priest who is having a breakdown under the stress of showering without really knowing whether he sinfully wills or combats pleasure. His therapist, a psychologist who cannot control the movements of one eye (and one wife) "cures" the priest by making excessive showering necessary for treatment, but unpleasant while questioning the priest's unquestioning acceptance of the motives of others (Haley, 1967).

In truth, the humorous psychotherapist must be a play or even ploy doctor ("he who teaches"). All others are too easily victimized and can't really take a joke without a diagnosis.

Summary

This paper explores the author's thinking, through research and clinical findings, of Freud's forgotten operational definition of maturity, the creator and/or appreciator of gallows humor. Research on paper and pencil tests of humor and wit have confirmed most of Freud's hypotheses on the maturity of the humorous attitude. These laboratory findings give no indication of ways of teaching humor (hence maturity?) in psychotherapy. It is suggested that the humorist learns to live with existential paradoxes. That is, he does not rigidly compartmentalize the world dualistically (self-other, religious-secular, sick-well, superior-inferior, doctor-patient, etc.), by trying to live in one realm and ignore the other. He can rapidly restructure his world so both extremes seem possible at times. The humorist sees as many realities as people. This remarkable tolerance, in the extreme case, is possible from humorist's high self-esteem and extensive social interest. He does not put impossible demands upon himself or others and does not act destructively to enhance his self-esteem at the expense of an understanding social interest. Examples of techniques of contemporary psychotherapists conducive to humor development are given.

REFERENCES

1. Adler, A. (1929) *Problems of neurosis.* New York: Harper, 1964. (a)

2. Adler, A. *Superiority and social interest.* Evanston: Northwestern University Press, 1964. (b)

3. Bateson, G., Jackson, D., Haley, J., & Weakland, J. Toward a theory of schizophrenia. *Behavioral Science,* 1956, 1, 251-264.

4. Ellis, A. *Reason and emotion in psychotherapy.* New York: Lyle Stuart, 1962.

5. Frankl, V. *The doctor and the soul.* New York: Knopf, 1955.

6. Freud, S. (1905) Wit and its relationship to the unconscious. In A. Brill (Ed.) *Basic writings of Sigmund Freud.* New York: Modern Library, 1938, Pp. 633-803.

7. Freud, S. (1921) Group psychology. In J. Rickman, & C. Brenner. *A general selection from the works of Sigmund Freud.* New York: Doubleday, 1947, Pp. 169-209.

8. Freud, S. (1928) Humor. In *Collected papers.* London: Hogarth, 1950, Vol. V, 215-221.

9. Greenwald, H. Adult play therapy. Division 29, Contemporary Masters of Psychotherapy Series, American Psychological Association Meetings, San Francisco, September 1968.

10. Haley, J. An ordeal for pleasure. *Voices: The Art and Science of Psychotherapy,* 1967, 3(3), 109-118.

11. Hardin, G. Three classes of truth: Their implications for the behavioral sciences. *ETC: A Review of General Semantics*, 1961, 18(1), 1-20.

12. Jackson, D. A suggestion for the technical handling of paranoid patients. *Psychiatry*, 1963, 26, 306-307.

13. Oliver, W., & Landfield, A. Reflexivity: An unfaced issue of psychology. *Journal of Individual Psychology*, 1962, 18, 114-124.

14. O'Connell, W. The adaptive functions of wit and humor. *Journal of Abnormal and Social Psychology*, 1960, 61, 263-270.

15. O'Connell, W. An item analysis of the wit and humor appreciation test. *Journal of Social Psychology*, 1962, 56, 271-276.

16. O'Connell, W. Resignation, humor, and wit. *Psychoanalytic Review*, 1964, 51, 49-56.(a)

17. O'Connell, W. Multidimensional investigation of Freudian humor. *Psychiatric Quarterly*, 1964, 38, 1-12. (b)

18. O'Connell, W. Humor of the gallows. *Omega*, 1966, 1, 32-33.

19. O'Connell, W. Organic and schizophrenic differences in wit and humor appreciation. *Diseases of the Nervous System*, 1968, 29, 276-281. (a)

20. O'Connell, W. Humor and death. *Psychological Reports*, 1968, 22, 391-402. (b)

21 O'Connell, W. Creativity in humor. *Journal of Social Psychology*, 1969, 78, 237-241. (a)

22. O'Connell, W. Maturity, sex, and wit-humor appreciation. *Newsletter for Research in Psychology*, 1969, 11, 14-15. (b)

23. O'Connell, W. Social aspects of wit and humor. *Journal of Social Psychology*, 1969, 79, 183-187. (c)

24. O'Connell, W. Teleodrama. *Individual Psychologist*, 1969, 6(2), 42-45. (d)

25. O'Connell, W. Humor: The therapeutic impasse. *Voices: The Art and Science of Psychotherapy*, 1969, 5(2), 25-27. (e)

26. O'Connell, W. Democracy in human relations. *Desert Call*, 1970, 5(2), 8-9.

27. O'Connell, W., & Peterson, Penny. Humor and repression. *Journal of Existential Psychiatry*, 1964, 4, 309-316.

28. O'Connell, W., & Covert, C. Death attitudes and humor appreciation among medical students. *Existential Psychiatry*, 1967, 6, 433-442.

29. O'Connell, W., Rothaus, P., Hanson, P., & Moyer, R. Jest appreciation and interaction in leaderless groups. *International Journal of Group Psychotherapy*, 1969, 19, 454-462.

30. O'Connell, W., & Cowgill, Sallie. Wit, humor, and defensiveness. *Newsletter for Research in Psychology*, 1970, 12, 32-33.

31. Shulman, B. The use of dramatic confrontation in group psychotherapy. *Psychiatric Quarterly Supplement*. 1962, Part 1, 1-7.

32. Worthen, R., & O'Connell, W. Social interest and humor. *International Journal of Social Psychiatry*, 1969, 15, 179-188.

Footnote
[1]Such truths can only be inferred validly by feedback from others. One had better believe he is a worthwhile person "on faith alone," but proof of interpersonal skill ("a great therapist") can come only from others commenting on behaviors. In any case, no one can force anyone to accept either his own person or attributes.

THE HUMORIST, AN IDEAL FOR HUMANISTIC PSYCHOLOGY (1969)

"Anyone who like Dostoevsky has tried to ponder upon the *significance of laughter,* upon the possibility of learning to recognize a man better from his laughter than from his life-attitude, anyone who went so far that he came upon the idea of *the accidental family,* where every member lives for himself, isolated from the other, and implanting in their children the tendency for still greater isolation, greater self-love, that man has seen more than can be expected or demanded from any psychologist" (Adler, 1959).

A short quotation from a newspaper column is part of my dreams. It reported, in effect, that we will be able to recognize the psychologist of the future immediately because he will be the happiest person in sight, a living expert on how to be socially creative (MacLean, 1969). This sounds very wonderful, yet if we "trust only movement" (Adler, 1956) we must admit that the psychologist, psychiatrist, and social worker of the present do not fit this prototype. What is more, they do not, as yet, grasp the importance of laughter and humor, and do not comprehend the universality and pathology of the "accidental family," as did Adler.

We are more likely to be preoccupied with endogenous and deterministic theoretical creations and busy ourselves with exact measurement of humanly insignificant matters. We are at once the by-products and creators of a satiating mechanistic sameness. But a healthier generation will reject and not emulate this ethos. Barring catastrophic power struggles, in some century we must enter the "Age of Cooperation" in which man learns where his individuality and responsibility begin and end. The fulminating evolution in communication now makes evil more visible. There will come a day when the rapid dissemination of world events will remove the defense that we are not aware of inhumane acts. Then another defense mechanism will be faced: the incomplete "span of humanity" which allows us to regard others as evil, infrahuman, and motivated only by pain-avoidance (Coser, 1969). The purpose of this paper is to hasten the day when the loving, breathing, decision-making person will be considered more worthy of scientific puzzlement.

Therefore two concepts which generate enthusiasm in our daily existence—the sense of humor and social interest *(gemeinschaftsgefühl,* communal feeling)—will be introduced as lively psychological terms for the future. At present very little has been written about the attitudes, goals, and behaviors of the person with social interest and humor. This paper will be an initial attempt to bring more substance to the two concepts of maturity. Then the sense of humor, primarily a Freudian concept, will be combined with the Adlerian ideal of social interest under the rubric of humanistic identification in hopes of stimulating further interest in the process of maturity.

The Humorist: Freud's Puzzle

The humorist was an enigma to Freud (1928). Here was his epitome of maturity paradoxically using pathological mechanisms of "denial of reality." The humorist was, in addition, a glaring exception to the Freudian faith in a totally prohibitive superego. Yet Freud's clinical description of humor seemed to be an apt one for his time. Unfortunately, his explanation, couched in an abstract displacement of energy and subsequent "inflation" of the superego, completely ignored the self-training and goals of the life style. Clinically, the hallmark of Freud's humorist was the production or appreciation of enlivening jests ("something fine and elevating" as well as "liberating" Freud, 1928) under conditions of severe objective stress, such as one's imminent execution. The object of the humor could be one's self, others, or all the vagaries of Mankind or the Universe, itself. In other words, the humorist endures and contributes rather than isolates and decompensates.

Even in the extreme examples encountered by Frankl (1955), concentration camp inmates dying alone, humor often shines. In such cases social interest and humor are present in the internal sentences one allows himself, a loving indefatigable "yes" to the Universe. Yet Frankl has not acknowledged social interest (and by extension, humor) where there are no other individuals physically present. This digression is necessary to note a possible distinction between the physical

199

and psychological bases of social interest and humor. Frankl and many Adlerians would require social interactions for humor, an unnecessary diminishing of social interest. The theory of Humanistic Identification (O'Connell, 1968b) points toward *psychological* relatedness with others, certainly seen in understanding life styles. To engage in body counts would transform the beauty of social interest to a drab and hectic social game. In fact, Thomas Merton comes to mind as a mature individual with optimal self-esteem and outsight, even though he seldom left his monastery grounds. Moreover, in our superficial examination of social life we overlook the tremendous energy we devote to "contemplation" or nonverbalized internal sentences, even when interacting with others. It is very rare that we give up our life style manipulations to feel, see, and hear through another's style of life (Adler, 1956), for we really "contemplate" (are "autistic") much of our life even when in the midst of others. We just don't usually upset ourselves and others too much with this subtle inner activity, hence most of us escape involuntary hospitalization.

Social Interest as Outsight

This gem of Adler's thought cost him the positive regard of the numerous influential medical and measurement-model people. It still does. But there are minor prophets in our fields who see the lawlessness of the individual as prognostic of national ruin (Brussel, 1969). The old laws have been those of gross control and power. They often make no other sense and offer no personal gain for most people. There is as yet no developed theory which is congenial, offers social satisfaction for mortals, and is championed by the Happy-Psychologist-of-the-Future. Yet, hope is not yet dead. A logical extension of Freud's theory of humor and Adler's view of social interest would lead one to more fruitful lands.

In the theory of Humanistic Identification are two main variables, self-esteem (or personal worth) and social interest. The latter indicates the number of people one can cooperate with as equals, experiencing their life styles. Superior-inferior abstractions about people disappear with the belief (Judeo-Christian-Democratic) that people can change. It then becomes one's task to "stroke-and-spit." That is, in a true democracy one "strokes" by communicating the worth of others to them.

He "spits" by giving feedback to others as to how and why they reject this gift of worth and what demands they are not putting on others. "Spitting" also means predicting what the other might do in frustration. For example. a patient in Action Therapy (O'Connell, 1966b) might remark that he needs confidence to get better. In role reversal he portrays what others must do to "cure" him. When auxiliaries then communicate this "confidence" to the patient he rejects the offer. A nimble director assists by having the patient report his inner goal-directed reactions through a soliloquy. Other possibilities to make public the attitudes or internal sentences are by empathic doubles or mirrors. Perhaps the patient rejects the success-bombardment and beams (or gives other recognition responses) when being given special service (Dreikurs, 1957). He demands this type of pampering and reacts with depressive and/or paranoid rejecting behaviors when dependency needs are frustrated—and the environment doesn't come across freely and plentifully on demand. What we often call mental illness seems to be the irresponsible demands of the hyperdependent. The greater the dependency the more I try to manipulate "objects" for signs that they esteem me (to the immature, others are objects, emotionally colored as good or bad). Dependency leads to greater frustrations; frustrations to self- and other-blame and further excursions of the useless side of life.

Our search for esteem is the psychological analogue to our physical need for oxygen. We all need it and suffer some kind of death without it. The mature one who has abundant self-esteem and outsightful harmony is truly grateful for what he gets. He understands others—and realizes he must very often give esteem (according to how the other defines "esteem") to harvest any from his outer world. He does respect and love himself in the process of giving encouragement to others. There are no complete dualisms of self-other, heaven-earth, child-adult in the universe of the psychologically mature.

Maturity implies a consciousness of choice: I can find evidence to hate or love myself and others. That decision is my key existential choice between good and evil, which again are not independent entities, as man is not. I must esteem and practice outsight, if I want to model the world as I wish it to be. I cannot *demand* proofs of worth if I value sanity and health. I can only work for it through my own loving behaviors.

The Humorist as Mature Ideal

Freud's romantic idealism led him to esteem the humorist, even though his closed constitutional system of personality development was a completely inadequate scheme for explanation. Adler's idealistic hope for growth led him to social interest, his trait of authentic actualization. In truth, it would be easy to combine the traits, as has been done implicitly in the theory of Humanistic Identification. Starting with Freud's basic attitude of the humorist, and ignoring his energy displacements, the similarity with Adler becomes apparent. The internal sentences (or "self-reinforcement") of the humorist's life style are "Look here! This is all that this seemingly dangerous world amounts to. Child's play—the very thing to jest about" (Freud, 1928). (It is of interest that these are almost the same words attributed to the 16th Century humanist and humorist, Thomas More, when threatened with pain and material deprivation.) (O'Connell, 1966a) The humorist's life style operates like all others except that the content differs: again, selective perceptions find what is looked for. Such a life-plan is based upon the communal love for others, the ability to perceive them as unique human beings. Demands are out of place where others are seen as also worthy of being made in the "image of God." The humorist approaches his destiny or existential conditions of imperfection and death without the emotional manipulations of the trapped, pampered child. The humorist is social interest personified: a cooperative, non-demanding individual, a living model of one who is concerned with the common inferiorities of mankind. But another variable in addition to social interest is needed for the humorist to develop. That is, high self-esteem or personal worth. Divorced from outsight or social interest, self-esteem leads to psychopathic callous behavior in which others are defeated. Adequate self-esteem is necessary for anyone to avoid hyperdependency. The search for esteem goes on unconsciously in all of us. Yet we all have within us an intuitive knowledge of what movements from others signify acceptance. We all search for worth; the racist finds it from the reactions of his fellow haters. The true humorist contents himself with giving and receiving feedback without demanding that people live by his advice. He is not the masochist who actively courts pain and frustration for the inferior esteem and a social control it offers. Rather he knows, as did Adler, that one is ultimately responsible for maintaining his own life style and that acquiescing silently to the power-cravings of others destroys responsible identity. See Lang's "mystification" where hyperdependency results from toadying to demands which are disguised as "love" (Lang, 1965).

The theory of Humanistic Identification recognizes the humorist's life style as the ideal of maturity. To repeat, two hypothetical dimensions are postulated to explain life styles: the extent of social interest as manifested behaviorally by outsight, and self-esteem or worth. The humorist combines the best of both. He gives and takes feedback ("spitting") and communicates hope and worth ("stroking"). He is empathic toward others and esteemed for this. He does not demand great demonstrations of affection because he has learned to esteem himself and understand and accept the life styles of others. Very little in this paper is contradicted by research. Freudian humor, the ability to produce or appreciate non-hostile jests in times of unavoidable stress, was demonstrated in psychologically healthy college students (O'Connell, 1960). It is greatest with community leaders (Worthen, 1967) and varies inversely with death fears (O'Connell, 1968a). Influential leaders in patient peer groups produce humor (O'Connell, 1969b) and do not appreciate and create hostile and resigned wit (Freud, 1928) as do hyperdependent patients (O'Connell, Rothaus, Hanson, & Moyer, 1969). College students high in humor appreciation are neither repressors nor sensitizers (O'Connell & Peterson, 1964). Freud did appear mistaken in equating humor appreciation and creation (O'Connell, 1969a). The latter seems more closely allied to maturity, giving credence to the Adlerian emphasis upon the actively social life style as the sign of psychological development.

Advantages of Humanistic Identification

The theory of Humanistic Identification offers the peculiar advantage of bringing under one roof the maturity concepts of psychoanalysis and Individual Psychology. The humorist, the sign of maturity in the theory of Humanistic Identification, creates optimal self-esteem and outsight. He feels of worth, part of the ongoing spectrum of mankind, past, present, and future. The emphasis on self-esteem and outsight highlights *process* rather than essence thinking. People are not drastically different because of the possession of essences, but by their uses of *processes*. Unfortunately, a kind of self-worth is created through the behaviors of sickness as well as maturity. Patients enhance symptomatic behaviors because they have decided they have no hope for any greater worth. If human life is seen as an interactional process of life styles, we all have the responsibility for increasing the humanistic (not symptomatic) self-esteem of others and deflating our neighbor's ploys to employ behaviors which depreciate himself and others for asocial power purposes.

Attention to esteem and outsight points out the futility of merely interpreting behavior as signs of repressed drives or hidden goals. To be mature one needs to love ("stroke and spit") himself and others, without the artificial distinctions of soil and blood. It is the therapist's duty to model maturity and point out behavioral manifestations of decreased outsight, low esteem, and uncooperative blame in the here-and-now.

Humanistic Identification highlights the interplay of the life style and environment. A person seeks esteem, to be confirmed as correct and important in his fictive interpretations of the world. *Outsight is a behavior; esteem an affect.* It therefore becomes theoretically possible, albeit unlikely, for one through ignorance to so choose or have as his destiny an environment so violent as to punish even a humanistic life style. His esteem can be low, while his outsight high. The reverse of this is more apparent. Psychopathology does not necessarily stem simply from low self-esteem. High self-esteem which enables a person to act with an increased radius of influence is even more catastrophic for the world than low self-esteem, if social interest is narrow and highly biased. Low self-esteem results in increased fantasy at the expense of concerted environmental behavior. True schizophrenia is a victimization of one's self by an existential choice to dwell in fantasy and *demand* to be left alone. Concerted planned antisocial acts therefore are not to be explained as epiphenomena of schizophrenic disease. Psychopathic behavior follows more from self-training in asocial actions which promise high self-esteem. For example, kill a controversial, mature national figure and win the material gain of money, fame, and respect from certain people. Who has the disease then!

There are still no fashionable behavioral measurements of basic social interest. In this humanistic system, one sign of its extent is the lack of negative nonsense (Ellis, 1962) or blame. Beyond that, the person with communal feeling listens, sees, and feels the life style of the other. He is not so overly dependent that he will not give feedback on autistic behaviors. But above all, the mature person (or humorist) respects the democratic right of one to be crazy, while communicating how and why one makes this hidden choice from unfortunate mistaken premises.

Summary

In these days of individual and social discord one often wishes for more theoretical-experimental understanding of the sense of humor and the sense of communal spirit or *gemeinschaftsgefühl*. These concepts, the late developing fruits of Freud and Adler, have hardly been touched. Undoubtedly we all could profit immensely from the knowledge of the inner-and outer-developmental factors leading to a happy nonviolent empathic contributor to mankind, the humorist. The theory of Humanistic Identification offers a framework for thought, with its view of humanistic maturity as high self-esteem and extensive social interest. The latter is dependent upon the knowledge that understanding the life styles of others (practicing outsight) decreases arbitrary demands, frustrations, and the myriad signs of untoward tensions. The mature individual is aware of his own need for esteem, loves himself and others. Behaviorally he "strokes and spits." That is, he communicates worth without duplicity and has the courage and independence not to be duped by subtle esteem games. He trusts only movement. The same behavior describes the humorist. Ideally he is not lacking in social interest and has the self-esteem necessary for action. He realizes to the end the importance of abiding by his existential decisions of demandless love and understanding. The humorous attitude thus represents the ultimate in the socially creative life style. In a few words, the humorist is active social interest or courage personified.

REFERENCES

1. Ansbacher, H. L. and Ansbacher, Rowena (Ed.) *The Individual Psychology of Alfred Adler.* N. Y.: Basic Books, 1956.

2. Adler, A., Dostoevsky (1918) In A. Adler, *Individual Psychology.* Patterson, N. J.: Littlefield, Adams & Company, 1959, 280-290.

3. Brussel, J. Decline and Fall of U. S. Begun. *Houston Post.* March 30, 1969.

4. Coser, L. The Visibility of Evil. *Journal of Social Issues,* 1969, 25, 101-109.

5. Dreikurs, R. *Psychology in the Classroom.* N. Y.: Harper & Row, 1957.

6. Ellis, A. *Reason and Emotion in Psychotherapy.* N. Y.: Lyle Stuart, 1962.

7. Frankl, V. *The Doctor and the Soul.* N. Y.: Knopf, 1955.

8. Freud, S. Humor. *International Journal of Psychoanalysis,* 1928, 9, 1-6.

9. Lang, R. Violence and Love. *Journal of Existentialism,* 1965, 5, 417-422.

10. MacLean, Kate. After Encounter—What? *Berkeley Barb,* 1969, 8 (9), 27.

11. O'Connell, W. The Adaptive Functions of Wit and Humor. *Journal of Abnormal Social Psychology,* 1960, 61, 263-270.

12. O'Connell, W. Humor of the Gallows. *Omega,* 1966a, 1, 32-33.

13. O'Connell, W. Psychotherapy for Everyman: A Look at Action Therapy. *Journal of Existentialism,* 1966b, 7, 85-91.

14. O'Connell, W. Humor and Death. *Psychological Reports,* 1968a, 22, 391-402.

15. O'Connell, W. Humanizing Religion, Race, and Sex. Paper read at Minnesota Society of Individual Psychology Symposium, Minneapolis, November 1968b.

16. O'Connell, W. Creativity in Humor. *Journal of Social Psychology,* 1969a, 78, 237-241.

17. O'Connell, W. The Social Aspects of Wit and Humor. *Journal of Social Psychology,* 1969b, 79, 183-187.

18. O'Connell, W., & Peterson, P. Humor and Repression. *Journal of Existential Psychiatry,* 1964, 4, 309-315.

19. O'Connell, W., Rothaus, P., Hanson, P., and Moyer, R. Jest Appreciation and Interaction in Leaderless Groups. *International Journal of Group Psychotherapy,* 1969, 19, 454-462.

20. Worthen, R. E. The Concept of Psychological Health Explored in Terms of the Value Orientations Direction and Centeredness. Unpublished doctoral dissertation, Baylor University, 1967.

THE ENIGMA OF BROTHERLY LOVE

There is probably no problem with more relevance for mankind as a whole than the definition and measurement of conditions conducive to the growth of brotherly love. Yet this topic is one which elicits mainly lip service at the most. Subtle disdain is more characteristic of the sophisticated 20th Century reaction to the word. For example, love itself, as the concept is used in our civilization, is an abstraction frequently connoting " a multitude of sins" or mixed meanings (e.g., greed, dependency). In the behavioral sciences, the person evincing curiosity and puzzlement about the genesis and value of brotherly love has all too often been regarded as a singular aberration suffering from "do-goodism" and puritanical repressions. Such a reaction would not prevail had we not unconsciously incorporated society's faith in the sanctity of the easily measurable and the physiological. Even these with a humanistic orientation occasionally dogmatically state that such a process as love intrinsically defies measurement.[1] Apparently such a protest overlooks the fact that psychological research is developing techniques for evaluating the single case in a longitudinal fashion rather than relying entirely upon group results. Yet it is my contention that love has not been explored by behavioral scientists principally from a failure to see its value in the realities of human existence. Until very recently psychological needs have not been considered,[2] while status and prestige went to the scientist who dealt with the time-honored physiological methodologies. Yet as Jung[3] aptly stated, there is no logical reason to assume that psychological needs are not ephemeral epiphenomena of the physical.

Since the disciplines of religion, psychology, and psychiatry are composed of people with varying theories or philosophies of man, depending upon their own experiences and training, it probably is unrealistic to expect unanimity of opinion on the present utility of specific scientific concepts.

Reprinted from *The Individual Psychologist*, 1968, 5, 6-9.

What is more logical and more healthy is to develop less rigidity and avoidance in conceptualization and more puzzlement about man in general. Heterogeneity with the disciplines is evidenced by the intellectual walls constructed and maintained by adherents of special theoretical interest. For example, witness the love-for-God vs. love-for-man issue in religion, and the physiological research-in-animals vs. psychological research-in-man dichotomy in psychology.

Since the concept of "Universal Man" is not a characteristic of our intellectual climate, it is naive to think in the generalities of "ministers believe . . . " or "psychologists maintain . . . " It is even more chimerical to think in such broad terms as "theologians and behavioral scientists agree that . . . " The main point of all this is to state that the views of people personally committed to the serious study of love are largely influenced by their personal experience, for better or for worse. This state of affairs will continue until science can tell us with incontrovertible evidence that one ethic communicated in such-and-such a manner will lend to desirable psychological developments (e.g., identities, value system of the individual). This may be one of the factors that has relegated love to a rather sterile cliche rather than dynamic force for human betterment.

One of the pioneers in this exploration, Erich Fromm,[4] offers a classification of love into the subtypes of mother, father, brother, erotic, and love for God. In his generic sense love has the attributes of respect, knowledge, care and responsibility. In the end, the concept is still highly abstract with little thought as to how these attributes are communicated to transform a "thing" into a "thou."

At the present time there seems to be no substitute for participation with the whole human being to impress one with the value of brotherly love and its concrete expression, good works. There is probably no better laboratory for this interaction than the controversial mental hospital, if one can break out of the confines of structured interviews and the splitting of man into glands, chemicals, isolated structures, and physiological drives. One cannot deny that the overriding importance of "matters of consequence" makes opportunities for this invaluable training for the minister and doctor extremely rare. We seem to be the victim of our techniques and are loath to venture far from their false securities.

Since I have been granted the chance for informal ex-
perimentation with methods of psychotherapy in a setting of
hospitalized schizophrenics over the last 13 years, [5] [6] I would
like to state a few tentative thoughts in hopes of putting
brotherly love and good works on solid interpersonal ground.

1) *Brotherly love and good works depend on the presence of
outsight* (understanding of the state of the *other* person's needs,
fears, and hopes). Traditional psychotherapy generally centers
on the *inner* state of the client. That is, the therapist assists the
client to arrive at insight into the history of his troubles and
the personal dynamics of his present unsatisfied needs in
hopes that liberation of positive forces for growth will result.
There is very little emphasis upon the neglected fact that
lowered self-esteem generates psychological disturbances and
self-esteem is built upon by the good will of others. Perhaps
we therapists have been guilty of a touch of grandiosity,
believing our incentive value to be so great as to buoy up any
or all feelings of unworth through a verbal "laying on of
hands." By learning to reduce psychological tensions of others
(e.g., need for understanding, need for belonging), one can
usually gain approval and esteem from others. It is a very rare
individual who can rely mainly upon inner approval for
satisfaction (following actions congruous with his value
system) rather than depend upon the good will of others. Of
course, if such inner-directed people harbor a non-
humanitarian value system, then mankind undergoes far more
suffering, as history amply demonstrates.

2) *How do I know if my works are Good or Bad?* This is
not an easy question to answer, except in the extreme case
when physical danger and suffering of the other are obvious. A
thorough search into this question would go far beyond the
scope of this paper and would involve intricacies of both
personality and learning theory. Many of the ills of the world
might be attributed to reliance upon the effects of punishment
rather than good example or identification model.[7] Punishment
might stop an act but only lead to more intensely hostile acts
and hatred of the arbitrary punisher.[8] Yet it is common to see
punishment passing for good works (under the guise of being
"therapeutic").

Learning theory tells us that when we reward an action (by reducing a person's tension), it is more likely to recur. So in every literal sense we are partially responsible for his actions. We are faced with the dilemma of whether such an action is good or bad, in the long view, for optimal development of an individual's potential for "love and work."

3) *Psychologists and ministers are faced with considerable ignorance about the effects of brotherly love and good works.* Psychotherapists, as a rule, are inclined to blame parents for the "lack of love" in child rearing. This hostility is precipitated chiefly by perceiving the blame to rest with hostile-sexual "unconscious wishes" on the part of the parents. Few of us[9] have been sufficiently explorative to see that parents, like the rest of us, have problems of esteem—and perhaps operate on a wrong theory of methods of communicating love and goals to others. In other words, honest ignorance instead of disguised malevolence might be operating in many regressive relationships.

We live in times of relative ignorance of human problems, and mankind has suffered by our failure to acknowledge this truth. Knowledge of love—its growth and value—will probably follow the efforts of those who are committed to its importance and are capable of accepting the insight of many disciplines. We also know little about how to apply brotherly love to help others, especially those whose life style is directed toward finding reasons for hating others. Just "love" is not enough?

Summary

The concept of brotherly love and its concrete expression have been examined for possible leads out of our present stage of relative ignorance. In addition to their theological importance, brotherly love and good works are therapeutic concepts which should be of paramount importance to all concerned with mental health. Lack of knowledge about these basic and neglected concepts will probably be overcome only by increasing research and making possible ease of communication between the helping disciplines.

REFERENCES

1. Stern, K. *The third revolution.* New York: Harcourt, Brace & Co., 1954.

2. White, R. Motivation reconsidered: the concept of competence. *Psychol. Rev.*, 1959, 66, 297-333.

3. Jung, C. *Modern man in search of a soul.* New York: Harcourt, Brace & Co., 1933.

4. Fromm, E. *The art of loving.* New York: Harpers, 1956.

5. O'Connell, W. Ward psychotherapy with schizophrenics through concerted encouragement. *J. Ind. Psychol,* 1961, 17, 193-204.

6. O'Connell, W. Practicing christianity and humanistic identification. *J. Human. Psychol,* 1964, 4, 118-129.

7. O'Connell, W. Identification and curability of the mental hospital patient. *J. Ind. Psychol,* 1962, 18, 68-76.

8. Bandura, A. Punishment revisited. *J. Consulting Psychol.,* 1962, 26, 298-301.

9. Lehrman, N. Anti-therapeutic and antidemocratic aspects of Freudian dynamic psychiatry. *J. Ind. Psychol.,* 1964, 19, 167-181.

DEMOCRACY IN HUMAN RELATIONS

Democracy, like love, is a psychological concept we seldom have tried to define and measure. Indeed, both seem to have much meaning in common. A democratic relationship is one in which the other is respected. Demands upon the other are minimal and open. This is the secret of psychological maturity: to be satisfied with relatively small degrees of attention and reward from others. The hub of the process is a well-practiced ability to love oneself *without* a self-centered and self-defeating lack of awareness and commitment to the psychological needs of others. The love that knows no dualisms is the basis of social interest.

Self-love without the love of others is characteristic of the "successful" psychopath who manipulates the immature dependencies of others. More socially unsuccessful are the neurotics and psychotics who find minimal esteem by being sick, victimized, isolated, and infrahuman. All these pathologies demand much from others but get little socially constructive esteem. The end result is the schizophrenic's unverbalized demand to be left alone in his created inner hell.

Love can be seen as an extension of the democratic process, implying more highly significant others. True love hangs in delicate balance. If the participants lack adequate social interest and lean too heavily for need-fulfillment upon only a few pampered others, the relationship can swing into gruesome hyperdependencies. In both democratic respect and the longing-for-closeness characteristic of love, the "revolt" is an inner one against our mistaken certainties about people, but not against ourselves. But this life style "revolt" must be stimulated by the failure of the environment to be victimized by self-centered needs. Those about us must democratically "stroke and spit." That is, against a background of giving time and effort to see people as important and worthy simply by

Dr. O'Connell's article is based on a paper he presented at the 1969 American Society of Adlerian Psychology Meetings in Wilmington, Delaware.
Reprinted from *Desert Call*, 1970, 26, 57-63.

"being," others should be able to detect and communicate the subtle grandiosities of the typical life style. In a democratic situation, dependency and its obverse, withdrawal, are never so great as to block mutual feedback. There is openness to communicate feelings about behaviors immediately, often loudly, but *without* classifying the other as forever evil, hopeless, and infrahuman.

Psychosocial democracy is predicated upon the ability to speak and listen while trying to understand the life style of the other. While political democracy is obtaining more votes for the previously disenfranchised, psychosocial democracy is suffering. The emphasis on "tell-it-like-it-is" is an intrapsychic search for and ventilation of frustrated demands. From the ghetto to the campus—and even to the sensitivity training laboratory—there is excessive focus upon one's reactive frustrations rather than on one's precipitating *demands*. The life-style needs of the other are not considered. For example, I have seen a famous figure in sensitivity training fight a group member who told him to "shut up," all the while deriving esteem from this behavior through the praise of dependent followers. He thought he was honest by "expressing his feelings." But this trainer was not telling anyone of his demanding dependencies upon others.

Sensitivity training (or human relations laboratories) with socially-oriented leaders who know the machinations of the life style can aid the democratic process immeasurably. Often accused by the far right of destroying "high morals and integrity," this training situation can be an effective method for personal examinations of esteem, demands, frustrations, and goals. Take a group out of its customary surroundings, isolate it as a potential community, and do not allow the usual avoidances and frenetic withdrawals to go unnoticed. All the while authentic leaders (demonstrating openness, democratic respect, and an eagerness to cooperate-as-equals) shape the interactions. The democratic process of responsibility for the awareness and the communication of life-style demands, frustrations, and goals is part of authentic sensitivity training. But human relations training laboratories can be easily diverted to the service of isolated asocial demands aimed at another's behavior. In addition to the "honest" dictatorial leader, there are grabbing, groping, stripping, and weeping participants who inspire a maudlin response from some others.

The incidental value of finding what behavior is personally shocking becomes the end of such "telling-it-like-it-is," intrapsychic groups. Acting out frustrations in the guise of honesty—while still hiding one's negative nonsense—is only a more subtle form of masturbation.

In the view of Teilhard de Chardin, a weakness of our political democracy is that each man becomes emancipated and thinks of himself as the only center of the universe. A psychosocial democracy is based on the laws of social interest and social hedonism. Authentic sensitivity training is of this kind, communicating both the worth and the mistakes of persons. With success, the other is perceived as a uniquely human innervating experience that each participant can sustain in his daily existence. But success demands honesty, openness, communication—at once the hallmark of democracy and of love.

PRACTICING CHRISTIANITY AND HUMANISTIC IDENTIFICATION *

The Great Fissure

The purpose of this paper is to explore the uncertain relationships between the behavioral sciences and religion by examining one of the etiological factors involved, a hopeful theory of reconciliation, and topics of ostensible disagreement.

It seems profitable for all that someone ask a metacommunicative, "What goes on here and why?" when psychotherapists are castigated by members of the priesthood for being callously immoral (Martin, 1962), at the same time they are being told that the world of morals, ethics, and values should be barred to them (Mowrer, 1962a). From the other side there are voices saying ethics and values are indigenous to the process of psychotherapy while eradication of religion would assist people to become more responsible individuals (La Barre, 1959; Ellis, 1960; Szasz, 1961). All this takes place while the popular impression is that harmonious interaction prevails, with the main problem of mental hygiene implementation being external financial ones.

A bit of the onus for the basic antagonisms between the science of man and religion must rest with the views of Sigmund Freud. While Freud cannot be blamed for the centuries of border warfare between science and religion, he did postulate his own value judgments about religion. These were

---

*Humanistic identification is used as a generic term for an advanced state of maturity in which the person feels that he is an integral part of mankind, sharing the past, and existential present and future problems with his universal "band of brothers." This developmental stage, an advancement beyond the narrow fixations of blood and soil (Fromm, 1959), makes unnecessary the continuous expenditure of energy for defensive measures in interpersonal relationships. It thereby allows for unique identification superimposed upon this feeling of relative well-being.

A practicing Christian, in this article, refers to one who makes the Judeo-Christian ethic part of his permanent value system and displays this approach to life in action rather than words solely. One can consider the practicing Christian to mirror in behavior a humanistic identification.

Reprinted from the *Journal of Humanistic Psychology*, Fall 1964.

eagerly accepted by many, perhaps more through the confluence of cultural perplexities and Freud's charismatic influence than by incisive thoughts and observations. In brief, the principal points which bring psychoanalysts (and myriad followers in the behavioral sciences) into collision with Judeo-Christian philosophy seem to be the following:

1. The Freudian analogy, frequently taken for identity, between a magical search for the father, obsessive compulsive neurosis and conventional religion (Freud, 1927, 1930, 1932).

2. Freud's "nothing but" method of reductionism which analyzed various kinds of love and other sublimations into the "real" elements, all of which had a pathological flavor (e.g., narcissism, sexuality, hostility) (Benda, 1961).

3. The eschewing of human values in favor of a more mental model based upon "reason." It is interesting to note in passing that Freud's epitome of maturity, the humorist, fails to abide with the still-vague dictates of Freudian reason (O'Connell, 1960).

Essentially, the Freudian model lent itself to a view of man as a detached individual (Rieff, 1961) whose values apparently followed automatically upon satisfaction of physiological needs. It appears that Freud's thinking, based on a sample of Victorian neurotics, led him to a few erroneous conclusions, the main one being a lack of differentiation between what philosophy of life is taught the child and the means of encouraging learning. The effects of harshness seen by Freud in his patients may have motivated his failure to make the important distinction between content and method of learning (Lehrman, 1962).

Yet it is possible that the rift between the two disciplines can be mended by focusing upon the adaptive assets of a combination of religion with humanism, existentialism, and learning theory.

Behavioral science is turning away from man as a hapless victim of mechanical universal frustrations motivated solely by unconscious animal drives. Values, responsibilities, and sins are becoming ultimate concerns. The crimes of dictators and bureaucrats have emphasized the defects of the gross neglect of philosophic questions in the scientific study of man. In other words, defining maturity in terms of societal norms has failed to spawn anything but justifications for selfish shortsighted gains. Ego drives are now becoming prominent in psychological investigations with further thought toward *inborn psychological* needs freed, so far, from physiological states (Fromm, 1955; White, 1959; Gilbert, 1961; Shoben, 1960). One can even read of inborn fears and possible inherited guilt which go beyond Freud's descriptions and into interpersonal methods of treatment (Reubenstein & Levitt, 1957).

All this does not mean that tomorrow or the next day psychiatrists, psychologists, and clergy will all peacefully break bread with each other and converse amiably in a common tongue. The time is merely closer, but not yet at hand, for any unanimity about the role for each in the mental treatment field. Agreement is slowly being reached on the ideal man of religion, psychology, and psychiatry. The province of psychiatry and psychology, it is supposed, may possibly be to point out through research the physiological and psychological influences necessary to mold this desired human being. The clergy, on the other hand, might be willing to incorporate these insights into their religious instructions. All this presupposes mutual interdisciplinary respect and an overcoming of professional delusions of omniscience.

Outsight and Identifications: A Possibility for Harmony

The writer would like to make a brief plea for a greater accent upon *future* oriented psychotherapy based upon a principle of *outsight* (Forer, 1961). This way of looking at the process of therapy does not remove the development of rapport and insight from the therapeutic picture, but does highlight the proposition that man is the social animal who develops his personal psychic concepts for better or for worse from the rewards and punishments administered by other people. Such a philosophy of treatment, developed from experiences in psychotherapy with severe neurotics, character disorders, and schizophrenics, places the psychotherapist in the role of active teacher rather than passive searcher for past traumata. In this approach, a premium is placed upon flexibility in the therapist. He must be able to become a tension-reducer for the patient in order to construct the significant relationship. He must be able to switch from the mother to father role (O'Connell, 1961, 1962) rewarding assertive, socially constructive behavior which will gain the patient self-esteem in extra-therapy situations. In this outsight type of therapy the anxiety of the patient is reduced in the initial phase, whereas it might even be raised by the therapist in the latter portion. With the therapist assuming these dual parent-like roles over time and bringing the outside world into consideration, some of the criticism of orthodox psychotherapy with schizophrenics may be answered. For example, Mowrer states that the schizophrenic's low self-esteem is justified by the way he behaves toward others (1962b). The second or the father role of reinforcing a *mutuality* or thoughtfulness toward the generalized-other is one way out of this apparent impasse.

It is postulated that most emotionally disturbed people are suffering from a lack of a humanistic identification so they do not feel as if they are part of, or belong to, the human race. They may hate, fear, and scorn others and, thus, in the long run suffer impairment to their own egos and bodies. Without humanistic identification one cannot progress to unique identification, or the urge to be different in a rewarding way, since his energies are usually dissipated in a defensive cold war with his fellow man. Since, in the formative stages of our psychic development we have an implacable need for the good-will of others, what is a better education from the point of view of future reward than to learn to understand the needs of others and to develop techniques for increasing self-esteem through rewards of others? It may be that when man's internal concepts and techniques for gratification are maturely developed, reward emanates mainly from within so that external rewards for increasing self-esteem are not as pressing; but still they seem to be present in attenuated intensity (Rapaport, 1958). All immature people appear to be either overtly or covertly crying for reward from others and it may be that man's existential concepts (responsibility, freedom, values, identifications, self-esteem) are merely labels for the product of one's interpersonal rewards and punishments.

The initial answer to Freud's pressing question as to why one should love his fellow man (Freud, 1930) is that this is the way one becomes a significant person or a model of identification for others. A lesser reward accrues to the tension-reducer himself, but it is a form of mental health insurance nevertheless. That is, energy expended upon others, given rather freely without too much demand, is not energy devoted to hypochondriacal and other narrow, long-term, non-rewarding actions. So in a real sense we are all responsible for the sanity of our brothers. If the panicky and withdrawn schizophrenic suffers from catastrophically low self-esteem and poor social skills (which precludes the development of a feeling of belonging outside of the hospital structure) we all appear to be partly responsible for this, as well as for the development of our ego autonomy.

Brotherly love in action (Fromm, 1959) may be the common ground on which religion and psychiatry will find their peaceful co-existence. A frequent response to the term of brotherly love is one of marking the user as a "do-gooder" or a hypocritical double-binder, since very rarely does the word have an authentic duplication in reality. Further discussion of the theory of brotherly love and its research implications will be reserved for future papers. But it must be added that it is not an instrumental behavior which is easily and habitually elicited as is its verbal counterpart. For the present, suffice to say it may be based upon the possessor being willing and able to reduce tension in the other. It presupposes knowing the needs of the other individual and behaviors which should be rewarded. Since this doesn't mean aiding the satisfaction of the other's *demands* but teaching him how to cope with anxiety in the context of other equally important people, limits are also a necessity. And in the time the client, patient, or student must learn the needs, hopes, and fears of the generalized other, rather than wallow interminably in enumeration of his own traumata and internalized sentences which habitually berate others (Ellis, 1962). So it is that active, self-disclosing therapists (or teachers) are one of many novel corollaries required for this outsight model of psychotherapy.

Adler saw hope in living the Judeo-Christian ethic (Adler, 1956); Freud perceived only sickness and pessimism in its precepts (Freud, 1930). Freud's theory did not allow for treatment of schizophrenics while Adler looked beneath the facade of "narcissistic neurosis" for motives amenable to personal intervention. It may be that in our stage of ignorance in the development of psychotherapy we should venture beyond Adler and wonder how love is communicated and learned. Any gains realized would be a service not only to religion and the behavioral sciences, but to mankind as a whole.

Current Controversies

From experiences in working with and speaking to clergy interested in the problems of mental health (perhaps a biased sample which might give me a more mercurial outlook) the writer has clustered seven lively topics, interposing deductions from outsight therapy.

FREE WILL AND DETERMINISM

Traditionally, clergy are regarded as the defenders of complete free will, while behavioral scientists stand as the ultimate in determinism to insure the workings of science. For the psychotherapist the dilemma has often been a very perplexing one, to the extent that the issue is suppressed as being an irrelevant topic. Perhaps one can solve preoccupation with the problem by means of a "soft" determinism, or an adherence to the malleability of man. Partly responsible for this potentiality for change is the fact that a person can frequently become significant to others by reducing his anxieties and tensions. This is the basis of what psychologists call "secondary reinforcement" (Mowrer, 1956). For example, mother becomes loved by reducing the child's needs, both psychological and physiological, or by being closely associated with such need reduction. Father, in helping to mold the child's character, might create tensions in later years by his demands, but also aids the adolescent in acquiring skills for gaining approved need reduction more independently. The father (or some significant person operating in his role) will also reward the child by approval for his motivation and performance. By displaying various forms of love (mother, father, brother, or erotic) (Fromm, 1959) and thereby reducing tensions and anxieties we become significant people. Thus we follow the precept of Jesus to "love thy neighbor as thyself." In this way people can change: they become less fearful, anxious, and become willing to incorporate viewpoints of significant others in our intrapsychic world. It may be that this is the prototype of much of our value development. As Goethe once said, we learn more from those we love.

If the individual has been fortunate enough to develop optimal self-love and love for others as individuals, he is not prone to regard the world as a nursery made for his support nor ultimately a den of willfully frustrating people. Then this love itself becomes a causal factor in deciding upon which overt or covert responses we shall make to the mass of stimuli. So our behavior is caused, but only in extreme cases is so fixated by habit or devoid of alternative responses as to become strictly determined, as in the case of infants and severely regressed schizophrenics.

Taken by itself the term free will can be quite meaningless. Complete "freedom from" signifies the ultimate in capriciousness. What is meant here by free will is the relative autonomy (Rapaport, 1958) of the person from unconscious and environmental factors, the conscious ego with humanistic values being the executive agent. This is our goal of psychotherapy.

IDEAL MAN

He is no longer a nebulous cultural ideal but one who is endowed with humanistic identification. That is, he feels related to all of mankind through common experiences, feelings, and fates. When this belief becomes an essential part of man he can then progress emotionally to allow for unique identification beyond the solace of humanistic belongingness. He is not hobbled by residual hates, demands, and incestuous fixations upon blood, soil, or profession. This again harks back to the Christian ethic and should be the treatment goal for psychotherapists as well. But the practicing Christian with a living ideology of generalized love-in-action without untoward demanding in return is a rarity, and probably the result of many fortunate factors. He has been exposed to pleasant anxiety-reducing experiences, helped by practicing Christians, or has learned through life experiences and deep intellectual and emotional conviction that practicing Christianity has its earthly rewards, while neurosis and psychosis can represent a temporal hell (Mowrer, 1961). Any psychotherapist can tell us that it is vitally necessary for man to have interests outside his own body and that selfishness and narcissism are not happy states of mind. And if we "do unto others" with love and support, others will, in the majority of cases, eventually do so unto us. Ideally, we should figuratively "turn the other cheek" and not supply an emotional instigator with objective reasons for hating us more. In addition, we realize the terrific toll on the body as well as on the personality of anxieties, hatreds, and fears and resolve to examine our own motives and values when these reactions interfere with our goals.

GUILT FEELINGS

Despite Freud's hope of founding a science of man without values, hidden beneath his complexes and structures was a very formidable moral: that honesty toward oneself is the best policy (Salzman, 1962). Recent controversy has centered about the honesty inherent in merely explaining away guilt in the psychotherapeutic hour (Mowrer, 1961). Hence, the question, "Is guilt real or imaginary?" And, ultimately, "If it is real is the person responsible for his sins?" Psychoanalytic treatment is often regarded as a method which perceives guilt and sin as stemming from neurotic scrupulosity. And in such a rigidly deterministic system no one is responsible. Now much of our psychotherapy is predicted with such a *Weltanschauung* in mind. That is, the therapist hopes the patient will in time develop a blame-free outlook on life and feel it unnecessary to punish the world and himself for past foibles. But this method can be reduced to pathos when through either imitation of, or identification with the therapist the patient faithfully recites the therapist's blame-free creed of faultlessness for the past, present, and future. In nine cases out of ten, the therapist now finds himself opposed to the onus-free view he previously espoused. What has transpired here? The therapist himself mind. That is, the therapist hopes the patient will, in time, determinism: he intellectually accepted the latter and emotionally believed variations of the former. And we do have considerable evidence to support the thesis that much of a patient's behavior is somewhat freely chosen with a *conscious* goal in mind (Adler, 1956; Bonime, 1960; Arieti, 1962). It is caused but not determined. It has elements of chosen behavior yet the patient is blind to its irrationality and the practicality of change. In this case the prime mover is fear or ignorance of the mundane pay-off or rewards of humanistic identification or practicing Christianity, not repression of conscience or impulse.

Or, it is equally likely that the therapist expected the determinism to be softened by identification with him. But in the example, what behavior pattern was to be incorporated beyond that of acting as if blameless? So it follows from accepting a free-will tenet that one also accepts the possibility of true guilt and responsibility. Yet the guilt behooves one to make restitution by present good works toward man rather than open old wounds in others by confessing to the world. Had our illustrative therapist believed this he would not have been preoccupied with trying to wipe out old accusations *ad infinitum,* but would have moved on to encouraging and reinforcing behavior which would be rewarding in the patient's future actions.

SIN

The topic of guilt naturally leads to the allied concept of sin. Throughout this paper the concern has been with humanistic identification in man or the horizontal religious component of man's relationship to man. The adaptive aspects of the man-God interaction has been left to Erich Fromm (1959) and the clergy. Despite this division of labor it is difficult to conceive of a practicing Christian inferring hatred for man from his love for God.

Sin is perhaps regarded as transcending guilt; the former would include behavior considered damaging to man with or without awareness on the part of the instigator of the act. Sin has had a poor reception in psychology because it frequently means an occasion to punish the "culprit" (Ellis, 1960). From the standpoint of a humanistic psychology man "sins" because of his fears and ignorance. He attempts to follow a course of action which is short-sighted and only leads to more future problems. He may or may not be conscious of the ramifications and etiology of his actions. To him, his behavior might be considered eminently appropriate even in the face of self-defeating neuroses or psychoses.

The central theme here is that use of the concept of sin as a precipitator for more punishment is morally wrong. Most of our psychiatric syndromes arise from reactions to low self-esteem, and feelings of worthlessness arising from "unpardonable sin" only cause further psychic damage. (This does not mean that we can explain the choice of the particular symptom or its formal mechanism by catastrophically low self-esteem). Now if a person once realizes the gains possible to him through a humanistic identification and believes he can carry out this style of life, he can gain self-esteem in a practical, perpetuating manner. Brotherly love may be at a premium, but it is not blind.

PLAYING THE GOD

Here is a derisive phrase to which no profession can claim sole possession. Ignorance and fear can cause many psychological illnesses and a person who finds self-esteem in one immature and insecure role will oftentimes react with defensive omnipotence and/or omniscience when faced with a perceived threat outside his anchor role. The point to be elaborated upon is that of both therapeutic and anti-therapeutic omnipotence. When a psychotherapist like Rosen (English, Hampe, Bacon, & Settlage, 1961) "plays God" he is doing so with a therapeutic end in mind which should call for much effort, care, and responsibility on his part. To the schizophrenic, Rosen is for a certain time, figuratively, a God. He is with him almost constantly, tries to communicate understanding, and be associated with need reduction so as to become a significant figure. Ideally he does so not to maintain this authoritarian role but only to obtain therapeutic ends. The most pernicious type of anti-therapy occurs when the individual who is seen as having the power informs the poor dependent one "There is no hope for you. And by fiat, I am the only one who has a say in your hopeless case." This is definitely anti-therapeutic omnipotence.

WHAT IS REPRESSED:
IMPULSE OR GUILT?

This question is one deserving of volumes rather than paragraphs. The implicit answer given by each psychotherapist is likely to dictate the strategy and tactics of the psychotherapy encounter. In turn this answer seems to be influenced mainly by the therapist's view of man and the etiology of deviant behavior.

Essentially the question is, in psychoanalytic terms, "What is repressed, the id or the superego? Is the task of the therapist that of encouraging impulse expression or helping the patient to acknowledge anti-social transgressions?" (Mowrer, 1961). While no simple answer can be forthcoming, perhaps a closer examination of the concepts involved will bring the issue to sharper focus.

It may be that in this day and age, repression has been too mechanical and overworked as a personality concept. Freud's idea of repression was mainly the exclusion and barring of ideation from consciousness (Freud, 1915). At other times a dual sort of a repression of both ideas and actions was suggested (Freud, 1936); yet main emphasis has always been upon the idea rather than the act. One might reason that an individual could repress hostility, for example, from *awareness* and yet his overt behavior prove to be of a very hostile nature, as long as he managed to blind himself about the meaning of his behavior. This type of repression of thoughts rather than actions seems to be more protean than a rigid dual variety unwittingly assumed to operate. In other words, as long as the person's awareness of the meaning of his action is blunted, his actions can conceivably be more overtly hostile than the original idea dictated.

More therapeutic gain seems possible when one questions the reasons for repressions and the leading of unrewarding lives. Fear of the consequences of actions can lead to repressions at any time in one's life but such qualms can be handled eventually by increasing self-esteem in the psychotherapy relationship. By considering the individual's world view to be of supreme importance in directing behavior, the emphasis on repression changes from its centrality in the Freudian system to a secondary effect ancillary to an individual's genotypical self-esteem. But other life experiences in addition to fear and anxiety can cause unrewarding behavior. Instead of using the "hidden-finished-object-in-the-basement" model of repression, it is possible to regard the superego as a "swiss cheese" or incompleted, "aborted" model of ideation and actions. These three ways of conceptualizing the superego are not mutually exclusive, for early repression can result in multiple gaps and a grossly incomplete system of values. Rather than dwell primarily upon an intrapsychic system of abstractions it might be more profitable to think in terms of actions which were learned from pathological identification models or out of avoidance and fear.

Research into creativity reflects another basic fault in our conceptualization of the superego. There has been extensive study of the prohibiting functions of the superego, but little rumination of the growth and function of the benign, humanistic superego. Given a person's lack of humanistic identification and prevailing feelings of weakness and fear or short-sighted unrewarding behavior, a union between Freud and

Mowrer's view of repression is ultimately possible. The contrasted notions of the content of repression are combined into one main operation when repression is seen as chiefly a denial of awareness or responsibility for one's impulse, while the derivative of the repressed impulse faithfully reflects the urge which was ejected from consciousness. It is hypothesized that in the majority of instances repression is not the central concept and is secondary to the failure to identify with humanistic models of behavior.

SICK RELIGION

Naturally there is sick religion as there is sick psychiatry, psychology, and what-have-you. Not that the professions are bizarre and weird in themselves but the certain ends—greed, power, hatred—might be disguised undesirable ones practiced by particular individuals. In our schizophrenic patients we see religiosity reflecting desires for magical power, derivatives of hostile impulses, and wishes for an encapsulated isolation. These are not examples of practicing Christianity, but represent nominal Christianity in its worst extreme. Whenever we stop searching for the kingdom of heaven within, start to give immature responses to immature people, forget the benefits of love, we lose sight of the goals of mental health and practicing Christianity. Perhaps there is more than a sparkle of truth to Shaw's remark that no nation has, as yet, been sane enough to try the way of Jesus (Shaw, 1916).

The Christian ethic is synonymous with an ideal end of psychotherapy, humanistic identification. Practicing Christianity here means that the individual has developed a feeling of belonging and responsibility toward the human race and shows this love in his actions. It is postulated that this feeling based on the use of outsight in psychotherapy is minimal in schizophrenics and severe neurotics. Outsight must be developed to insure that one will be rewarded with needed self-esteem outside of the psychotherapy interactions. Seven topics for discussion are presented: free will and determinism, ideal man, guilt, sin, playing God, repression, and sick religion. These seven are a few of the zones of contention likely to appear in intellectual interchanges between students of psychiatry and religion.

REFERENCES

1. Ansbacher, H. L. and Ansbacher, Rowena (Ed.) *The individual psychology of Alfred Adler.* New York: Basic Books, 1956.

2. Arieti, S. Psychotherapy of schizophrenia, *Arch. Gen. Psychiat.,* 1962, 6, 112-122.

3. Benda, C. "Narcissism" in psychoanalysis and the "love of oneself" in existential psychotherapy. *Dis. Nerv. Sys.,* 1961, 22, 1-9.

4. Bonime, W. "Depression" as a practice: dynamic and psychotherapeutic considerations. *Comprehensive Psychiat.,* 1960, 1: 3, 194-198.

5. Ellis, A. Mowrer on "sin." *Amer, Psychol.,* 1960, 15: 11, 713-714.

6. Ellis, A. *Reason and emotion in psychotherapy.* New York: Lyle Stuart, 1962.

7. English, O., Hampe, W., Bacon, C., & Settlage, C. *Direct analysis and schizophrenia.* New York: Grune & Stratton, 1961.

8. Forer, B. Schizophrenia: the narcissistic retreat. *J. Proj. Tech.,* 1961, 25, 422-430.

9. Freud, S. (1915) Repression. In *collected papers,* Ernest Jones (Ed.), London: Hogarth Press, 1950.

10. Freud, S. (1927) *The future of an illusion.* New York: Doubleday, 1957.

11. Freud, S. (1930) *Civilization and its dicontents.* New York: Doubleday, 1958.

12. Freud, S. (1932) *New introductory lectures on psychoanalysis.* New York: Norton, 1933.

13. Freud, S. *The problem of anxiety,* New York: Norton, 1936.

14. Fromm, E. *The sane society.* New York: Rinehart & Co., 1955.

15. Fromm, E. *The art of loving.* New York: Harper, 1959.

16. Gilbert, G. Toward a comprehensive biosocial theory of human behavior. Paper presented at Interamerican Congress of Psychol., Mexico City, 1961.

17. Krasner, L. Behavior control and social responsibility. *Amer. Psychol.,* 1962, 17, 199-204.

18. La Barre, W. Neurotic defense mechanisms in supernatural religion. *Amer. Human, Assoc. Publication Series No.* 102, 1959.

19. Lehrman, N. Moral aspects of mental health. *Amer. Human. Assoc. Publication Series, No.* 128, 1962.

20. Martin, A. The moral man. *Friar,* 1962, 17: 1, 11-19.

21. Mowrer, O. Two-factor learning theory reconsidered, with special reference to secondary reinforcement and the concept of habit. *Psychol. Rev.*, 1926, 63, 114-128.

22. Mowrer, O. *The crisis in psychiatry and religion.* New York: Van Nostrand, 1961.

23. Mowrer, O. Even these, thy hand. *Chic. Theol. Sem. Reg.*, 1962, 52, 1-17.

24. Mowrer, O. Personal communication, 1962.

25. O'Connell, W. The adaptive functions of wit and humor. *J. Abnorm. Soc. Psychol.*, 1960, 61, 263-270.

26. O'Connell, W. Ward psychotherapy with schizophrenics through concerted encouragement. *J. Ind. Psychol.*, 1961, 17, 193-204.

27. O'Connell, W. Identification and curability of the mental hospital patient. *J. Ind. Psychol.*, 1962, 18: 1, 68-76.

28. Rapaport, D. The theory of ego autonomy: a generalization. *Bull. Menninger Clinic*, 1958, 22: 1, 13-35.

29. Reubenstein, B. & Levitt, M. Some observations regarding the role of fathers in child psychotherapy. *Bull. Menninger Clinic*, 1957, 21: 1, 16-27.

30. Rieff, P. A schema of therapeutic types. Paper read at Amer. Psychol. Assoc. meetings, New York, 1961.

31. Salzman, L. Morality of psychoanalysis. *Pastoral Psychol.*, 1962, 13: 122, 24-29.

32. Shaw, G. *Androcles and the lion, over-ruled, pygmalion.* New York: Brentanos, 1916.

33. Shoben, E. "Love, loneliness, and logic." *J. Ind. Psychol.*, 1960, 16: 1, 11-24.

34. Szasz, T. *The myth of mental illness.* New York: Hoeber-Harper, 1961.

35. White, R. Motivation reconsidered: the concept of competence. *Psychol. Rev.*, 1959, 66: 5, 297-333.

HUMANIZING RELIGION, RACE, AND SEX

Humanistic Neglect

It is axiomatic in Adler's organismic outlook that Man cannot be chopped up into some autonomous personality parts or independent behaviors (Adler, 1956). He is seen as a *gestalt*, operating in an environment which is made conscious only when filtered through his life style. All people are constantly in quest of feelings of esteem and worth. The immature use evasive or irresponsible behaviors to gain minimal asocial esteem. The truly mature have a great deal of self-esteem in a relatively demandless giving of time and effort toward understanding others. It is therefore redundant to define humanism in different areas of life—religion, race, sex—for in all facets it is ultimately the same: one's esteem is gained by faith in the worth of the individual.

Judging by the time, effort, and puzzlement expanded on its behalf, humanism is of little consequence to Man. No crash programs are operating for existential explorations, yet it may well be that our world will finally expire in consequence of our frenetic efforts to avoid curiosity about our inner nature and its social needs and responsibilities. Man has always resisted taking his own nature seriously. Here is true insanity indeed. To this end, consciousness and responsibility have been analyzed away by an intense faith that the true answer to problems in living will be discovered by automatically redistributing molecules and/or material goals.

The paper is not a cry to cease physiological and sociological research. It is rather a curiosity about Man's faith in discovering Utopia by measuring the more easily quantifiable things while reducing himself to zero as a mover of the

Paper presented as part of a symposium entitled "The War Between the Generations," co-sponsored by The American Society of Adlerian Psychology and The Minnesota Society of Individual Psychology, Minneapolis, Minnesota, November 9, 1968.

Reprinted from Pew, W. (Ed.), *The War Between the Generations*, Minneapolis: Alfred Adler Institute, 1968, 17-32.

world. As we squander our resources in repressing others and seeking to prove our own greatness, we approach the ultimate Freudian apocalypse. Man feels himself isolated while striving for "health" through expression of narcissistic, hostile, and sexual "drives." His actions reflect a demand to be loved (a word which he cannot define) by others (whose beneficial potentialities he cannot admit). In a world where saints, heroes, and altruism are "nothing but" reaction formations, bags, and hangups, we naturally find repression of thought, speech, action, and flight from cooperation with others (seen only as potential rivals or jailers). "The typical ideal of our time is still the isolated hero for whom fellow men are objects" (Adler, 1966). Consciousness is drugged (by alcohol, LSD, etc.) because it is too painful, focused as it is upon our self-hatred and meaningless vacuous existence. Responsibility is a hollow word adding to our pain. Through it we have for ages ferreted out the poor scapegoat and burned the hapless heretic.

How different all this would have been had we in the helping professions listened to Alfred Adler (1956, 1966), and had institutionalized religion not silenced Pierre Teilhard de Chardin (1964). Perhaps they were subjected to a deafening silence because they would not reduce consciousness and responsibility to epiphenomena of some "more real" activity. Both saw Man as responsible for the evolutionary process, an ideal which, while giving super-meaning to life also brought a depressing chill. For as long as Man views himself as diminutive and unworthy he will create external Gods which he can manipulate, as he kills and dies for them.

Evolution of Gemeinschaftsgefühl (and Humanistic Identification)

Yet in spite of all our self-hatreds and denials, Adler and Teilhard are with us more than ever. The increased emphasis upon problems-in-living at the expense of medical models has decreased Man's passive-dependency upon rigidly deterministic extra-psychic factors. The death of God movement in theology has re-emphasized the Judeo-Christian tradition of growth through loving good works as opposed to traditional blind and narrow obedience to a wrathful, distant God. Can we imagine what organized religion would be like, stripped of its bureaucratic magical-egotistical uses (Birnbaum, 1961)? Supposing instead of Hell-Fire-and-Damnation techniques—which only exacerbate the sins of narrow selfhood and other-blame—religion had focused upon Man as made in the image of God. This ideal is different completely from "made *as God*," the goal which drives us out of paradise and makes Hell on Earth. What if we really believed we were made in the image of God in the sense that potentially, we shared His creative powers of Grace? That is, by our loving activity toward others we could help persons to grow. This philosophy would not lead to unbridled conceit because we share this creative potential *equally* with all mankind, and are a band of brothers. It would sharply decrease the masses of alienated and hyperdependent followers. Yet this change seems impossible until we *experience*, not alone read or write about, our own personal worth in the social context. Conscious of our personal worth, we would realize the importance of responsibility defined as, first, the ability to admit mistakes and choose behavioral alternatives without telling oneself "I . . . , they . . ., etc. . . ., are no good forever"; and to live up to implicit and explicit promises. This conscious responsibility is what is lacking most strikingly in the "mentally ill." Are there any mental patients who do not try with their private logic to solve the problem of responsibility by assuming either powerlessness or all the powers of God? We unhospitalized ones do not swing to such extremes, but do waste a good deal of energy in wrestling unsuccessfully with the limits of one's responsibility.

Until the world has the moral courage to define courage as active social interest, as did Adler, we will have our violence and despair in king-sized packages. Sex, race, and religion can all be used as magical-egotistical ways to subdue and conquer the other. And then the victim seeks to victimize the aggressor often by more devious means of self- and other-punishment. It almost appears that the world has actively conspired against looking at Man as the paragon of the animals, or God's fondest creation. There must be someone to blame, whip, burn or we tear at ourselves (Freud's idea of pernicious human nature—which only encourages cynicism and misery). We unwittingly work hard at molding ourselves into the image of wrathful Gods (isolated in the clouds of personal preoccupation).

Humanism today "has been one of the code words for softheaded thinking, pornography, and the collapse of authority"

(Novak, 1968). The democratic humanistic system of cooperation-as-equals may be destroyed by the ethics of pseudoindependence, and populating our inner and outer worlds with hard sin and various implacable devils. Humanism has always been threatened by man-made devils created for projection of our unwanted desires and responsibilities upon those we want to think of as inferior. So far, we have been remarkably successful at filling mental hospitals, jails, and cemeteries with such rejects. In our rush to independence we do not acknowledge our psychological needs for responses from others. Even though we supply our personalized meaning for events, others give us the responses to be molded. In a relationship of mutual affection, they offer encouragement and accurate feedback which prevents the growth of autistic, antisocial runaways. It is crucial that someday, somewhere we must show humanism as it is—a tough courageous task—rather than a cowardly flight from "manly" shoot-outs.

Humanistic Identification

Imagine for a moment that Man's phenomenological existence is valid and receives motivating force from such psychological needs as relatedness, rootedness, transcendence, stable sense of identity, and frame of devotion (Fromm, 1955). While Man has an innate potentiality for love or social interest, the expression and development of this ability depend upon its rewarding by significant others. A person associated with the satisfaction of one's psychological and physical needs becomes a significant other (provided one's life style does not distort the happening) (O'Connell, 1968). We ever strive to increase our feelings of worth (belonging, self-esteem, or power) in the sense that we can convince ourselves that we are able to influence others to do our will. But we do not automatically extend the need to belong to social intercourse with all other people (see Table 1). This may be our prime disease: the satisfaction of our need for worth by the rewards of few select others. Contrast this with the ideal mature one who has few, if any, encumbering gruesome-twosome demanding relationships. "Social feelings require a different ideal," (from that of an isolated hero) "namely that of the saint, purified, to be sure, from fantastic clinkers originating from superstition" (Adler, 1966). He can honestly love himself and realizes that positive

232

Table 1

Do-It-Yourself Method of Mental Illness
(Based on the Theory of Humanistic Identification)

The Main Tent: You've Got to Accentuate the Negative

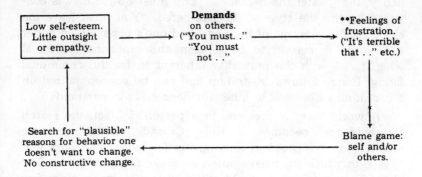

Low self-esteem.
Little outsight
or empathy.

Demands
on others.
("You must. ."
"You must
not . .")

**Feelings of
frustration.
("It's terrible
that . ." etc.)

Search for "plausible"
reasons for behavior one
doesn't want to change.
No constructive change.

Blame game:
self and/or
others.

The less the esteem, the more the search for perfection (lack of the courage to be imperfect). Patient hides "short-comings," doesn't want to be "humiliated," "embarrassed," etc. In the end the patient doesn't realize that he is punishing himself directly, or indirectly through withdrawal from human race (and esteem of others). He loses main sources of belonging and personal worth (i.e., esteem) by failure to relate to others and by punishing self with negative nonsense. The more one hides feelings and withdraws, the more the tension, the more retreats, etc.

(**Mutual giving and receiving of responsible verbal feedback—without making negative generalizations—may stop the development of "mistaken certainties" or self-defeating generalizations about self and others.)

The Side Show: Symptomatic Complaints

Patient now uses his symptoms (feelings he doesn't like—or behaviors that bother others) to get a little self-esteem. These are "the games people play" or "the art of one-upmanship." Patient generally not aware of these goals of attention, power, revenge and, or special service (Dreikurs, 1957). Moral: Even "passive" patients are active, making decisions. It's work to be crazy. Don't reward symptomatic behavior by allowing oneself to be put one-down (through thwarted demands upon patient).

meaning develops through outsight as well as insight. The ideal of social interest or humanistic identification is one who can relate to the whole human race—past, present, and future—by giving instead of demanding (O'Connell, 1965, 1968).

Immature dependency is inspired by our alienated way of evaluating people and is tenaciously maintained to gain some esteem by controlling the movements of others. Operating unwittingly on the principle that some reliable source of esteem is better than none, the victim does not change: his demands merely victimize others who need him. The greater the dependency, the greater the demands. "You must do for me" is conveyed by the life style of the pampered. "You must leave me alone" is the message of the neglected one's behavior. In either case there is certain to be tension and emotional upheaval when faced with the mutuality inherent in fruitful communal living. Blame follows frustration and can be conceptualized on a continuum from self to other (or depressive to paranoid).

A world view is precious to a person. In fact, the search for evidence becomes a Holy Crusade. Often awesome creativity is evidenced in finding fuel for hatred and hopelessness with which to enslave others or make life stimulating. The client lives in a narrow world with brittle self-esteem since few satisfy his arbitrary demands. When others do so they usually demand reciprocal satisfaction of their neurotic needs. Mother, for example, may laud a prepsychotic child for his concern about her, but then she will demand that he cater to her narcissism, and her's alone.

The humanist, be he psychotherapist, teacher, or clergy had better be aware of this, and not himself demand requited love and tolerance from other persons. He "strokes," really believing in the worth and uniqueness of the individual. But he also "spits" on target (O'Connell, 1967). For not having demands to be loved by the client, the therapist can talk at length about the hidden goals of attention, power, revenge, and special service (Dreikurs, 1957) as they appear in therapy. All the while, self-righteous indignation at being an object of manipulation is tempered by the therapist's belief that such immature dependence follows from the patient's socially learned and defective identification. Restrictions on feelings of social worth and importance lead to these crippling dependencies on others, and vice versa. The more the self-loathing and alienation, the greater the magical demands upon others. The narrower the world view encouraged by the "rewarding" ones, the more prejudiced the developing outlook of the "rewarded" ones. As Adler pointed out many times, if the child is not encouraged to seek relationships with many people, he is prone to pampering or neglect by a few. While pampering may eventuate in high self-esteem, its base is too narrow socially, and outsight is limited. In the end, both pamperer and pampered fail to develop into human beings with social souls. Society suffers eventually from the temper tantrums of the pampered who have a much greater radius of destructive action than the neglected isolate.

Beyond Gemeinschaftsgefühl

The great hope inherent in Teilhard's writing is his emphasis upon love in the social sense as the motive-power for future evolution and his refusal to dichotomize the sacred and profane. Western religions have always been plagued with sterile dualisms and God-given essences, ignoring our present lives as mere by-products of external forces. Heaven-earth, my soul-other souls, clergy-laity, etc., all profoundly separated and isolated, are incapable of any quality change through social interaction. (The same curse haunts Western psychiatry with its traditional emphasis upon self-other, inner-outer, sick-well, and the reified "essence" of mental illness.) Because Man's relationship to Man, as a sign and precondition of sanctity, has been officially ignored for so long, the Catholic Church has been shaken to its foundations by the new importance given to Man's acquired social identification or life style as a prime mover. Like psychoanalysis, the Church has glorified the biological and disdained the psychological needs and goals in its evaluation of behavior. There still exists in both systems such growing sexual preoccupations and hang-ups that the here-and-now maturation of social interest has not been considered worthy of serious study. Yet it is heartening to realize that there are now many voices raised against Christian Quietism and fear of Modernism.

"If we affirm the priesthood of all believers and the newly-emerging lay ministry, we see that every Christian is called in some degree to be a therapist. To be effective, we must recognize people's need for love, and discern behind their many and varied requests, a cry for it. This certainly was one of Jesus' great secrets in dealing with people. He did not see a drunk or a prostitute or an uncouth fisherman. He saw persons desperately looking for love whose outward appearance was frequently a poor substitute for what they really wanted and needed.

. . ."We are tested by people who make requests of us. When we are approached on the street by a dirty, foul-smelling drunk, we may react to the obviously unlovely and repulsive symptoms, or we may see behind the man's symptoms a child seeking the love he has never found." (Larson, 1967)

One of the most pathetic signs of Church disruption comes from witnessing the plight of the rebels who yearn to actualize the undefined love for one's neighbor which is at the heart of authentic Christianity. Many humanistically motivated priests, sisters, and ministers have been easy prey for anti-cognitive, narcissistic offshoots of "sensitivity" training (Argyris, 1967). While such methods can give a person some recognition-shock of fears of closeness to others, they fail to provide a logical theory of personality change. Often, crying and rubbing become status symbols with little effective transfer to the movements of real life. The participant becomes overly prone to vocalize his feelings without realizing their *demand* quality upon the other. One must admit some truth in the radical right views of sensitivity training (O'Connell and Hanson, 1968). At times unemotional moral behavior is debunked as "really" a defense against either latent hostility or "authentic" crying and rubbing. To date there is no popular theory to give definitions or behavioral directions to abstractions of love, hope, and charity.

It is exceedingly simple to find "reasons" to generalize hatred. It is much harder to be tolerant and creative in giving and discovering proof of worth. The paucity of interpersonal love, in spite of one's efforts to create and perceive it, works to the disadvantage of the incipient humanist. He's going to have to find contentment in giving more affection than he receives from others. Therefore there is pragmatic value of being in a state of Grace (e.g., believing that one is important enough to accept unconditional love from God). To be able to freely give, one needs to love himself without, at the same time, isolating himself from potential sources of interpersonal rejection. Few help the humanist to love himself authentically. That is why ex-humanists are so plentiful. The earth-bound humanist will surely object to any mention of deity. He will say we must educate Man to love himself and others in spite of all mistakes—without support from any other power. All this sounds wonderful—but can Man ever love himself without looking for proof (if not reasons) from others? I say he can't. Premises about ourselves are always followed by a search for proof, our unscientific way of being human. Hunting for social proof of his Being by his irrational ways gets the psychotic declared "crazy." If social self-esteem is so crucial in my existence, I would do well to accept the free gift of God's love, making certain I also have the Grace to grant it to all humans *sub specie aeternitatis.*

If these humanistic yearnings are to be satisfied they will probably be reached through an extension of the spirit of Adler into heretofore wholly theological areas of concern. Viktor Frankl (1955) made such a move when he re-evaluated *gemeinschaftsgefühl* in terms of actualizing spiritual values, such actions having transpersonal meaning. Yet as Ansbacher (1966) has pointed out, *gemeinschaftsgefühl* has always carried the meaning of "general connectedness" not restricted to the present social community. Had Teilhard been aware of Adler's *gemeinschaftsgefühl* he probably would have considered it synonymous with his metaphysical concept of radial energy, that evolutionary explosive power source resulting from a "tangential" closeness with other existents. In this era of social awareness, Adlerian psychology finds itself able to be of incalculable assistance to religious movements if it is willing to take the risk of rubbing elbows with theology.

We may pull heaven down to earth and find that such concepts as grace, sin, and agape relate to social interaction between people. Pragmatically, it seems acceptance of a "general connectedness" with a loving social God can increase some people's self-esteem and social interest tremendously. The dangerous syndrome of asocial behavior with high self-esteem (a frequent symptom of the "successful" psychopath) is precluded if the mystical relationship of Grace means to the recipient that his social love and tolerance is both the precondition and *sine qua non* of this metaphysical deistic relationship.

A recurrent theme in institutional Christianity has been that Man should not think of gain (i.e., live pragmatically) for doing good (another ill-defined term). So this suggestion of "insurance" for one's self-esteem and social interest through belief in a loving God will be repugnant to the *pre-aggiornamento* personality. The presence of psychological and physiological needs in such people often means a flaw in the mythical independence they cherish.´Yet for the purpose of stabilizing high self-esteem and wide social interest the belief in a loving God is valuable. Note here that this "illusion" is ´not compensatory, for in this case Man is not avoiding his main tasks in life and this kind of a God is not his, his family's, or his country's alone. No theological issues are broached since there is no scholarly concern with the issue of whether God exists. In effect, the cause of one's personal worth and social commitment is advanced by this belief. In this particular era, humanism is not often socially rewarded. If it is true that one must look for proof of worth and is not so detached and isolated as to try to do it alone (except in the case of the psychotic), what are the dangers of going beyond *gemeinschaftsgefühl* or Humanistic Identification?

Sin, in an Adlerian theory of Humanistic Identification, would be equivalent to blame or negative nonsense (Ellis, 1962). This is false faith or negative overgeneralizations about people, regarding the self and/or others as worthless, hopeless, incurably and socially damned now-and-forever. The "sinner" is helped to self-esteem by tactfully demonstrating the behavior which leads to self- and other-hatred.[1] In this system, sin is not an isolated act of overlooking a ritual but rather selecting perceptions and ideas which lead to alienated actions.

Both therapist and clergy alike often find themselves striving for an "unconditional positive regard" or *agape* which is frequently translated into self- and other-pampering (O'Connell, 1967a). That is, we aim to be God, rather than made in the creative image of God. When the therapist realizes that an agape which accepts any act rewards pampering, he is jolted into receptivity for a stroking-and-spitting orientation (O'Connell, 1967b). Therefore the therapist must teach himself and the patient the fine art of differentiating between actions and the generalizations about people which follow these actions. If the therapist cannot see himself in this light, his therapeutic career will be short and disasterous. If he does not look at his patients as unique persons, worthy of making decisions in their own right despite many mistakes, he would do better to work with animals. Unfortunately, the definition of agape and positive regard which sticks with us is that one must be completely unruffled by any actions of the other. We'd have more contented professionals if we'd deal with right-wrong (or healthy-sick) actions from a Teilhard-Adler perspective. That is, will the behavior in question lead to more love and acceptance of persons, *sub specie aeternitatis?*

Authority, Race, and Sex

Throughout all facets of our existence we find an ever-growing reaction to accepting arbitrary authority—with a predictable backlash from more conservative and repressive forces. While some of us feel a need to commit ourselves to vaguely defined humanistic changes, others want to have a static world in which slaves will always be willing slaves for the sake of their own magical-egotistical power needs. This phenomenon has been called "The Dark Ages of Quietment" when applied to our practice of silencing those who make us impatient (O'Connell and Hanson, 1968). Because we have failed miserably to define Man's needs and goals in a socially profitable way, the protesters, when they are victorious, bring as much misery upon us as do the dictatorial repressors—and very often they react in the same dehumanizing way toward the verbal expressions of others.

When we get to the moon we will be no closer to understanding the vicious cycle of self-hatred—demands upon others—frustration and blame. Drugs may quiet this dissonance but won't substitute loving behavior. We need to stop and think about *our* existence and its goals.

In questions of race we can do no better than the advice of Adler in not dominating or being irritated or enslaved by the "stupidity" of others. In this country we are evolving toward a choice-point in which repression vies with revolution for the main stage. Unfortunately while all concerned want to "tell it like it is," very few involved Americans want to listen and accept the right of the other to have personal attitudes, hopes, and fears. The social responsiblities toward persons are lost in the mania for catharsis as an end in itself. Radicals of Right and Left do not impress one as being committed to solving the meaning of social interest of "building the earth." Social protests and counterprotests move more to the tune of asocial selfish themes than any democratic chorus. The private practice of searching for scapegoats in the reconstructed past is impotent in the face of overwhelming social needs for tolerance and mutual concern. Here is a challenge which the Adlerian, through interest, aptitude, and training, is well-suited. If not he, who else?

The humanistic view of sex is, by now, obvious. If behavior follows from cognitive attitudes in service of one's goals, one either becomes a humanist or does not, depending on the state of his demands toward others. Shulman (1966) has classified the dehumanizing uses of sex as motivated by demonstrating success or failure, mischief, distance, domination, suffering, vanity, revenge, and proof of abnormality. The panacea for Man's ills is to be found not in unbridled sexual release upon other "objects" but in discovering the social and asocial uses and goals of behaviors.

Summary

Humanism today is often regarded as a soft, confused philosophy of moral weaklings. Until this view is reevaluated it is doubted that Man will live in harmony with himself and others. A humanistic science and philosophy of Man will have roots in Teilhard's Christianity and Adler's psychology. According to this thought, Man is the culmination of the evolutionary process, creating, by his loving behavior, the conditions necessary for a better world. In this sense, humanism is not a detached escapist philosophy, for it is easier and more fashionable in our times to find reasons to compete and hate than to understand and love. Humanistic Identification (a psychological theory of humanism) assumes that this human love can only be lived by "stroking-and-spitting." That is, to be a significant other one must often work hard in his "stroking" spending time and effort to understand the other through his verbal and physical actions. "Spitting" implies an ability to avoid partiality toward persons. Being maturely independent, one can inform the other of his asocial learned tactics to gain short-sighted attention, power, revenge, and special service. Stroking and spitting in another context is similar to proper feedback in authentic sensitivity training. Such behavior is congruent with courage in the Adlerian sense (active social interest) and in the popular meaning (ability to stick to a punishing task).

It is the key assumption of this humanistic system that nondefensive love of the self, inseparable from the social love of others, is absolutely necessary. To stimulate this authentic love and self-esteem, a nontheistic belief in a loving God is encouraged. Some humanists would maintain that this is a sick delusion since Man should be able to have faith in his worth, irrespective of environmental factors. Yet, telling Man that he is worthy, as well as pointing out his asocial goals, does not seem to complete the education in maturity. One exists precariously, subject to extensive potential stress, as long as he *demands* to be loved by others *before* he can love himself. Yet, even if he is able to arrive at mature self-love, Man is not completely detached, and restlessly searches and creates some kind of *personal* proof of worth. This intelligent activity in the asocial and immature can be wasteful of psychic energy and stimulate rejection from others who are not aware of strained methods of searching for worth. Self-love is not an easy task. Therefore trust in any impersonal source is valid if this faith does not preclude Man's active social interest (understanding and encouraging hope in others).

REFERENCES

1. Ansbacher, H. L. and Ansbacher, Rowena (Ed.) *The Individual Psychology of Alfred Adler.* New York: Basic Books, 1956.

2. Adler, A. The Psychology of Power. *Journal of Individual Psychology,* 1966, 22, 166-172.

3. Ansbacher, H. Gemeinschaftsgefühl. *Individual Psychology Newsletter,* 1966, 17, 13-15.

4. Argyris, C. On the Future of Laboratory Education. *Journal of Applied Behavioral Science,* 1967, 3, 153-183.

5. Beecher, W. Personal Communication. November 28, 1968.

6. Birnbaum, F. Frankl's Existential Psychology from the Viewpoint of Individual Psychology. *Journal of Individual Psychology,* 1961, 17, 162-166.

7. Dreikurs, R. *Psychology in the Classroom.* New York: Harper and Row, 1957.

8. Ellis, A. *Reason and Emotion in Psychotherapy*. New York: Lyle Stuart, 1962.

9. Frankl, V. *The Doctor and the Soul*. New York: Knopf, 1955.

10. Fromm, E. *The Sane Society*. New York: Holt, Rinehart, Winston, 1955.

11. Larson, B. The Gift of Love. *Christian Herald*, 1967, 2, #3, 21-23.

12. Novak, M. Beyond the Fringe: Why Wallace? *Commonweal*, 1968, 89, 78-79.

13. O'Connell, W. Humanistic Identification, A New Translation for Gemeinschaftsgefühl. *Journal of Individual Psychology*, 1965, 21, 44-47.

14. O'Connell, W. A Defense of Mowrer's Eros. *Insight*, 1967, 6, #2, 66-67 (a).

15. O'Connell, W. Stroking and Spitting. *The Individual Psychologist*, 1967, 5, #1, 29-31 (b).

16. O'Connell, W. Humanistic Identification: A Theory of Persons. *Journal of Existentialism*, 1968 (in press).

17. O'Connell, W., and Hanson, P. Anxieties of Group Leaders in Police-Community Confrontations. Paper presented at American Psychological Association Meeting, San Francisco, September 1968.

18. Shulman, B. The Uses and Abuses of Sex. *Journal of Religion and Health*, 1967, 6, 317-325.

19. Teilhard De Chardin, P. *The Future of Man*. New York: Harper and Row, 1964.

FOOTNOTE

[1]Willard Beecher (Beecher, 1968) has raised an interesting question on the validity of self-hatred. "I do not believe that such a thing exists as 'self-hate' . . . Do you really believe that it is possible for one to really 'hate himself'? (We only hate others—*for opposing us.*) It is this concept that separates Freud and Adler. . . ." It may be best to look at self-hatred from two frames of reference, the phenomenological and the external observer of the life style. People "possess' self-hatred, or so they report on the feeling level. But the "use" function is something else, according to the observer of life style tactics. To Adler self-hatred gave the person an excuse to avoid responsibly fulfilling his life tasks. In my theory people are always striving for an increase of self-esteem, therefore they never consider themselves completely worthless. People may be unaware that, at times, they are esteemed by seeing themselves as the tragic hero (experientially, it's better than nothing). They also can get at least minimal esteem from others in this role and goal through attention, power and revenge, struggles, and special service (see Table 1). Self-hatred, like guilt, is often a "legitimate" excuse for self-pampering and avoidance of possible error. One is "not responsible," hence cannot lose self- and other-esteem. The direction of such development is enhancement of the self through devious asocial means, hence is pathological. The phrase "apparent self-hatred" might be more suitable than "self-hatred" alone, since Man cannot live in a completely esteem-less state.

HUMANISTIC IDENTIFICATION: A NEW TRANSLATION FOR GEMEINSCHAFTSGEFÜHL

It may be that future generations will regard *Gemeinschaftsgefühl* to be Adler's most penetrating and basic concept, a legacy often ignored because of the uninspiring English substitute, "social interest." Interest appears too mild, volitional, and intellectual; social too narrow, compliant, and tethered by conventions and mores. In an effort to highlight the importance of Adler's concept for all facets of personality development, "humanistic identification" is offered as a more harmonious uniter of seemingly diverse concepts and professions.

In essence, humanistic identification refers to a process (not completed at the age of six or 60) characterized by a feeling of brotherly love or close kinship with other human beings in the present, as well as a strong affinity for the human race as a whole, past and future. Humanistic identification is demonstrated intellectually by "outsight," a commitment toward understanding the psychological needs of others and the tension generated by their lack of fulfillment; and by an active movement toward satisfying such needs and becoming a significant other.

Rather than use the phrase "mental illness" to label the patient's dissatisfaction with his behavior and/or society's discontent with the patient's actions, a construct based upon the client's position on a continuum from skin-tight identification to humanistic identification is recommended. In other words, mental illness must eventually be inferred from behaviors which prevent mankind from moving toward the molding of brotherly love *Gemeinschaftsgefühl*, or humanistic identification for all.

Reprinted from Journal of Individual Psychology, Vol. 21, 44-47, May 1965.

It goes without saying that these few words merely point out possible directions for research and that at present we have little definitive work on such inner processes and the necessary behavioral correlates. The postulated development of humanistic identification depends upon the presence of tension reducers, and even tension creators, who will tutor the client or helped-one in the art of outsight. One's style of life is maintained with tenacity, and the therapist, parent, or other person high in humanisitc identification must be in reality, a tutor of values in word and action. Here we see the transcending of one spurious dichotomy, that of the educator and psychotherapist: both are dealing in human values. In this outline a few additional advantages of the humanistic identification idea follow.

1. *Attention to the content of social interest.* Humanistic identification avoids the picture of a desperate dowager trying to create a better personality image without real commitment to the human needs beyond the superficial calm of social niceties. Unfortunately, in many circles the Adlerian is perceived as one who lives by the maxim of "Don't make waves." If the authentic Adlerian and the person high in humanistic identification are synonymous, ideally such a person makes no inordinate personal demands on others. But this in no way assumes that he cannot disapprove of narrow, skin-tight identification in others if he is willing to offer support and optimistic encouragement to the effect that actions can be learned which will result in more happiness if one will weather the anxiety of change.

2. *An end to an isolated concept.* Since isolation is the bane of Adlerians, even a concept such as *Gemeinschaftsgefühl* must be anchored in a field of ongoing research such as humanistic identification promises to do. The external and internal conditions, internalized sentences of Ellis,[2] which strengthen and maintain both broad humanistic and narrow skin-tight identifications are a fertile, relatively unexplored field but one of promise for the Adlerian in psychology, sociology and education.

3. *Self-esteem revisited.* Perhaps we have been too content with the equation of the primacy of low self-esteem equals mental illness. Does not high self-esteem in a narrow inept role mold the schizophrenic-prone individual? Left alone in the

world, his misunderstanding of others would eventuate in low self-esteem, but first, in many cases of pampering, is the conditional "love" of the mother. And the lack of humanistic identification in one who has high self-esteem in skintight identification pursuits, can be a dictatorial menace to the world. The potential schizophrenic can manipulate mother at the price of his freedom: he learns that the world is evil beyond mother. The "successful" sociopath is well practiced in the reduction of tensions and becomes significant to many, but he reinforces hatreds in others. For the present we are left with an angel-and-pin analogy: how many significant others and of what degree of humanistic identification must one identify with before one generalizes like a paranoid or a practicing Christian?[3]

4. *Humanistic identification as a precondition for authentic religious practice.* Institutionalized religion is usually wary of "psychologizing," although there is no common anchor for this term. Perhaps it is taken to mean the "reality" of id impulses and/or "irrationality" of religious motives. Western religions gravitate toward the spiritual end of a spurious spiritual-human dichotomy, devoting their energies toward refining the rituals for man's devotion to God. The cause of man's needs and relationships is generally relegated to a minority of humanists within the churches, or to popular humanistic organizations which are held together by hatreds of authoritarian religion and philosophical concern for the nebulous goals of mankind. All of this strife would be closer to solution if more emphasis were placed upon the untapped humanistic resources of the Judeo-Christian tradition, following the example of Adler.[3] For the humanistic identification concept assumes that an authentic religious orientation is predicated upon Adlerian courage: concern for humanistic identification models propagating their values by assisting in the psychological need reduction of others. Without this broad human base there is only the magical-egotistical religiosity,[1] itself so responsible for persecutions, wars, and the distrust of humankind.

By substituting humanistic for social one can circumvent Frankl's error of making some of value-actualization independent of man.[1] Frankl paradoxically conceives of man as existing without the *sub specie aeternitatis* imperative. Only a person with narrow identification can abstract himself intellectually from the human race; but even emotionally he feels isolated from past, present, and future. He is cursed with his narrowness, since humanistic self-esteem is predicated upon outsightful actions, and his very withdrawal reflects the influence of people, which is never really by anyone. A quote from St. Augustine is a warning against religious fixations and an entreaty for humanistic identification. "To love each person as though you had love for him alone and to love all as though all were one."

Summary

"Humanistic identification" is suggested as a better translation of Adler's *Gemeinschaftsgefühl* than "social interest" in that it affords a wider reference than "social" and avoids the connotations of conformity and gregariousness; and is not restricted to the mild, volitional, intellectual character of "interest." It covers the intellectual, affective, and behavioral aspects of the optimal relationship to others, namely understanding, empathizing with, and acting in behalf of others. It would seem to lead more directly to avenues of research and common ground with religion.

REFERENCES

1. Birnbaum, F. Frankl's existential psychology from the viewpoint of Individual Psychology. *J. Indiv. Psychol.*, 1961, 17, 162-166.

2. Ellis, A. *Reason and emotion in psychotherapy.* New York: Lyle Stuart, 1962.

3. O'Connell, W. Practicing Christianity and humanistic identification. *J. humanist. Psychol.*, 1964, 4, 118-129.

INDUCTIVE FAITH:
THE CONFLUENCE OF RELIGION
AND HUMANISTIC PSYCHOLOGY

Our generation has been privileged to exist in the most accelerated period of human change. Yet to many people their present lot is comparable to taking over the unfamiliar controls of a spaceship in which the pilot has suddenly disappeared and the course and destination are unknown. Man has not been trained by home, school, or church to be open to the opportunities of change. In this void, even the disappearance of time-honored prejudices is often mourned as the triumph of malevolent external forces over defenseless individuals.

For religion regarded etymologically (i.e., "re-ligio": that which binds us together), the present state of institutional disruption is herein regarded as a harbinger of growth rather than the throes of death. The current emphasis upon process-thinking and personology in Catholicism brings us closer to humanistic psychology. Adlerian psychology, with its emphasis on the fruits of creative social interest is a bulwark against the destructively narrow theories which spawn neurotic hatreds and pessimistic alienation (O'Connell, 1967). Ignored tenets of Christianity, possibly excommunicated by the holders of institutionalized power, will be reexamined in the light of contributions of existential-humanistic thinking.

The resurrected faiths in *analogia entis,* good works (viewed from the interpersonal growth rather than from the compulsively mechanistic), and basic poverty of spirit (or self-esteem), when combined with the Adlerian concepts of self-esteem and social interest will be called inductive faith. Inductive faith removes the absolute dualism between heaven and earth, the eternal and the profane. It looks for the conditions which create "man fully alive" and sees within the process its model of God. This novel way to hope in the human community is built upon personal experience (Stern & Marino,

Reprinted from Desert Call, 1973. 8 (1).

1970) rather than from static, abstract, and secondary views of man, so prevalent in institutional religions and theologies. Stern and Marino, for example, illustrate "the psychospiritual imperative to love," comparable in spirit to the social interest of Alfred Adler. This here-and-now interpersonal accent of inductive faith is quite foreign to institutionalized emphases upon exclusive denominational "truths" inherent in other-worldly duties and rituals. Inductive faith has relevance for today's youth who find a theory of man deduced from platonic concepts too schizoid and autocratic.

Crises of Faith

Traditional Christianity, even more than descriptive psychiatry, has been convulsed by the intrusion of dynamic process-thinking into its faith in a static universe of fixed essences and isolated categories. Progressive Christianity has been striving to overcome the heaven-earth dualism and in this process has focused upon the ancient, but lost, tradition of the growth of the "soul" through human interactions. The impetus has been for less angelic concern and more devotion to the development of self-esteem and social interest in the here-and-now of eternity. This type of action-conscious belief is unconscionable to ossified institutional concerns.

While the churches crumble as monolithic autocratic institutions, religion as a tolerant binding force faces another danger. Such a threat comes from mysticism-without-social-interest, the "voyage within" tactic instead of a cooperation-as-equals strategy for mankind. For all the value he possesses as a gadfly to dehumanized psychiatric practices, R. D. Laing (1967), for example, unfortunately champions religious movements which loosen and do not bind. Any mysticism which does not progress through stages of insight and outsight into life styles of self and others is almost certain to be destructive.

A case in point is the Manson-type mysticism which appears to be in the service of a narcissistic and grandiose search for rationalizations which sanction a dictatorial lack of social interest. Although the hippie movement disclaims veneration of materialistic goals, it is fertile ground for the idolatry of the isolated self. The failure to consider social interest leads to esteem through such useless goals or demands from others as attention, power, revenge, hero-martyr-saint, or special service

248

motives. In spite of all the intense efforts one cannot "dissolve the ego," but can only control the vagaries of his self-esteem and social interest by his behavior in life's tasks. Mere refusal to be duped by material possessions and mechanized rituals does not guarantee maturity. The latter is a consequence of social interest, the only goal which cannot be pursued to excess or ultimate insanity (Adler, 1964).

The modern movement in Catholicism, which is really as ancient as the first impulse to define love and put it into action, is personified by the works of Pierre Teilhard de Chardin and Johannes Baptist Metz, both of whom have been unknowingly Adlerian in spirit.

Teilhard: Evolution Through Love

The late French priest-paleontologist was profoundly concerned with highlighting the importance of the person and his interdependence upon the physical and interpersonal world. Teilhard (1959, 1965) believed that evolution now takes place only through psychic or radial energy, the within or interiority of man, rather than via the tangential energy (the without) of material evolution. Cosmic evolution reaches its peak in the self-reflectiveness of man, progressing "as if" the universe followed, unwittingly and with countless regressions, a principle of unity and self-realization culminating in man's socialization. Man is himself responsible for his "auto-evolution." It is his decision to love that converts tangential energy into radial, creative energy.

The future cosmic evolution will be decided by the developmental process of "the sense of earth," and how many persons will decide to follow this "grand option" rather than suicide, repression, and hyperindividuality. Teilhard articulated his views in what he called his hyperphysics, a natural and necessary extension of traditional science. The move beyond orthodox science was impelled by Teilhard's need to take account of the primacy of thought in the universe and the organic unity of mankind, seen as a biological growing atom. All the before-mentioned has an Adlerian ring of responsible and optimistic process-thinking. Teilhard's addition of an omega point of Universal Christ toward which mankind converges is extra-psychological and theological. But since the other-worldly addition does not increase hostility, inactivity, and hopelessness, its presence does not do injustice to Adlerian psychology. The following gives a clue as to Teilhard's closeness to social interest, that feeling of closeness to all of mankind which, in Adler's thought, was the hallmark of maturity:

> The phrase "Sense of Earth" should be understood to mean the passionate concern for our common destiny which draws the thinking part of life ever further onward. In principle there is no feeling which has a firmer foundation in nature, or greater power. But in fact there is also no feeling which awakens so belatedly, since it can be explicit only when our consciousness has expanded beyond the broadening, but still far too restricted circles of family, country, and race, and has finally discovered that the only truly natural and real human Unity is the Spirit of Earth (Teilhard, 1965, p. 43).

Metz: Poverty of Spirit

Johannes Metz (1968), Catholic existential theologian, emphasizes man's ontological poverty of spirit, and his provisional and finite nature in the face of inevitable death. The poverty of spirit is akin to low self-esteem, the innate state of worth according to Adlerian, but not Freudian theory. Orthodox psychoanalysis implies that children operate from primary narcissism, supposedly a state of high self-esteem (Blum, 1953). Adlerian theory regards the child in his world of giants and rivals, as a creature of low self-esteem, ever striving to maximize feelings of self-worth while minimizing attempts to extend social interest. According to Metz, the poverty of spirit (or low self-esteem) is only assuaged by an open acceptance of mystery and a commitment to the traditionally neglected categorical imperative of Christianity, love of the self. Metz emphasizes that the only biblical account of mankind's final judgment involves the question of man's active love for his fellows. True damnation is "richness of spirit" (or high self-esteem) in chronic isolation from needs of other men (low social interest). Heaven is accepting one's true poverty in the Pauline spirit of finding perfect strength in acceptance of one's basic weaknesses in isolation from others. Metz's theology works itself out in relationships of love, a practical mysticism which is constructed on a solid base of social interest, not on the cynicism of private logic. "Every authentic religious act is directed toward the concreteness of God in our human brother and his world (Metz, 1968, p. 35)."

Analogia Entis and Good Works

Oden (1964) has compared the unconditional divine love of God with the outgoing concern of the effective therapist. Following the Protestant principle of *analogia fidei*, "faith's analogy between the activity of God and the ontological presuppositions of the counselor (p. 69)," Oden sees in both the concern of God and the therapist an impetus toward learning to value and care for others. In spite of my background of theological ignorance, *analogia entis* (Pegis, 1948) will be nominated by me as a religious concept with tremendous therapeutic potentiality for humanistic psychology. In other words, one's radius of action is increased with greater love, if one believes he himself is an integral and functional part of a greater reality (along with all others) than merely being accepted by God.

To appreciate the value of the before-mentioned concepts of being and works, one must imagine a world which directs its energies to increasing self-esteem and social interest (Ansbacher, 1968; O'Connell, 1968). If the concepts of love, poverty of spirit, and *analogia entis* are examined on the behavioral plane, we would see them working in harmony toward the development of authentic, open, and demandless persons. Supposing *analogia entis* (analogy of being) were to be taken seriously: men would then see operating within themselves, through love, the dignity and power of a loving creative God. By practicing and incorporating love they could, even in vastly diminished form, create like God. To be more behavioral, to "feel-with" humanity, to encourage, and to give, and receive feedback of feelings from others would be love—and also social interest (O'Connell, 1964, 1970). To believe one's self worthy of being made in the image of God—and that this luck is shared with all mankind—is an "as if" philosophy conducive to the development of self-esteem and social interest. The beliefs do not isolate and do point to the practice of loving and understanding movements. They are diametrically opposed to the self-pampering and hostility-inspiring view that one is alone the favorite child or made *like* (not analogous to) God. This unbinding conviction "is Satan's slogan . . . *the* temptation . . . to reject the truth about humanity (Metz, 1968, p. 15)."

Perhaps the main reason why the above description has remained a pious sentiment greeted with cynical smiles is that no institution teaches love or Adlerian cooperation-as-equals. As yet love is not regarded as the learned ability to treat others with dignity, encouragement, and self-determination. Love is not valued highly enough to replace a study period or football coach.

Good works has been another hidden Catholic belief as opposed to the Reformation emphasis on faith alone. In practice, of course, it has been primarily an institutional prerogative. Hierarchical religions have displaced the practice to benefit their material and time demands from individuals. Inductive faith would direct good works toward human encouragement, as seen in the socially learned skills of giving and receiving feedback. The day is not yet with us, but one can imagine the tremendous growth in humanity which would ensue from creating, rather than repressing, human potential to love self and extend this movement toward others. We psychologists suffer from a trained incapacity to deal with—or even be puzzled by—the large human dilemmas posited by inductive faith. Perhaps we can at least empathize with, or be embarrassed by, the words of Bertrand Russell (1953): "The root of the matter is a very simple and old-fashioned thing, a thing so simple that I am almost ashamed to mention it, for fear of the derisive smile with which wise cynics will greet my words. The thing I mean . . . is love, Christian love or compassion (p. 59)."

REFERENCES

1. Adler, A. *Superiority and social interest.* Edited by H.L. & Rowena R. Ansbacher, Evanston, Ill.: Northwestern University Press, 1964.

2. Ansbacher, H. The concept of social interest. *Journal of Individual Psychology,* 1968, 24, 131-149.

3. Blum, G. *Psychoanalytic theories of personality.* New York: McGraw-Hill, 1953.

4. Laing, R. *The politics of experience.* Baltimore: Penguin, 1967.

5. Metz, J. *The Poverty of spirit.* New York: Newman, 1968.

6. O'Connell, W. Practicing Christianity and humanistic identification. *Journal of Humanistic Psychology,* 1964, 4, 118-129.

7. O'Connell, W. Individual psychology. In the *New Catholic Encyclopedia.* New York: McGraw-Hill, 1967, 7, 472-474.

8. O'Connell, W. Humanizing religion, race, and sex, In W. Pew (Ed.), *The war between the generations.* Minneapolis: Alfred Adler Institute, 1968, pp. 17-32.

9. O'Connell, W. Democracy in human relations. *Desert Call,* 1970, 5(2), 8-9.

10. Oden, T. A theologian's view of the process of psychotherapy. *Journal of Individual Psychology,* 1964, 20, 69-78.

11. Pegis, A. (Ed.) *Introduction to Saint Thomas Aquinas.* New York: Modern Library, 1948.

12. Russell, B. *The impact of science upon society.* New York: Simon & Schuster, 1953.

13. Stern, E., & Marino, B. *Psychotheology.* New York: Newman, 1970.

14. Teilhard de Chardin, P. *The phenomenon of man.* New York: Harper & Row, 1959.

15. Teilhard de Chardin, P. *Building the Earth.* Denville, New Jersey: Dimension, 1965.